T0351365

What Is Cognitive Psychology?

WHAT IS COGNITIVE PSYCHOLOGY?

Michael R. W. Dawson

 AU PRESS

Copyright © 2022 Michael R. W. Dawson
Published by AU Press, Athabasca University
1 University Drive, Athabasca, AB T9S 3A3

https://doi.org/10.15215/aupress/9781771993418.01

Cover design by Sergiy Kozakov
Printed and bound in Canada

Library and Archives Canada Cataloguing in Publication
Title: What is cognitive psychology? / Michael R. W. Dawson.
Names: Dawson, Michael Robert William, 1959– author.
Description: Includes bibliographical references.
Identifiers: Canadiana (print) 20220254389 | Canadiana (ebook) 20220254400 | ISBN
9781771993418 (softcover) | ISBN 9781771993425 (PDF) | ISBN 9781771993432 (EPUB)
Subjects: LCSH: Cognitive psychology.
Classification: LCC BF201 .D39 2022 | DDC 153—dc23

We acknowledge the financial support of the Government of Canada through the
Canada Book Fund (CBF) for our publishing activities and the assistance provided
by the Government of Alberta through the Alberta Media Fund.

Canadä   Alberta
                   Government

This publication is licensed under a Creative Commons licence,
Attribution–Noncommercial–No Derivative Works 4.0 International: see
www.creativecommons.org. The text may be reproduced for non-commercial
purposes, provided that credit is given to the original author. To obtain permission
for uses beyond those outlined in the Creative Commons licence, please contact AU
Press, Athabasca University, at aupress@athabascau.ca.

Contents

Chapter 5: Questioning Foundations

Acknowledgements

Many people offered support while I wrote the book. My colleagues Michael Carbonaro, Ben Dyson, Dana Hayward, and Peggy St. Jacques kept me on track. Many students in my laboratory offered feedback: Kezziah Ayuno, Nick Huber, Helen Ma, E. J. Meneses, George Nassar, Arturo Perez, and Stephanie Zawaduk. I would like to dedicate the book to Anna, Aubrey, and Wren.

I would never have written this book without Albert Katz's influence. Albert's many contributions to my career include introducing me to cognitivism when I was his student at the University of Western Ontario. This book reflects my journey from my first class with Albert to my current research in cognitive science.

What Is Cognitive Psychology?

Introduction

_____

Nineteenth-century psychology began the experimental study of consciousness (Boring, 1950). Two competing early-20th-century North American schools of psychology, structuralism and functionalism, continued this tradition. A new school, behaviorism, attacked psychology's mentalism, reacting against both structuralism and functionalism (Watson, 1913). "The time seems to have come when psychology must discard all reference to consciousness; when it need no longer delude itself into thinking that it is making mental states the object of observation" (Watson, 1913, p. 163).

Behaviorism soon dominated 20th-century psychology, changing the field's topics and inspiring new methodologies. Behaviorism aimed to "remove the barrier from psychology which exists between it and the other sciences. The findings of psychology become the functional correlates of structure and lend themselves to explanation in physico-chemical terms" (Watson, 1913, p. 177). For behaviorists, behavioral theories explained, but mentalistic theories did not (Skinner, 1950, 1977, 1990).

Cognitive psychology began to replace behaviorism in the 1950s, bringing mentalism back to psychology (Glenberg et al., 2013; Leahey, 1992; Miller, 2003; Sperry, 1993). Discoveries in cybernetics and computer science inspired the cognitive revolution (Miller et al., 1960; Newell & Simon, 1956, 1961). Cognitivists argued that behaviorism could not explain phenomena such as language (Chomsky, 1959). Cognitivists claimed that behaviorists viewed humans as passive responders. Cognitivists instead viewed humans as active information processors.

Cognitivism dominates modern psychology. For example, my department lists 73 courses in its 2020–21 undergraduate calendar; nearly half (33) explore cognition, with titles such as "Cognitive Psychology," "Spatial Cognition," "Introduction to Cognitive Neuroscience," "Social Cognition," and "Theory and Learning in Comparative Cognition."

The cognitive revolution ended decades ago. As the debate between cognitivism and behaviorism faded into history, cognitive psychology's theoretical foundations also seemed to become forgotten. What is cognitive psychology?

I often ask students to define cognitive psychology to begin my third-year "Foundations of Cognitive Science" course. My students understand cognitive psychology's core topics (e.g., attention, memory, and thinking), and they know typical methods for studying these topics. However, my students do not know cognitive psychology's basic assumptions. They do not understand why we can use computers to model cognitive processing. They cannot describe differences between behaviorist and cognitivist explanations.

Why might my students understand cognitive psychology as a practice, as studying core topics via particular methods, but not understand cognitive psychology's theoretical foundations? Modern textbooks present cognitive psychology in exactly this way.

Modern texts first describe cognitive psychology's history and then provide several "topics" chapters. Topics move from sensation and perception (cognitive neuroscience, perception, attention) through middle-level topics (different kinds of memory) and end with central processing (language, thinking, problem solving). Modern texts depict cognitive psychology as experimental results about core topics.

Modern texts also define cognitive psychology as using four "approaches": experimental psychology, cognitive neuroscience (studying normal brains via brain imaging), cognitive neuropsychology (studying psychological deficits arising from brain injury), and simulated cognition using computers. Unfortunately, using such approaches to define cognitive psychology plays fast and loose with theoretical foundations.

For example, cognitive psychology's theories are functionalist, appealing to what processes do, not to their physical causes. Functionalism makes computer simulations of cognition plausible, even though computers and brains are physically different. However, problems emerge when one endorses functionalism while promoting cognitive neuroscience. Which theoretical foundations permit the physical brain not to matter, but also to matter, at the same time?

The philosophy of science uses functional analysis to answer this question (Cummins, 1983). Functional analysis explains agents as organized systems of functions. Each function is broken down into sub-functions. A functional analysis becomes explanatory by describing physical causes of its simplest functions.

Functional analysis proposes an approach to scientific explanation different from the one used by behaviorism and permits cognitive psychology's four different approaches to be related. However, cognitive psychology textbooks rarely mention the philosophy of science. In short, students do not understand cognitive psychology's theoretical foundations because the foundations are not presented in the discipline's texts.

Why has cognitive psychology reached this state? When cognitive psychology arose, it constantly defended attacks against its core assumptions. Cognitive psychologists were forced to justify their approach. However, after vanquishing behaviorism, cognitive psychology has not faced serious challenges from competing schools of thought. Thus, it is complacent about its theoretical foundations.

In this book, I explore those foundations to address cognitive psychology's complacency. The book takes a historical perspective but is not a history. It examines classic studies in cognitive psychology because the assumptions underlying classic studies arose while cognitive psychology actively defended its foundations against behaviorism.

As a result, this book offers a different treatment of cognitive psychology. If you want to survey cognitive psychology's topics, then read a different book, such as a modern survey text. However, my hope is that, if you read this book first, you will better understand traditional topics presented in survey texts.

An older anti-survey text, Richard Mayer's *Thinking and Problem Solving: An Introduction to Human Cognition and Learning* (1977), inspired my work in this book. Each chapter in Mayer's wonderfully short book explores a different assumption about cognition (e.g., thinking as hypothesis testing, or as restructuring problems, or as searching semantic memory, or as information processing). Each chapter then shows how core assumptions are revealed in experimental studies.

Inspired by Mayer, I answer in this book the question "What is cognitive psychology?" by examining the theoretical foundations of cognitive psychology as follows.

Cognitive psychology assumes that cognition is information processing. Chapter 1 uses formal games to introduce information processing and describes similar processing in computers. Thus, Chapter 1 relates computer science to cognitive psychology.

Cognitive psychologists explain cognition in the same manner that computer scientists explain programs. However, cognitive psychologists cannot directly observe cognitive processes. Chapter 2 therefore describes methods for inferring unobservable processes and relates general experimental psychology to cognitive psychology.

Behaviorists criticized cognitive psychology's mentalistic theories as providing descriptions, not explanations. Chapter 3 describes a different approach, functional analysis, to show how mentalistic theories can explain. The chapter discusses how such analysis affects cognitive psychology's methods. Thus, Chapter 3 relates the philosophy of science to cognitive psychology.

The first three chapters introduce cognitive psychology's theoretical foundations by relating cognitive psychology to computer science, to experimental psychology, and to the philosophy of science. These foundations do not restrict cognitive psychology's variety. Chapter 4 describes a diversity of cognitive theories and relates them to the primary goal of functional analysis: identifying primitive functions, called the cognitive architecture. Thus, Chapter 4 illustrates how the ideas detailed in earlier chapters lead to competing theories, all of which seek the cognitive architecture.

Cognitive psychology not only permits competing architectural ideas but also allows many debates about its theoretical foundations. Chapter 5 introduces those debates. Each section explores a foundational question. Thus, Chapter 5 uses debates about core assumptions to reflect on cognitive psychology's current state.

These five chapters introduce cognitive psychology by examining its theoretical foundations. The book introduces cognitive psychology to undergraduates but should also interest graduate students and established cognitive psychologists.

What is cognitive psychology? The book offers a definition that recognizes that theoretical foundations affect methodology: *cognitive psychology is the branch of general psychology that explains psychological phenomena by using functional analysis to describe information processing.*

To understand this definition, we must first understand cognitive psychology's theoretical foundations. To begin, let us consider what "cognition is information processing" means.

What Is Information Processing?

Many scientists use mechanical analogies to achieve insights. For example, imagining the universe as a clock drove the scientific revolution. Similarly, imagining the heart as a pump helped in understanding the circulatory system. According to 18th-century philosopher Giambatisto Vico's (1710/1988) *certum quod factum* principle, "one is certain only of what one builds." Vico's principle explains the utility of mechanical analogies. We understand clocks or pumps because humans invented them. Well-understood mechanical analogies help us to gain new understanding of the world. Cognitive psychologists also use a mechanical analogy to guide the study of human cognition: thinking is imagined as being similar to how computers process information. Our understanding of computers, another human invention, makes the analogy fruitful. In this chapter, I introduce the computer analogy by reviewing the basic properties of information processing. The chapter relates information processing to board games. It then describes a simple information processor called a Turing machine. The chapter then relates the Turing machine to modern electronic computers, whose power attracts cognitive psychologists to the computer analogy. The chapter ends by claiming that the computer analogy shapes the methods that cognitive psychologists use to study human cognition.

1.1 Formal Games

Cognitive psychologists believe that human thinking is information processing. What does "information processing" mean? To provide an answer, let's explore the parallels between information processing and chess. We play chess on a board divided into an 8x8 pattern of alternating light and dark squares. Figure 1-1 illustrates a chess board labelled with a coordinate system.

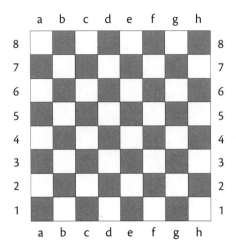

Figure 1-1 A chess board along with the coordinate system used to label its squares. Each row is labelled with a number, and each column is labelled with a letter.

Playing chess involves moving chess pieces, or *tokens*, on the chess board. One player, White, uses light-coloured tokens. The other player, Black, uses dark-coloured tokens. Chess uses six different token *types*. Each type has a different name and a distinctive shape. Figure 1-2 shows the token types available to both players.

King   Queen   Rook   Bishop   Knight   Pawn

Figure 1-2 The different chess tokens available for Black (top row) and for White (bottom row).

Different rules govern different token types in chess; rules define a token's possible moves. To know how to move a particular token, a player must identify the token as belonging to a particular type (Queen, Rook, etc.). Chess is a *formal game* because a player identifies a token's type by examining the token's shape or *form*. For example, Figure 1-3 shows the eight squares to which White's King on square d5 could move. Importantly, the eight possible moves presume that a King, and not some other type, is on d5.

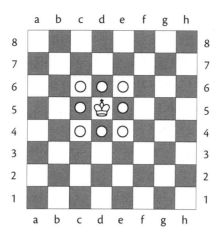

Figure 1-3 The white circles indicate eight squares to which the King at d5 could move.

If the token on d5 belongs to a different type, then different rules apply. Figure 1-4 shows the squares to which a Knight could move from d5.

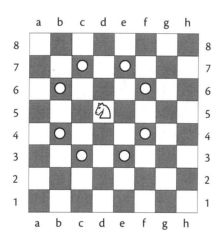

Figure 1-4 The white circles indicate eight squares to which the Knight at d5 could move. Compare Figure 1-4 with the possible moves of the King provided in Figure 1-3.

After the chess pieces are placed on their starting squares (Figure 1-5), a game begins when White moves one token to a different square. Black replies by moving one of her pieces.

Figure 1-5 The configuration of the chess pieces before a game begins.

Figure 1-6 presents the chess board's state after both players make three moves in a game. White has moved a Pawn, a Knight, and a Bishop. Black has moved a Knight and two Pawns. The only differences between Figure 1-6 and Figure 1-5 are chess token positions.

Figure 1-6 The chess piece positions in an example game after both players make three different moves.

In chess, a player can remove a token from the board. If a player moves a token to a square already occupied by the opponent's token, then the opponent's token is captured. A captured piece disappears from the board. Capturing a piece is illustrated in Figure 1-7. With her fourth move, White moves the Bishop from b5 to c6 to capture Black's Knight already on c6; that Knight vanishes from Figure 1-7.

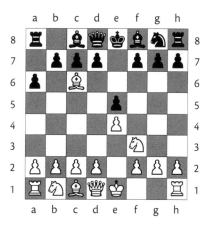

Figure 1-7 The Bishop at b5 in Figure 1-6 moves to c6, capturing the Knight at c6 in Figure 1-6.

Black responds by using her Pawn at d7 in Figure 1-7 to capture the Bishop at c6, producing the chess board shown in Figure 1-8. Note that the chess board in Figure 1-8 has two fewer pieces than the one in Figure 1-5.

Figure 1-8 The arrangement of chess tokens after Black's fourth move, the capture of White's Bishop by Black's Pawn.

How does chess relate to information processing? Information processing involves manipulating symbols stored in memory. A chess board is an example of memory. The chess board illustrated in Figure 1-1 is an empty memory, holding no tokens.

An information processing system also uses a finite set of tokens, or a finite alphabet of symbols, for storing in memory. In chess, the tokens for storage—for placing on the board—are illustrated in Figure 1-2.

An information processor uses operations to manipulate symbols in memory. One operation adds a new symbol to memory. In our chess example, this operation is illustrated in Figure 1-5; to create the chess game's starting positions, 32 different chess tokens appear in Figure 1-1's empty memory. The "add a token" operation executes 32 different times.

A second operation rearranges symbols by moving a token from one memory location to another. Figure 1-6 demonstrates how chess piece positions change after each player makes three different moves. Each move causes a token to change its location from one square to another; each move rearranges symbols on the chess board memory. Restrictions apply to token rearrangement in memory. Different rules apply to different token types (Figures 1-3 and 1-4). An information processing system must distinguish one token type from another to determine which rules can be applied.

A third operation deletes a symbol from memory. Figures 1-7 and 1-8 illustrate a token's removal from the board after being captured.

A fourth operation changes a token from one type to another. We could use this operation to describe capturing a piece. For example, when Black's Pawn captures White's Bishop at c6 in Figure 1-7 to produce Figure 1-8, two different operations occur. First, we delete Black's Pawn at d7. Second, we change White's Bishop at c6 into a different token, Black's Pawn.

The chess example illustrates two properties of any information processor: a *data structure*, which is a memory for storing different types of symbols, and a set of *rules* or operations used to manipulate the symbols in the data structure. Another basic property is *control*. Control determines "what to do next." At any given moment, an information processor must choose which rule to apply and which symbol to manipulate. Control permits an information processor to apply its rules in a particular order to accomplish a task.

Chess also involves control. In chess, we try to defeat an opponent by capturing her King. Chess players range in ability from mere amateurs to grandmasters and world champions. What makes a grandmaster better than an amateur? The grandmaster has superior control—she makes better decisions about what move to make next.

How does a grandmaster make better decisions about the moves to make in a chess game? She has more knowledge about playing chess and uses it to make better decisions about which move to make next by predicting her opponent's next moves, by identifying weaknesses in her opponent's position, and so on.

However, we are not immediately concerned with such details. For now, we need only understand that an information processor has three basic components: a data structure, rules for manipulating the symbols stored in the data structure, and a control procedure for deciding which rule to apply to the data structure. Chess illustrates the three components. Information processing is rule-governed symbol manipulation; it is like playing a formal game.

1.2 Form and Function

The Figure 1-2 chess pieces represent the Staunton design. In a Staunton chess set, Rooks look like castle towers, Knights look like horses, and Bishops, Queens, and Kings all have distinctive hats or crowns. However, many alternatives to the Staunton design exist. Some designs use cartoon or *Sesame Street* characters or American Civil War figures. Chess pieces can also be made from wood, plastic, stone, or other materials.

The many chess piece designs illustrate a *many-to-one relationship*. In a many-to-one relationship, many (seemingly) different things all belong to the same type. For instance, one type of chess token—the King—could resemble a Staunton piece with a crown, Abraham Lincoln, or Homer Simpson. We could also construct the King from many different materials. Yet the King's different shapes, built from different materials, belong to one type: the King.

How, then, do we define the chess King? We cannot define the King as a specific form in a particular chess set or the material from which it is built. To do so would rule out possible Kings. For example, defining a King as a wooden Staunton piece ignores the possibility that the King could take another shape or be built from another material. In short, we cannot define a King using *physical* properties; such definitions restrict us too much. Instead, we must define a King by its *function* in a chess game. A functional definition focuses on what something does, not on its physical properties. In chess, a King is the token to which the King's rules apply (Figure 1-3). Functional definitions permit assigning chess pieces of different shapes or materials to the same type, having the same function in a game.

We almost always explain information processors functionally, not physically. Cognitive psychologists liken human thinking to a computer running a program. What makes such an analogy possible given physical differences between brains and computers? The analogy works by being functional, not physical. Like different designs for chess pieces, brains and computers can perform identical functions even while being built from different materials.

1.3 The Formalist's Motto

Processing information is playing a formal game. A chess game's characteristics illustrate information processing's core properties. However, playing chess and processing information differ on one key property. Useful information processors manipulate *representations*—symbols with meanings, symbols referring to things in the world. Information processing conveys new meanings by creating new symbol combinations. Formal games do not.

Chess tokens do not represent meanings. A chess move has no content because chess pieces do not represent anything; formal chess moves depend only on token shapes. Chess piece positions do not communicate meanings.

To distinguish an information processor's formal properties from its meanings, we borrow two words from linguistics. Linguists use the word *syntax* to describe a sentence's grammatical structure. Syntax is a set of rules for distinguishing grammatical sentences from ungrammatical sentences. The rules governing token movements in a formal game are analogous to a syntax.

In contrast, linguists use the word *semantics* to describe a sentence's meaning. Claiming that a symbol has meaning is claiming that a symbol stands for something else; a symbol refers to something in the world. For instance, the string of letters *dog* is meaningful because it represents or stands for a particular animal in the world. When a symbol represents meaning by referring to something in the world, we call the symbol *intentional*.

Philosopher Franz Brentano (1874/1995) used intentionality to distinguish the physical from the mental. For Brentano, mental states could be intentional, but physical states could not, separating syntax from semantics. Consider linguist Noam Chomsky's famous example "Colorless green ideas sleep furiously," a meaningless sentence with proper syntax. Meaningless sentences can still be grammatical.

Separating syntax from semantics makes mechanical information processing possible. Information processors manipulate symbols using formal operations;

information processors do not understand what symbols mean. However, formal operations can be meaningful.

Although chess tokens do not have meanings, symbols used in other formal systems do. For example, mathematics uses formal rules to manipulate symbols. But mathematical symbols represent meanings. Engineers manipulate symbols to determine whether a bridge will stand, or whether an airplane will fly, using symbols to represent real-world properties such as force, gravity, or mass. Logic also manipulates meaningful symbols. In logic, a symbol represents a real-world property's truth or falsehood.

Mathematical or logical operations, though meaningful, do not themselves understand what symbols mean, for they are as formal as the rules governing chess. For example, one rule in mathematics permits replacing the string $x + x + x$ with the string $3x$ but does not know x's value or what x represents. The rule only requires recognizing symbol shapes (e.g., x, +) to permit symbols to be manipulated in a particular way.

Amazingly, mathematical operations preserve meanings. For instance, the preceding example of replacing one set of symbols with another ($x + x + x = 3x$) operates without knowing what x means. However, in the real world, whatever x is, when added to itself three times, the result will be three times its value. The formal operation preserves meanings, even though it does not understand them.

Philosopher John Haugeland (1985) notes that a symbol in an information processing system possesses dual properties. One property is the symbol's shape or form, which permits the symbol to be manipulated by formal operations. The other property is the symbol's meaning. Haugeland points out that information processing systems are powerful because their formal operations on symbols—operations not sensitive to meaning—still preserve meaning and therefore can produce new meanings. Haugeland summarizes this notion in *the formalist's motto*: take care of the syntax, and the semantics will take care of itself.

The formalist's motto makes modern information processors, such as computers, possible. Basic information processing operations provide a formal syntax for manipulating symbols. The syntax works independently of what the symbols represent. However, the syntax preserves the meanings of symbols, making modern computers useful information processing devices.

1.4 Demonstrating the Formalist's Motto

The formalist's motto claims that information processors formally manipulate symbols, but still preserve meanings, even without understanding what symbols represent. We will now consider one example to illustrate the formalist's motto.

In the 1930s, mathematician Alan Turing (1936) proposed an idea now known as a *Turing machine*. A Turing machine is a very basic information processing device with two different components (Figure 1-9). The first is an infinitely long *ticker tape* memory. The tape is divided into a series of individual cells. Each cell can only contain a single symbol. The ticker tape cells in Figure 1-9 contain a 0, a 1, or a B (for blank).

A Turing machine's second component is a *machine head* for manipulating the symbols on the ticker tape. The machine head includes methods for moving along the tape (one cell at a time), for reading the symbol in the current cell, and for writing a symbol into the current cell. The machine head also includes a register to indicate its current physical condition or *machine state*. Finally, the

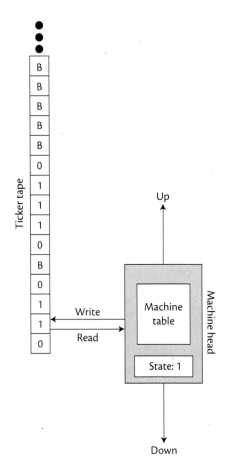

Figure 1-9 A Turing machine's basic components.

machine head contains operations, the *machine table*, for manipulating the ticker tape's contents.

To use a Turing machine, we ask a question by writing some symbols on the ticker tape. The symbols on the Figure 1-9 tape provide an example question. Next, we place the machine head at a starting cell on the ticker tape, and we assign a starting machine state. The starting cell for the Figure 1-9 machine head is the lowest cell containing a 1, and the starting machine state is 1. Finally, we activate the machine, which starts to read and write symbols on the tape, moving along the tape one cell at a time. Eventually, the machine halts. When halted, the symbols written by the machine on the tape give the machine's answer to the original question.

How does the machine head manipulate the symbols on the ticker tape? The machine head contains formal operations. The machine reads the symbol from the current cell on the tape, noting the current machine state. Combined, the symbol and the machine state tell the machine which operation to perform. At each processing step, the Figure 1-9 machine writes a symbol (0, 1, or B) to the tape or moves one cell up or down.

Table 1-1 contains one special instruction. If the machine head reads a 0 while in State 6, then the Turing machine executes an operation called HALT. When HALT occurs, the tape holds the Turing machine's answer to the original question. Figure 1-10 shows the Turing machine's answer to the question shown on the tape in Figure 1-9.

A Turing machine's information processing behaviour does not require understanding what the ticker tape's symbols represent. The interested reader can confirm this by starting with the Turing machine as laid out in Figure 1-9 and then following the machine table's steps. The reader—like the Turing machine itself—can produce the Figure 1-10 ticker tape without knowing what the tape's symbols mean. What question does the tape hold in Figure 1-9? What answer does the tape hold in Figure 1-10? If the reader can pretend to be the machine, but cannot answer such questions, then she has acted as a formal system.

Importantly, the ticker tape contents in Figures 1-9 and 1-10 are meaningful. In both figures, the tapes represent integer values by placing a certain number of 1s between two 0s. The integer 2 is coded "0110," the integer 3 is coded "01110," and so on. A tape can hold more than one integer, separating different integers with a blank cell.

Knowing the tape's encoding, we see that the ticker tape in Figure 1-9 represents two different integers (2 and 3) and that the ticker tape in Figure 1-10 represents a single integer (5). The Table 1-1 machine table provides instructions for adding two

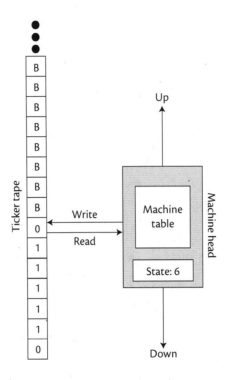

Figure 1-10 The state of the Figure 1-9 Turing machine when the machine head executes HALT.

integers together. Thus, the question in Figure 1-9 is "What is the sum of 2 and 3?," and the machine's answer in Figure 1-10 is "The sum is 5."

Our example Turing machine operates without understanding ticker tape meanings. But the Table 1-1 operations preserve meaning and will correctly add any two integers written on the tape. The Turing machine takes care of the syntax only, while the ticker tape's semantics takes care of itself.

1.5 A Universal Machine

The Turing machine in Section 1.4 performs only one task: summing up two integers. It does not solve any other information processing problems. A specialist, the Turing machine accomplishes only one thing.

Many other specialist Turing machines can exist. For example, one machine might (only) subtract one integer from another. Another machine might (only)

Table 1-1 A machine table for the Turing machine in Figure 1-9

Current State	Symbol Read	Write	Move	Next State
1	B	1		6
1	0	B		2
1	1		UP	1
2	B		UP	2
2	0	B		3
3	B		UP	3
3	0	B		4
3	1	B		5
4	B		DOWN	4
4	1		UP	6
5	B		DOWN	5
5	1		UP	1
6	B	0		6
6	0		HALT	6
6	1		UP	3

Note: B represents a blank cell.

multiply two integers together. To create a different Turing machine, we must create a different machine table to take the place of Table 1-1. Every specialist Turing machine has its own distinct machine table.

However, we can create a general information processor. Consider a reader pretending to be the Turing machine in Section 1.4. If that section provided a different machine table, then the reader could pretend to be the different machine as well, by following any instructions like those in Table 1-1. Therefore, she could pretend to be any Turing machine. She would be a generalist, not a specialist.

In the 1930s, Turing designed a Turing machine pretending to be any other Turing machine, called the *universal Turing machine*, which operates like the reader who uses Table 1-1 to simulate the Figure 1-9 machine. A universal machine's ticker tape holds different information (Figure 1-11). One part of the tape holds data—where one writes the to-be-answered question. Another part describes the Turing machine that the universal machine pretends to be. A third part serves as a temporary memory or scratchpad.

When observing a universal Turing machine behave, we might recognize that it operates like a reader who simulates Table 1-1. The universal machine's machine head moves back and forth between the data on the ticker tape and the machine description on the ticker tape. The universal machine reads a data symbol, goes to the machine description to find out what to do to the symbol,

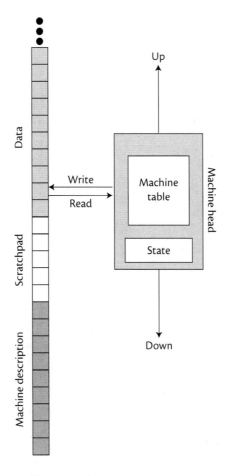

Figure 1-11 A universal Turing machine.

and then goes back to the data to perform the operation. The scratchpad remembers important information (e.g., the current machine state of the device that it is pretending to be). Eventually, the universal machine will HALT, with the answer to the question written on the ticker tape region for holding data.

However, the universal Turing machine does not understand the ticker tape's meaning and does not know that the ticker tape holds different information at different places. A universal Turing machine is purely formal, and it works like any other Turing machine by reading a symbol, noting the current machine state, and picking an operation from the machine table. The operation will involve either writing a symbol or moving along the tape, and it will determine the machine head's next state.

In short, a universal Turing machine also illustrates the formalist's motto. With respect to syntax (formal operations), a universal Turing machine is just another Turing machine. With respect to semantics (the interpretation of its behaviour), a universal Turing machine simulates another machine described on the ticker tape.

Importantly, the universal Turing machine changes behaviour without needing its own machine table to be altered. To change the behaviour of the universal Turing machine, we simply write a new machine description on the ticker tape. A universal Turing machine's ability to simulate any other Turing machine also means that it is an exceptionally powerful information processor. A universal Turing machine can answer any formally expressed question. It can answer any question that a modern computer can answer.

1.6 Why Is the Turing Machine Important?

The Turing machine was one of the 20th century's most important ideas. In mathematics, the Turing machine was important because its computational power originated from simple operations (Section 1.5). Therefore, it could be included in mathematical proofs because its mechanisms were simple and non-controversial (Hodges, 1983).

The Turing machine was central to proving that some mathematical statements are undecidable (Turing, 1936). For an undecidable statement, no method exists to decide whether the statement is true or false. For such a problem, a Turing machine never HALTs; instead, it enters an infinite loop. Turing's proof revolutionized the field because, prior to Turing, most mathematicians believed that all mathematical statements were decidable.

Created to be used in mathematical proofs, the Turing machine affected other fields as well. It provided the essential foundation for modern computers. The

Turing machine's core components (Figure 1-11) describe the basic properties of computers: a data structure, a basic set of operations, and a method of control.

The modern computer behaves like a Turing machine but far more efficiently. For instance, modern computers use random access memory, permitting immediate access to symbols stored anywhere in memory. A Turing machine accesses memory far less efficiently and must move through a sequence of tape cells to obtain information from a different memory location.

Although modern computers solve problems faster than Turing machines, they are not more powerful. Modern computers cannot answer any question that a universal Turing machine cannot also answer. The Turing machine's power—the breadth of questions that it can answer—explains its impact on studying cognition.

A Turing machine can solve some psychologically interesting information processing problems. For example, a Turing machine can determine whether a symbol string written on the ticker tape is grammatical or not. One example of such behaviour comes from studying an extremely simple-looking artificial grammar (Bever et al., 1968). Sentences from the grammar contain only two different "words": a and b. The grammar that Bever et al. studied was $b^N a b^N$, where N gives the number of b's in the string. According to this grammar, strings such as a, bab, and $bbabb$ are grammatical, but strings such as ab, $babb$, bbb, and $bbabbb$ are not. A string is grammatical only if the same number of b's appear before and after the a.

Bever et al.'s (1968) grammar exhibits embedded clauses: each b before the a is paired with another b after the a. A Turing machine can evaluate grammaticality if strings contain embedded clauses. Humans can as well because natural human languages have embedded clauses. We know that in the sentence "The dog who did not like cats who liked mice ran" the verb *ran* is associated with the noun *dog* because of our ability to process embedded clauses.

Less powerful information processors, such as the *finite state automaton*, cannot deal with embedded clauses in grammars. A finite state automaton is like a Turing machine because it processes a ticker tape with a machine head. However, a finite state automaton can only read symbols, cannot write to the tape, and can only move in one direction along the tape. It reacts to each symbol that it reads: the machine state represents the reaction. When the finite state automaton reaches the end of the question, it stops; its final state represents the answer to the question.

A finite state automaton cannot judge whether symbol strings were generated by a grammar such as $b^N a b^N$ (Bever et al., 1968). Because the device cannot move in both directions along the tape, it cannot track the pairings of b's that define embedded clauses. Thus, if human cognition is information processing, then cognitive operations must be like those performed by a Turing machine and not like those of a finite state automaton. Processing the embedded clauses of human grammar, for instance, cannot be accomplished by simpler information processors. When cognitivists assume that "cognition is information processing," they also assume that cognition can be described with a universal Turing machine.

1.7 The Modern Computer

Turing proposed the Turing machine as a hypothetical device to include in mathematical proofs. The Turing machine was never intended to be built; its simplicity made it impractical. However, the Turing machine inspired a more practical device, the digital computer, developed to meet the challenges of the Second World War.

British engineer Tommy Flowers built the first electronic computer, Colossus, in 1943. Colossus deciphered encoded German military messages. In 1946, John Mauchly and J. Presper Eckert created the first American electronic computer (ENIAC) at the University of Pennsylvania; ENIAC created artillery firing tables for the United States Army.

In 1951, the world saw the first commercial computers. The University of Manchester received the first, the Ferranti Mark I, in February. Soon after the University of Toronto purchased a similar machine. The advent of commercial computers permitted researchers to explore which problems computers could solve (Boden, 1977; Feigenbaum & Feldman, 1963; Hofstadter, 1979; McCorduck, 1979; Nilsson, 2010).

Early research focused on programming computers to play board games such as chess or checkers. Formal games provided ideal test cases for exploring machine intelligence. As we have seen, the rules for formal games are simple, but they can create complex game situations to challenge even the best human players. If computers could play high-level chess or checkers, then perhaps machines could achieve human-like intelligence.

The first successful game-playing programs appeared in the early 1950s (Samuel, 1959). Arthur Samuel developed the first checkers program in 1952. By 1955, his program could learn to improve performance by playing against itself. His program would eventually become a good, but not an expert, player.

Four decades later the Chinook program developed at the University of Alberta by Johnathan Schaeffer became the world checkers champion (Schaeffer et al., 1992; Schaeffer et al., 1995; Schaeffer et al., 1993). In 1994, Chinook defeated the reigning human champion, Dr. Marion Tinsley. Similar stories can be told about computers playing other formal games. IBM's Deep Blue defeated world chess champion Gary

Kasparov in a match in 1997 (Campbell et al., 2002). Google's AlphaGo defeated world go champion Lee Sedol in 2016.

Computers also produced intelligent behaviour outside the realm of games. In the mid-1950s, Herbert Simon, Allan Newell, and John Shaw created a program, the logic theorist, for developing logical proofs (Newell & Simon, 1956). It successfully derived 38 proofs in Russell and Whitehead's *Principia Mathematica*. An undergraduate class taught by Simon in 1956, attended by artificial intelligence pioneer Edward Feigenbaum, was told that, "over Christmas, Allan Newell and I invented a thinking machine" (Grier, 2013, p. 74). Simon was talking about the logic theorist.

Many early computer scientists believed that intelligent machines were inevitable. Alan Turing wrote a landmark paper in 1950 to propose how to identify machine intelligence. Two decades into the 21st century, we live in the age of intelligent machines. Computers perform many complex tasks. Banks rely on artificial intelligence to decide about investments and fraud protection. Computers—including our smartphones—translate the spoken word into text. Security systems identify objects and recognize faces. Medical programs diagnose diseases and process huge amounts of patient data. Most domains of human life come into contact with computer programs performing tasks that seemingly require intelligence.

Yet modern computers are formal symbol manipulators no different in kind from Turing machines. Clearly, the formal manipulation of symbols permits machines to behave intelligently. As a result, many researchers believe that symbol manipulation also underlies human intelligence. Perhaps brains perform operations similar to those performed by computers.

1.8 Explaining How Computers Process Information

Cognitive psychology adopts a key working hypothesis: human thinking involves formal operations like those of chess, Turing machines, and electronic computers. Thus, explanations of human cognition will be similar to explanations of computers. How do we explain a computer's information processing?

We explain computers at different levels of analysis (Chomsky, 1957; Marr, 1982; Pylyshyn, 1984). Each level involves asking a different question and then using a distinct method to answer the question. The most abstract is the *computational level of analysis*. At the computational level, we answer the question "What information processing problem is the computer solving?" Typically, we express answers to computational questions as proofs, using formal methods such as mathematics and logic.

For example, consider the Section 1.4 Turing machine, which—like any other Turing machine—receives a question and then produces an answer. The computational level of analysis defines which question is being answered. Computational accounts define the mapping from the initial question to the final answer.

The computational level of analysis expresses explanations using mathematics or logic because of a many-to-one relationship. Many different question-answer pairings all belong to the same information processing problem. For instance, $2 + 3 = 5$, $1 + 6 = 7$, $4 + 9 = 11$, and so on all involve calculating integer sums. In fact, an infinite number of different examples of adding integers exist; the Turing machine of Section 1.4 could handle each and every one.

Rather than providing an infinitely long list of question-answer pairings, computational explanations are far more compact. For instance, the Section 1.4 Turing machine deletes the string 0B0 separating the 1's of the two integers on the initial tape and then moves all the symbols down three cells to fill in these three deleted values, creating a single integer (the sum of the original two). Describing the machine in this way proves that it adds two integers; the proof provides a computational account of the Turing machine.

A second approach examines a computer at the *algorithmic level of analysis*. An algorithm or program is a sequence of operations for accomplishing a task. An algorithmic account of a computer explains its behaviour by describing the program being executed. The computer behaves one way when executing a word processing program, but it behaves differently when executing a web browser program. An algorithmic account of a universal machine would focus on the "machine description" on the ticker tape, which serves as the program that the universal machine is executing. If we change the machine description on the tape, then the universal Turing machine's behaviour will change.

A third approach to explaining a computer occurs at the *architectural level of analysis*. The architecture consists of the properties built into a computer to process information. Architectural accounts answer questions such as "What serves as the device's memory?" "Which symbols can the device store?" "Which basic operations manipulate symbols?" "How are these basic operations selected?" An architectural account of a universal Turing machine would focus on symbols on the ticker tape, on possible machine states, and on machine table contents.

We call a computer's architecture *primitive* because the architecture belongs to the machine's physical structure. Later we will see that identifying an architecture—an information processor's primitives—converts cognitive descriptions into cognitive explanations.

Physical properties bring a computer's architecture into being. As a result, the *implementational level of analysis* provides a fourth approach to explaining a computer. An implementational account explains how the computer's physical properties create primitive information processing properties (the architecture). How do physical mechanisms produce the primitive operations used to manipulate symbols?

In summary, we can explain a computer at four different levels of analysis: implementational, architectural, algorithmic, and computational. A complete explanation requires appealing to each level: explaining which problem is being solved, which algorithm is being used, which basic operations make up the algorithm, and which physical mechanisms bring primitive operations to life. When we assume human cognition to be information processing, human information processing must be explained in a similar fashion. Cognitive psychologists try to explain human cognition in the same way that computer scientists explain computers.

1.9 A Hierarchy of Levels

The different types of analysis for explaining information processors are hierarchically organized; a many-to-one relationship exists from one level to the level above it (Dawson, 1998, 2013).

A many-to-one relationship exists from the algorithmic level to the computational level. Different algorithms can solve the same problem. Consider calculating the product of two integers, x and y. One algorithm adds x to itself y different times. A different algorithm computes the logarithm of x, computes the logarithm of y, adds the two logarithms together, and takes the antilogarithm of the sum. Both algorithms determine the product of x and y but are very different from one another.

Another many-to-one relationship exists from the architectural level to the algorithmic level. Different architectures can run the same algorithm. Imagine multiplying two integers together using the logarithmic algorithm described above. The algorithm could be carried out by the specialized machine table of Turing machine Z. But a Turing machine with a very different architecture could execute the same algorithm: the universal Turing machine simulating Turing machine Z.

Finally, a many-to-one relationship exists from the implementational level to the architectural level. Different physical mechanisms can bring the same architecture to life. Consider constructing an architecture to define a particular Turing machine. We might imagine an architecture with an electromechanical tape head for processing a paper ticker tape. But other physical designs are possible. Turing machines have been constructed from LEGO, Meccano, wood, and toy train sets (Ferrari, 2006; Stewart, 1994).

Figure 1-12 illustrates the many-to-one relationships between levels, showing that one architecture can be implemented by many different physical implementations, many different architectures can be used to program one algorithm, and many different algorithms can carry out the same computation.

When we explain information processing, we must consider relationships between levels. Explanations must detail how particular operations are primitive, how operations are organized to create an algorithm, and how the algorithm solves an information processing problem. Comparisons between two systems (e.g., between a computer simulation and a human subject) must also be made at different levels. Do the two systems solve the same problem? Do the two systems use the same algorithm? Do the two systems use the same architecture?

However, comparing systems at the implementational level is not a priority. Provided that two systems bring the same architecture into being, we need not worry whether they do so with different physical mechanisms, provided that we endorse

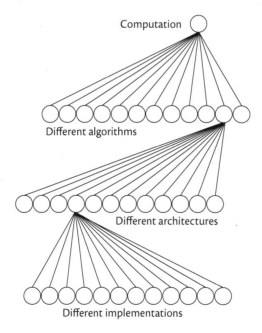

Figure 1-12 An illustration of the various many-to-one relationships between different levels of analysis.

functionalism (Section 1.2). Indeed, computer simulations of cognition make sense only when we ignore implementational differences between computers and brains.

1.10 Explaining Human Cognition

Computers use formal operations to manipulate symbols stored in data structures. Computers preserve meanings, or create new meanings, even though formal operations ignore what symbols represent. Computers bring the formalist's motto to life by taking care of the syntax while letting the semantics of symbols take care of itself.

Cognitive psychologists assume that they can explain human cognition just as we would explain a computer's information processing. How do we explain a computer? We could detail the properties of its data structures, of its basic operations, and of its control. When we assume that cognition is computation, we must assume that the same approach can be applied to human thinking. Alternatively, we could examine a computer at multiple levels: computational, algorithmic, architectural, and implementational. Cognitivists believe that human cognition can be explained at these different levels.

However, there is an important difference between computers and humans, making human cognition much harder to explain.

Consider asking a programmer to add new features to a computer program. Computers have operations to permit the programmer to see a program's properties. The programmer can list the program's steps or examine the data files that the program processes. In other words, the programmer can directly observe the computer's information processing.

Psychologists cannot examine human cognition in the same fashion. For a cognitive psychologist, a human participant is a *black box*. Researchers can directly observe stimuli presented to a participant as well as a participant's responses. However, cognitive psychologists cannot *directly* observe internal processes of converting stimuli into responses. These psychologists assume that human thinking is rule-governed symbol manipulation but cannot directly observe human information processing's data structures, operations, or control.

In response, cognitive psychologists design clever experiments to permit them to observe subtle relationships between stimuli and responses. Armed with such data, they *infer* the properties of the information processing that cannot be directly observed. Cognitive psychologists create models of human information processing and use the fine details of experimental data to validate their models. Chapter 2 introduces the reader to this research strategy.

1.11 Chapter Summary

According to Vico's *certum quod factum* principle, we are only "certain of what we build." Science exploits Vico's principle by using the properties of well-understood human devices to illuminate less-understood phenomena. For instance, cognitive psychologists treat thinking as analogous to the operations carried out by computers. They hope that the well-understood properties of computers will help us to understand human cognition. Computer performance fuels their hope because computers can perform many tasks that ordinarily require human intelligence.

If computers can produce intelligent behaviour, then computer-like operations might provide the foundation for human intelligence. Thus, cognitive psychologists assume that cognition is computation, where "computation" is rule-governed symbol manipulation.

To explain a computer's information processing, we could detail data structures, basic operations, and control. We could also examine a computer at multiple levels of analysis. What information processing problem is being solved? Which algorithm is used to solve the problem? What are the operations used by the algorithm? Which mechanisms bring the operations into being?

Cognitive psychologists aim to explain human cognition the same way. What are the properties of the data structures, operations, and control of human cognition? How can we explain human cognition at the four different levels of analysis?

However, cognitive psychologists encounter a difficult problem when answering such questions. Unlike computer programmers, cognitive psychologists cannot directly observe the core properties of human information processing. Instead, they can only observe stimulus-response relationships mediated by human information processing. Clever experiments must be designed to permit cognitive psychologists to infer information processing details from observable behaviour.

We can now explore the research strategies used by cognitive psychologists. Chapter 2 provides example experiments conducted by cognitive psychologists to support the assumption that cognition is computation. With these examples in hand, Chapter 3 introduces the philosophical foundations of theories of human cognition.

Inferring Cognitive Processes

Cognitive psychologists view cognition as information processing: rule-governed symbol manipulation. The information processing assumption is attractive because symbol manipulating machines—digital computers—can produce intelligent behaviours. Why else might we assume that cognition is information processing? In this chapter, I explore this question by introducing some research methods invented during cognitive psychology's early years. Cognitive psychologists observe how various manipulations affect human behaviour and then infer properties of human information processing. Cognitive psychologists infer such properties without directly observing internal processing. Chapter 2's examples demonstrate the use of psychological experiments both to defend and to elaborate the information processing hypothesis. The chapter's examples provide a focus on cognitive psychology's early studies of human memory, which permitted inferences about different kinds of memories and their properties. Each memory uses different symbols, manipulates symbols with different processes, and uses different methods of control for deciding the order in which to execute processes.

2.1 Using Symbols

Do humans differ from animals and machines? Many scholars argue that humans are special because they use mental representations, a view rooted in 17th-century philosophy. Descartes (1637/1960) argued that only humans possess a soul or consciousness, and the soul's essence is only to think. His notion of thinking resembles modern information processing. Modern echoes of Descartes are easily found. Bronowski writes that "man is distinguished from other animals by his imaginative gifts" (1973, p. 20). Bertalanffy argues that "symbolism, if you will, is the divine spark distinguishing the poorest specimen of true man from the most perfectly adapted animal" (1967, p. 36).

Modern computers refute using symbols to grant humans special status. We live in an age in which the difference between humans and machines has become blurred. Perhaps we should consider the advantages provided by representations not only for humans but also for animals or machines.

Philosopher Karl Popper (1978) proposed that representations aid survival. Thinking permits actions to be modelled, evaluated, and discarded *before* being performed so that humans do not rashly undertake dangerous acts. For Popper, reasoning allows our hypotheses to die in our place. Cognitive psychology also presumes that *planning* plays a critical role in cognition. Cognitive psychologists hypothesize that humans perceive information, construct mental models of the perceived world, and then manipulate models to plan and evaluate potential actions. We call such processing the *sense-think-act cycle*.

Cognitive psychologists emphasize "thinking" in the sense-think-act cycle and treat thinking as rule-governed symbol manipulation. Earlier we considered evidence supporting the information processing assumption: information processing machines produce seemingly intelligent behaviours. What other evidence supports viewing cognition as computation, as manipulating mental representations? Chapter 2 provides several examples from cognitive psychology to illustrate how observing human behaviour supports inferences about human information processes, which we cannot observe directly.

Chapter 2 focuses on the multi-store memory model central to early cognitive psychology (Shiffrin & Atkinson, 1969; Waugh & Norman, 1965). That model explains memory as multi-stage information processing. Each stage involves a different memory store with unique properties. Properties include the symbols used to store information, how long symbols exist in the store, the capacity of the memory, how information in the memory is maintained, and how information can be transferred to another memory.

Although the multi-store memory model was important historically, many modern revisions to and elaborations of it exist (Baddeley, 1986; Conway, 1997; Eichenbaum, 2002; Tulving, 1983). If more modern memory theories exist, then why do I use older research to introduce cognitive psychology's methods?

Cognitive psychology reacted to behaviorism (Flanagan, 1984; Gardner, 1984; Leahey, 1987; Miller, 2003). Behaviorism characterized psychology as a natural science by excluding mentalistic terms from theory and by focusing on the relationships between observable stimuli and behaviours (Watson, 1913). Cognitive psychology aimed to return mentalism to experimental psychology.

The behaviorist dominance of psychology caused problems for early cognitive psychologists, who encountered difficulties publishing research in mainstream journals because editors thought that the research was too mentalistic (Mandler, 2002). Furthermore, cognitivists challenged the status quo by openly rejecting all behaviorist assumptions (Bruner, 1990; Sperry, 1993). "We were not out to 'reform' behaviorism, but to replace it" (Bruner, 1990, p. 3). To succeed in a behaviorist environment, cognitive psychologists needed methodologies to withstand intense behaviorist scrutiny. Cognitive psychology's research on memory, which produced the multi-store memory model, used methodologies tempered in the crucible of behaviorist criticism.

The multi-store memory model also adheres to a philosophy of science called functional analysis. Functional analysis defines cognitive psychology's explanatory goals and opposes the philosophy of science followed by behaviorists. I will detail the properties of functional analysis in Chapter 3 by building upon the material discussed in Chapter 2.

2.2 Partial Report and Iconic Memory

The sense-think-act cycle begins with sensing. For psychology, sensing is *transduction*—converting something from one form into another form. In cognitive psychology, sensing transduces energy received from the world into mental representations or symbols.

George Sperling (1960) conducted an early and influential study of transduction. He wanted to determine how much information could be seen in a single brief exposure. In one study, participants saw an array of letters and numbers (Figure 2-1) for a mere 50 milliseconds (ms). After the display disappeared, participants reported as many characters as possible. Participants retrieved characters from memory because the display had vanished. Sperling called his method the *whole report* condition because participants attempted to report the whole character set.

```
7  I  V  F
X  L  5  3
B  4  W  7
```

Figure 2-1 An example stimulus from Sperling's experiment.

A participant in the whole report condition recalled three or four characters. However, she also reported seeing other characters but could not recall them. A limitation prevented all items from being retrieved. For instance, the *memory traces* of the characters quickly decayed, making them unavailable for recall if participants needed a long time to report all the items.

Sperling tested this possibility with his *partial report* method. Participants in a partial report task experienced a display like that in Figure 2-1, again for only 50 ms. However, immediately after the stimulus disappeared, participants heard one of three possible sounds, each a signal about which characters to report. Participants reported only the characters in the display's bottom row (low tone), or the display's middle row (medium tone), or the display's top row (high tone). Participants knew that their task was to report a subset of display characters but did not know which subset in advance. The tone that they heard caused them to direct *attention* to the appropriate subset in memory.

In a partial report task, participants again only reported three or four characters from a row. However, because participants did not know in advance which row to report, Sperling inferred that a participant's memory held about 9 of the 12 characters. He reasoned that most of the display remained in memory because participants could retrieve three or four items from any display row. The partial report technique indicated that display memory had a larger capacity than predicted from the whole report method. Presumably, participants could report only a small number of items before the whole memory disappeared.

Sperling varied the partial report method to infer further details about the memory for brief visual displays, called *iconic memory* (Neisser, 1967). For example, Sperling delayed the tone signalling the to-be-reported row; a 1-second delay caused partial report accuracy to fall to the same level as that observed using the whole report technique. He concluded that items persisted in iconic memory for less than a second.

Other variations of the partial report method permitted Sperling to conclude that iconic memory represents the visual properties of characters. In a typical partial report condition, the display disappears by being replaced with a dark visual field. However, if the display is replaced with a bright visual field, then performance is poorer. The bright stimulus following the display erases or *masks* memory contents. Brightness masking uses a bright stimulus to erase iconic memory's contents.

Sperling also discovered that iconic memory did not encode other display character properties. He conducted a partial report experiment that cued participants to report only the letters (or the numbers) in a display. Sperling found partial report performance to be no better than whole report performance. Iconic memory represents visual properties of characters but not abstract properties such as character type. Iconic memory illustrates a *sensory register*, which holds information briefly in some sensory format (e.g., visual, auditory). Other sensory registers, such as echoic memory for auditory information, also exist (Neisser, 1967). Sensory registers represent sensory information and do not encode more abstract properties, such as character type.

Sperling's partial report method provides a pioneering example of using experimental observations to infer properties of mental representations. Sperling measured only how many characters participants could correctly report from the memory of a brief display. But he inferred many properties of iconic memory, and he described iconic memory as a high-capacity visual representation that persists for less than a second.

2.3 Primary Memory and Acoustic Confusions

To be used in the sense-think-act-cycle, information must persist for a longer duration than is offered by iconic memory. Psychologist William James wrote that "all the intellectual value for us of a state of mind depends on our after-memory of it. Only then is it combined in a system and knowingly made to contribute to a result" (1890, p. 644). He examined his own experience to argue for different kinds of memory, calling one *primary memory*. We consciously experience information in primary memory as part of the psychological present.

Pioneering studies in cognitive psychology investigated primary memory's properties. One famous study by Conrad (1964) explored the format—the symbols—used to store information in primary memory. Conrad hypothesized that primary memory uses acoustic properties to represent items.

To test this hypothesis, Conrad presented sequences from a 10-letter alphabet. Five letters (B, C, P, T, and V) defined one group that sounded similar to one another when pronounced. Five other letters (F, M, N, S, and X) defined a second group with similar sounds. The two groups, however, did not sound similar to one other. Conrad predicted that, if primary memory stored items acoustically, then much confusion would occur between letters belonging to the same group, and less confusion would occur between letters belonging to different groups.

Conrad presented participants with six-letter sequences from his alphabet. Each sequence was presented visually, one letter at a time. A new letter appeared every 750 ms. Thus, Conrad used much longer display durations than those that Sperling used. As a result, Conrad was not studying iconic memory. After the sixth letter was presented, participants wrote the sequence down—from memory—in order. Conrad used recall accuracy as his dependent measure. A correctly recalled letter was written in the correct location in a six-letter sequence.

A participant made an error when she confused the correct letter with an incorrect one. Conrad summarized recall errors in a *confusion matrix* like that in Table 2-1. Each row in the matrix corresponds to a presented (correct) letter. Each column corresponds to an (incorrect) response to the presented letter. The numbers in a row indicate how many times participants made a particular error. For instance, the top row indicates that B was incorrectly recalled as C 13 times, incorrectly recalled as P 102 times, incorrectly recalled as T 30 times, and so on.

Conrad used results like those in Table 2-1 to note that participants confused a presented letter with a letter in its sound-alike group more frequently than with a letter in the other group. For example, consider the total number of confusions (790) between letters all belonging to the first sound-alike group. The total sums

Table 2-1 The frequency that a presented letter was incorrectly recalled as a different letter in Conrad's (1964) study of immediate memory

		Recalled Letter								
		B	C	P	T	V	F	M	N	S	X
Presented Letter	B	–	13	102	30	56	6	12	11	7	3
	C	18	–	18	46	32	8	6	7	21	7
	P	62	27	–	79	30	14	8	5	11	2
	T	5	18	24	–	14	5	5	1	2	2
	V	83	55	40	38	–	31	20	19	9	11
	F	12	15	15	18	21	–	16	28	37	30
	M	9	3	8	14	15	12	–	167	4	10
	N	3	12	8	14	11	13	146	–	12	11
	S	2	35	7	8	11	131	15	24	–	59
	X	0	7	7	10	5	16	5	5	16	–

up the numbers in the grey area in the upper left of Table 2-1. In contrast, only 233 confusions occurred between letters in one group and letters in the other group (the sum of the white area in the upper right of the table). We see similar results when we compare the sums of the other two quadrants in Table 2-1.

Conrad also compared the confusion matrix from his (visual) recall study with another one from a study in which participants heard spoken letters. He added white noise to each letter's pronunciation to make each letter hard to hear correctly. Conrad found a very high correlation between Table 2-1 and the confusion matrix for the spoken letters, providing strong evidence that the recall errors in Table 2-1 reflect letter sounds.

His study again illustrates using behavioural observations to infer cognitive processes. Conrad summarized recall errors in a confusion matrix. By examining errors, he realized that confusion was more likely between sound-alike items and not between look-alike items. Conrad used his observations to infer that primary memory represents items with a code for how an item sounds when pronounced. In short, he collected evidence to answer questions about primary memory's basic information processing properties.

2.4 Delaying Recall from Primary Memory

Why might primary memory encode sounds when representing items? We often use *rehearsal* to preserve information in memory. Rehearsal involves saying items aloud to keep them in primary memory and is easier if the format of primary memory makes items easier to say aloud. In short, primary memory's acoustic representation supports a particular process, rehearsal.

How important is rehearsal for maintaining items in primary memory? Peterson and Peterson (1959) challenged primary memory by preventing rehearsal. In a given trial, participants heard one item to remember (a consonant syllable), followed by a number. Participants then counted, aloud, backward from the number by threes until the researcher signalled them to stop. Counting out loud prevented them from rehearsing the item. When signalled, participants tried to recall the item presented at the start of the trial.

Peterson and Peterson manipulated the length of the delay—the length of time that participants counted out loud—before participants tried recalling an item. Peterson and Peterson discovered that an item's probability of correct recall dramatically decreased as the delay increased. They used an exponential function to relate recall probability to amount of delay; the equation is provided and illustrated

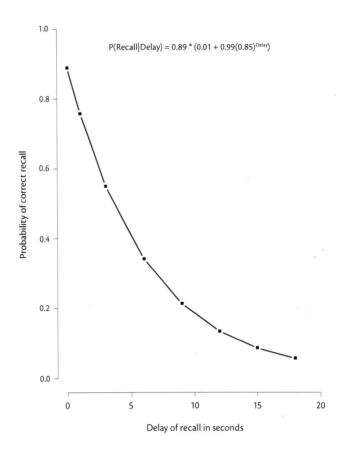

$$P(\text{Recall}|\text{Delay}) = 0.89 * (0.01 + 0.99(0.85)^{\text{Delay}})$$

Figure 2-2 The equation that Peterson and Peterson used to fit their experimental data relating recall probability to delay.

in Figure 2-2. The figure shows that, without rehearsal, items are likely forgotten after a few seconds of delay. Rapid forgetting without rehearsal is another primary memory property inferred from behavioural measures.

2.5 Primary Memory and Recoding

In Sections 2.3 and 2.4, I described how cognitive psychologists infer the properties of primary memory. Conrad demonstrated that primary memory stores items in an acoustic format. Peterson and Peterson discovered that items in primary memory are forgotten in seconds without rehearsal.

Another property is capacity: how many items can primary memory hold? One measurement of capacity is the *span of immediate memory*, the longest digit sequence that someone can recall after hearing the sequence only once (Gates, 1916). It is measured with the *digit-span task*, which presents digit sequences of different lengths to participants to determine the longest sequence that a participant can remember. Gates used the digit-span task to determine that humans have a span of immediate memory of between seven and eight digits.

Many later studies confirmed the results from Gates, as summarized by George Miller (1956) in his famous paper "The Magical Number Seven, Plus or Minus Two." Miller concluded that primary memory holds only between five and nine different items—the magical number. But he famously argued that researchers define the term "item" poorly. For instance, they often vary the digit-span task by presenting different stimuli, such as letters and words. Such studies reveal that the span of immediate memory is smaller for words than for letters (Bousfield & Cowan, 1964). But is the capacity for words really smaller?

Imagine the finding that primary memory can hold seven letters but only six words. However, if each word contains at least three letters, then remembering six words means that a participant also remembers eighteen letters. Which is a more appropriate "item," words or letters used to construct words? Miller proposed that we cope with primary memory's limited capacity by *recoding* items into *chunks*. He argued that "chunks" are more appropriate for measuring capacity than "items."

Recoding organizes or combines many items into a single chunk. "There are many ways to do this recoding, but probably the simplest is to group the input events, apply a new name to the group, and then remember the new name rather than the individual input events" (Miller, 1956, p. 93). For Miller, primary memory could hold about seven chunks, but each chunk could represent many individual items, extending memory capacity. He wrote that recoding is "the very lifeblood of the thought processes" (p. 95). Miller argued that we constantly use recoding, which primarily involves translating information into a verbal code. The next section illustrates recoding, teaching the reader how to recode digit sequences into words.

2.6 Example: Recoding Digits into Chunks

How might we use recoding to cope with primary memory's limited capacity? Consider one approach to coping with the digit-span task, a *mnemonic technique*, or memory aid, for recoding digits into chunks represented as words. The *major method*, from the 1830s, recodes each digit into a consonant sound (Lorayne & Lucas, 1974). Table 2-2 provides the mapping from digits to consonant sounds. In order to use the major method, the reader must memorize the sounds associated with each digit.

Some simple memory aids help you to memorize Table 2-2. For example, the lowercase letter *n* possesses two feet, which is why its sound is associated with the digit 2. Similarly, the lowercase letter *m* possesses three feet, which is why its sound is associated with the digit 3. Typical memory aids for remembering the major method mappings are provided in Table 2-2. If you take a few minutes to use these rules to remember the mappings, then you can perform an impressive memory feat by the end of the chapter.

The major method begins by using the Table 2-2 mappings to recode to-be-recalled digits. For example, consider one 10-digit sequence used in the study by Gates: 2574638197. The major method converts the 10 digits into a consonant sound sequence: *n-l-k-r-sh-m-v-t-b-k*. Consult Table 2-2 to see the rules used to generate the sounds.

The major method's second step converts sounds into chunks, where each chunk represents several digits. Vowel sounds are inserted between consonant sounds

Table 2-2 The major method for recoding a digit as a consonant sound.

Digit	Sound	Memory Aid
0	*s*	the word *zero* starts with *s* sound
1	*t* or *d*	1 long stroke in *t* or *d*
2	*n*	*n* has 2 legs
3	*m*	*m* has 3 legs
4	*r*	*r* is last letter in *four*
5	*l*	a hand makes an *L* when thumb is extended
6	*sh* or *ch* or soft *g* or *j*	6 looks like an upside-down *g*
7	*k*	7 looks like a *K* if you add a small line
8	*f* or *v*	*V*8 juice
9	*p* or *b*	9 can look like a *p* or a *b*

to combine multiple consonant sounds into a single word. We use vowel sounds because vowels do not represent any digits, so they can be added freely.

For instance, consider one grouping for the consonant sound sequence for 2574638197: *n-l, k-r-sh, m-v, t-b-k*. By adding vowel sounds, we convert the consonants into a four-word sequence: *nail, crash, movie, tobacco*. Each word chunks two or three consonant sounds together to represent two or three digits in a single item. Four words are easier to remember than are 10 digits.

We recall a digit sequence by reversing the major method. First, we recall a word from memory. Second, we extract the word's consonant sounds. And third, we convert the consonant sounds into digits—our responses to the experimenter's running a digit-span task. We repeat the process for each word held in primary memory.

Recoding and chunking using the major method become faster and easier with practice. Table 2-3 provides some additional examples of using the major method for several other digit sequences studied by Gates. The examples in Table 2-3 suggest a second recoding stage to make the major method even more efficient. In this second stage, we chunk the words in the third column into a single image to be remembered. For instance, *chin* and *foam* bring to my mind an image of a great deal of foam dripping from someone's chin. *Lake* and *neighbour* can be combined into a single image of my neighbour Al standing in front of his dock at Hastings Lake.

Table 2-3 Examples of using the major method to recode and chunk other stimuli studied by Gates.

Digit	Sound	Words
6283	ch-n-f-m	chin foam
57294	l-k-n-b-r	lake neighbour
241738	n-r-t-k-m-v	antarctic movie
2170463	n-t-k-s-r-g-m	antiques regime
27985543	n-k-p-f-l-l-r-m	kneecap fail alarm
9627	p-sh-n-k	passion ache
41852	r-t-f-l-n	art felon
38471629	m-v-r-k-t-ch-n-b	mover catch honeybee

2.7 Functional Dissociations of Serial Position Curves

Recoding copes with primary memory's limited capacity. However, recoding requires additional cognitive resources. For instance, the major method requires knowing different words for chunking consonant sounds. We must also know how to map digits to sounds. We cannot store this additional knowledge in primary memory alone. Instead, we must store such general knowledge in a different, larger, and longer-lasting memory, called *secondary memory* by William James (1890).

Psychologists Shiffrin and Atkinson (1969) called secondary memory the *long-term store* and theorized, with appropriate processing, that information can be transferred to it from primary memory. For Shiffrin and Atkinson, "the long-term store is assumed to be a *permanent* repository of information" (p. 180).

Excellent evidence supporting the existence of different memories, primary and secondary, comes from observing *serial position curves*. A serial position curve plots data from a *free recall* experiment. In a free recall experiment, an experimenter presents participants with an item sequence to remember. At the end of the sequence, participants recall as many items as possible and in any order—hence the name free recall.

Although a free recall experiment does not constrain recall order, item order is important when researchers summarize participant performance. A serial position curve graphs an item's recall probability as a function of the item's position in the sequence, its *serial position*. Serial position curves ordinarily look like a flat-bottomed U. Figure 2-3 illustrates serial position curves for four different sequence lengths (10, 20, 30, and 40 items). A mathematical model, used to fit real experimental data (Murdock, 1962), generates each curve. The model, which predicts recall probability from an item's serial position (x) and the list's length (L), is also provided in the figure.

Serial position curves routinely show a higher probability for recalling the first three or four items presented in a sequence, the *primacy effect* (see Figure 2-3). Similarly, the last three or four items presented in a sequence also have a higher recall probability, the *recency effect*. The remaining (middle) items in a sequence have much poorer recall probability, producing the bottom of the U-shaped serial position curve, which increases in width as the sequence increases in length.

How do serial position curves provide evidence of the existence of both primary and secondary memory? Cognitive psychologists believe that primary memory causes the recency effect, and that secondary memory produces the primacy effect. For example, Glanzer and Cunitz (1966) incorporated the Peterson and Peterson (1959) paradigm into the free recall task. At the end of a to-be-remembered list,

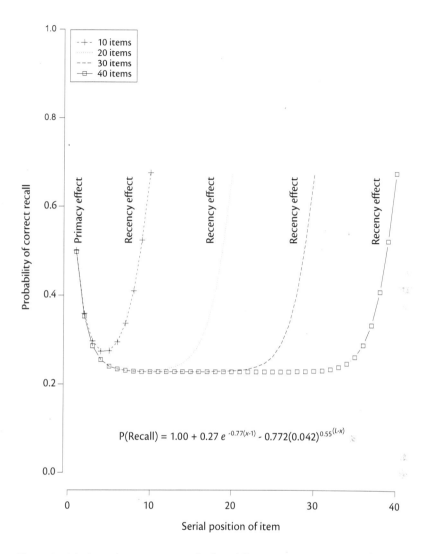

Figure 2-3 Ideal serial position curves for four different lists composed of different numbers of items.

participants performed mental arithmetic to prevent rehearsal. Preventing rehearsal reduced the recency effect, which even disappeared with sufficiently long recall delay. Crucially, delaying recall did not alter the primacy effect.

Glanzer and Cunitz's result supports the hypothesis that primary memory produces the recency effect. For instance, when participants can recall items in any order, they recall the most recent items first, reporting items currently being rehearsed. Preventing rehearsal means that participants cannot report such items, nor can they recall items from primary memory if a delay causes forgetting. Furthermore, finding that preventing rehearsal does not change the primacy effect indicates that the items presented the earliest are held in a store different from primary memory.

Glanzer and Cunitz (1966) reduced the primacy effect by presenting items more quickly and increased the primacy effect by repeating items. Both manipulations did not change the recency effect. Glanzer and Cunitz hypothesized that having longer times to process items, or having items repeated, aids encoding items in secondary memory. However, both independent variables do not affect the recency effect, which involves recall from primary memory, a system governed by processes (e.g., rehearsal) different from those of secondary memory.

Discovering that different manipulations affect the primacy effect and the recency effect illustrates a *functional dissociation*. When different factors alter a serial position curve's different parts, we infer that the different parts reflect qualitatively different information processing. Functional dissociations permit cognitive psychologists to infer that different memory stores exist, even though the memories cannot be directly observed.

2.8 Rehearsal and the Primacy Effect

Glanzer and Cunitz (1966) found that the primacy effect diminishes with increases in the presentation rate for to-be-remembered items. What causes this decrease? Glanzer and Cunitz hypothesized that rote learning transfers information from primary memory to secondary memory. One form of rote learning involves rehearsing aloud items from primary memory, without any more detailed processing. We call such rote learning *maintenance rehearsal*.

Maintenance rehearsal preserves items in primary memory. Plausibly, items remaining for longer durations in primary memory have higher likelihoods of transfer to secondary memory. Longer item rehearsal increases recall probability (Mechanic, 1964; Rundus, 1971). Increasing the presentation rate reduces rehearsal, diminishing the possibility of transfer to secondary memory and decreasing recall probability.

To illustrate, consider the list of words below. If we present the list one word every 4 seconds, then participants have ample opportunity to rehearse repeatedly the first few words. Only when the middle of the list is reached will rehearsal become difficult, because participants do not have sufficient time to place all the presented items into a *rehearsal loop*, the set of primary memory items currently being rehearsed.

- piano
- snake
- clock
- pencil
- lobster
- cigar
- star
- house
- pipe

In contrast, presenting the same list at a faster rate (e.g., one word every second) makes maintenance rehearsal more difficult. First, there is less time available to rehearse items. Second, the rehearsal loop will be filled faster than with a slower presentation rate. Difficulties with maintenance rehearsal decrease the likelihood that items are transferred to secondary memory and reduce the primacy effect.

Other processes of control can transfer items from primary memory to secondary memory, such as *elaborative rehearsal* (Craik & Lockhart, 1972). Elaborative rehearsal involves thinking about what items in primary memory mean. Such thinking requires linking new items to existing information in secondary memory. Elaborative rehearsal connects representations in primary memory to representations in secondary memory.

The list presented above permits elaborative rehearsal. Each word in the list is a *concrete word* used in a free recall study (Paivio & Csapo, 1969). We can easily generate mental images for concrete words. Elaborative rehearsal of these words could use secondary memory to provide a mental image for each item.

One could also enhance elaborative rehearsal by using mental images to chunk items together. For instance, we could imagine a piano played by a snake, a clock with pencil hands, a lobster smoking a cigar, and so on. Such recoding again requires knowledge already present in secondary memory.

Elaborative rehearsal involving mental imagery provides a powerful technique for improving item recall. Compare recall of concrete words (as above) with recall of more *abstract words* (below) (Paivio & Csapo, 1969). Participants have much more difficulty generating mental images for abstract words than for concrete words. Paivio and Csapo found, in a free recall task, significantly better memory for concrete words compared with abstract words. Elaborative rehearsal, via mental images, is easier for concrete words.

- justice
- ability
- ego
- moral
- bravery
- amount
- theory
- freedom
- grief

The major method for recoding digits offers another example of elaborative rehearsal. To succeed, secondary memory must already hold the major method. Similarly, secondary memory must also provide the words used to chunk consonant sounds together as well as the images used to combine different words into a single chunk.

Note, too, that elaborative rehearsal will be disrupted by speeding up the presentation rate in a free recall experiment. Elaborative rehearsal will be more effective if we have more time to think about the meanings of items. Faster sequence presentations reduce the opportunity to perform elaborative rehearsal. As a result, the transfer of items from primary memory to secondary memory is impaired, reducing the primacy effect in a serial position curve.

2.9 Sentence Verification and Secondary Memory

Evidence such as the functional dissociation of the primacy and recency effects permitted researchers to infer the existence of secondary memory. Cognitive psychologists agree that secondary memory stores concept meanings. But how does secondary memory encode and organize meanings? New techniques answered such questions.

One such technique is the *sentence verification task* (Collins & Quillian, 1969). In that task, a participant presses one of two buttons to indicate whether sentences such as "A canary is a bird" are true or false. Researchers measure *response latency* or *reaction time*—the time from sentence presentation to button press. The sentence verification task was developed to test a particular model of secondary memory (Quillian, 1967, 1969). Quillian's model uses a network to represent relations between concepts by encoding category membership (Figure 2-4). A

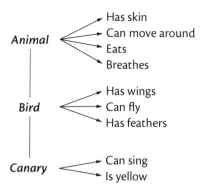

Figure 2-4 An example representing concepts and concept properties in a hierarchical network.

network node represents each concept (the words on the left in Figure 2-4). Links between nodes represent whether one concept belongs to a higher-order category (e.g., canaries are birds). The organization of the network is hierarchical. Quillian's model also represents concept properties by linking nodes to features. For instance, the features attached to the "Canary" node in Figure 2-4 represent that canaries can sing and are yellow.

The principle of *cognitive economy* governs Quillian's network. Cognitive economy minimizes duplicate features. Rather than storing the property "Has feathers" with each node for a different bird, the network stores the property once, attached to the node "Bird." Thus, to determine whether a canary has feathers, we find the property "Has feathers" from the "Bird" node to which "Canary" is linked.

In Quillian's model, verifying a sentence such as "A canary breathes" involves searching the network to determine whether, starting at the "Canary" node, we can reach or retrieve the property "Breathes." When testing the model, Collins and Quillian (1969) assumed that retrieving a property directly connected to a node takes a constant time, as does moving from one node to the next in the hierarchy. They also assumed that times are additive, so following more links to find a property takes longer. The sentence verification task tests Collins and Quillian's predictions. In a hierarchically organized secondary memory (Figure 2-4), some sentences should be faster to verify than others.

For instance, verifying "A canary is yellow" should be faster than verifying "A canary has wings" because the first sentence only involves retrieving a property from the current node, whereas the second sentence requires retrieving a property after moving from the current node to another node in the hierarchy. Verifying "A canary has skin" should take even longer because it requires retrieving a property from a node two links above "Canary." Collins and Quillian's (1969) results supported the predictions. Typically, participants would take 75 ms longer to verify a sentence such as "A canary has wings" than to verify a sentence such as "A canary is yellow." And they would take on average about 150 ms longer to verify a sentence such as "A canary has skin" than to verify the sentence "A canary is yellow."

Collins and Quillian (1969) concluded that secondary memory has a hierarchical organization. However, they also raised new questions. For instance, participants took longer to verify false sentences than true sentences, a result that Quillian's model could not predict. Such questions led other researchers to conduct further studies by varying the sentence verification task. New results inspired alternative secondary memory models.

For instance, category size affects sentence verification (Wilkins, 1971). Participants take less time to verify sentences involving categories with fewer members (e.g., musical instruments, sports) than sentences involving categories with more members (e.g., birds, diseases). Wilkins also found that word occurrence frequencies in language affect sentence verification speed. Sentences including higher-frequency concepts or properties take less time to verify than do sentences including lower-frequency words. Note that Quillian's model does not represent properties such as category size and word frequency.

Similarly, the preceding stimulus affects sentence verification time. A high degree of semantic relatedness between the two sentences reduces the time for verifying the current sentence (Ashcraft, 1976), an example of a *priming* effect. Again, Quillian's theory does not explain priming.

The concept or property *typicality* also affects sentence verification times (Ashcraft, 1978). Researchers measure typicality by having participants generate examples of a stimulus. For example, participants could generate different examples of the stimulus "Bird." The more typical an example, the more frequently different participants will generate it. Participants generate "Robin" as an example of "Bird" more frequently than "Duck."

Ashcraft (1978) found faster verification for sentences containing typical concepts or properties ("A robin has feathers") than for sentences containing atypical concepts or properties ("A duck has a bill"). Note that Collins and Quillian (1969) would predict that both sentences produce the same verification time because both "Robin" and "Duck" are the same distance away from "Bird."

When new experiments produced problematic results for Quillian's model, the model was revised (Collins & Loftus, 1975). As revised by Collins and Loftus, the model was a *semantic network* (similar to that in Figure 2-4) composed of interconnected nodes. However, the semantic network abandoned the logical structure of concepts used by Collins and Quillian (1969). Instead, the semantic network of Collins and Loftus represented the semantic similarity or *semantic relatedness* of concepts. Two concepts with high semantic similarity share many properties. A semantic network represents semantic relatedness by having two concepts connected to many of the same nodes (the shared properties).

Spreading activation serves as the basic process in a semantic network. When nodes in the network activate, activation travels as a signal to other connected nodes, increasing activity in nodes that receive the signal. When a participant is presented with a sentence such as "A robin has feathers," the nodes for both "Robin" and "Feathers" activate, and activation spreads from them. If activity from "Robin" and "Feathers" intersects or collides in the network, then the sentence is true.

The semantic network model addressed many limitations of the original Quillian network. For instance, the higher the semantic relationship between the two nodes, the faster the signals intersect, because the number of potential routes for activity to intersect increases with increases in semantic relatedness. The revised model also explains typicality effects because more typical concepts or properties have more links to other nodes. Priming effects can be explained by hypothesizing that network activity takes time to decay, meaning that activity produced by a previous stimulus might still exist in the network, facilitating the verification of a related sentence.

The semantic network revised Quillian's original model. Other researchers abandoned network representations, proposing radically different secondary memory models. For example, *set-theoretic models* represent each concept as a collection or set of features (Rips et al., 1973). Rips et al. replace spreading activation with a process of feature comparison. To verify a sentence such as "A robin is a bird," we compare the features for "Robin" to the features for "Bird." If the two concepts share a sufficient number of features, then the sentence is true. Sentence verification speeds up as the number of shared features increases, which accounts for many of the results obtained from the sentence verification paradigm.

Even when researchers agree on set-theoretic representations, they dispute other details. For instance, Rips et al. (1973) presume that we represent concept categories (e.g., "Bird," "Fish") as feature sets, but a category member must possess particular features. For example, all birds have hearts. Requiring particular features to belong to a concept is known as the *classical theory* of concepts.

In contrast, *prototype theory* does not represent categories with definite features (Rosch, 1975; Rosch & Mervis, 1975). Prototype theory instead defines categories using the *family resemblance* between category members, because some members better represent a category than do others. Prototype theory represents each category member as a set of features varying in *cue validity*. A feature with high cue validity occurs more frequently in category members than does a feature with low cue validity. A *prototype* possesses many features with high cue validity. In prototype theory, we classify a new instance as belonging to a category if the new instance has high family resemblance to a category's prototype. Family resemblance is determined by comparing the features of the instance with those of the prototype using a process sensitive not only to which features are shared but also to cue validities (Tversky, 1977).

We cannot directly observe secondary memory. We must infer its properties from other observations, such as results provided by the sentence verification task. By measuring the time taken to determine the truth of a sentence of the form "An x is a y," and by manipulating the relationship between x and y, cognitive psychologists can infer properties of secondary memory.

However, the inferences that cognitive psychologists make must be re-evaluated constantly when new experimental results are obtained. New sentence verification results required existing models to be revised, producing new theories. Progress in cognitive psychology depends on developing more sophisticated techniques for evaluating whether one proposal (e.g., a semantic network) is more plausible than another (e.g., a set-theoretic model). I consider the logic of comparing theories in more detail in Chapter 3.

2.10 Associations, Verbal Learning, and Secondary Memory

In the previous section, I used the sentence verification task as a context for examining secondary memory. However, researchers use many other methods to study secondary memory. Results from such methods in turn support many different theories about cognitive processing. Below I briefly consider one example, *associationism*.

Associationism proposes links or associations between concepts; thinking of one concept causes us to think about another. Associationism originated in the writings of Aristotle in 350 BC (Sorabji, 2006). Experimental psychologists have had a long interest in associationism (Warren, 1921). Associationism also inspired a model of secondary memory called HAM, for human associative memory, which arose at the same time as the models introduced in Section 2.9 (Anderson & Bower, 1973).

A particular form of associationism inspired behaviorism. Behaviorists did not study associations between ideas; rather, they studied *habits*, associations between environmental stimuli and behavioural responses (Thorndike, 1932). Behaviorists aimed to make psychology a natural science by focusing only on directly observable entities (stimuli and responses) and by removing unobservable mental terms from psychological theory (Watson, 1913).

However, through the first half of the 20th century, several factors increased interest in studying an older idea, the associations between ideas. These factors included the rise of information theory, growing interest in the study of human learning and memory, and the impact of linguistics on psychology (Cofer, 1978). In studying the associations between ideas, psychologists returned to investigating unobservable mental properties, leading to experimental psychology's *verbal learning tradition*. That tradition modified behaviorist methodologies to study the learning of verbal materials (Andresen, 1991; Deese, 1965; Deese & Hulse, 1967; Hunt, 1971). Although verbal learners proposed associations between mentally represented concepts, they studied objective stimulus properties (Cramer, 1968).

Stimulus *meaningfulness* provides an example property. Researchers measure meaningfulness by having participants generate associates of stimulus words (Noble, 1952). A word that produces many associated words has higher meaningfulness than a word that produces fewer associates. Note that cognitive psychologists define meaningfulness not by using internal semantics but by using observable behaviour. Verbal learning experiments demonstrated that words with higher meaningfulness have higher recall probability in memory experiments (Deese & Hulse, 1967).

The *paired-associate learning task* provided a key methodology to the verbal learning tradition. That task, invented by Mary Whiton Calkins in 1894, presents participants with pairs of unrelated words to remember (e.g., *House-Tree, Robin-Dog*, etc.). Typically, the paired-associate learning task uses the *anticipation procedure* (Pennington & Waters, 1938). In that procedure, a researcher presents the first word of a pair, and participants try to recall the second word. (On the first trial, the second word must be guessed.) After responding, participants see both members of the pair. Thus, each trial provides both a test and a learning opportunity. Researchers measure performance by counting how many times the list must be presented before a participant recalls the words perfectly. The paired-associate learning task was popular because various independent variables, such as the meaningfulness, frequency, and similarity of stimulus items, could be manipulated easily (Goss & Nodine, 1965; Underwood & Schulz, 1960). Also, the task seemed to test most directly associationist ideas of interest to verbal learners (Deese & Hulse, 1967).

The verbal learning tradition bridged waning behaviorism and rising cognitivism. Early on, verbal learners had difficulty publishing results in mainstream journals because the verbal learning approach seemed to be too mentalistic (Mandler, 2002), a problem solved when Charles Cofer founded the *Journal of Verbal Learning and Verbal Behavior* (Cofer, 1978; Virues-Ortega, 2006).

However, as cognitivism flourished, the verbal learning tradition became more mentalistic and emphasized principles governing secondary memory's organization (Tulving et al., 1972). For example, HAM modelled human associative memory by forming associations between nodes representing the hierarchical structure of linguistic propositions (Anderson & Bower, 1973). We will see in Section 2.11 that verbal learners also became more cognitive because paired associate learning experiments demonstrated that unobservable properties of representations were the most powerful predictors of memory performance. The verbal learning tradition finished its conversion into modern cognitivism in 1984, the year that the *Journal of Verbal Learning and Verbal Behavior* changed its title to the *Journal of Memory and Language*.

2.11 Imagery and Secondary Memory

The previous section introduced the verbal learning tradition as well as a key method, the paired-associate learning task. The verbal learning tradition proposed that secondary memory encodes associations between concepts. Section 2.10 noted that the verbal learning tradition helped psychology to transition from behaviorism to cognitivism. The paired-associate learning task pushed verbal learning theories toward cognitivism by demonstrating that the most important predictors of memory performance could not be directly observed.

In particular, the paired-associate learning task re-established experimental psychology's interest in another potential encoding in secondary memory, *mental imagery*. When we experience a mental picture, we experience a mental image. The idea that we encode concepts as mental images is as old as associationism. Aristotle believed that images represent ideas (Cummins, 1989). The first mnemonic techniques attributed to the Greek poet Simonides also used mental imagery (c. 500 BC) (Yates, 1966).

We can generate mental images for some concepts easier than we can generate images for others (Paivio, Yuille & Madigan., 1968), as we saw earlier in the two lists of words on pages 45 and 46. Such concepts are high in *imagery*. We measure concept imagery by having participants rate how easy or difficult it is to create a mental image for a concept (Paivio et al., 1968).

The paired-associate learning task can demonstrate that imagery predicts recall better than do traditional verbal learning variables (Paivio et al., 1968). Paivio et al. even conducted one study that controlled stimulus imageability while varying stimulus meaningfulness. The study demonstrated that meaningfulness did not affect recall performance. In fact, increasing meaningfulness decreases memory performance when imagery is controlled!

In general, Paivio's research demonstrates that imagery is one of the best predictors of performance in memory tasks (Paivio, 1969, 1971). Paivio's results led to another proposal about the nature of secondary memory, *dual-coding theory* (Paivio, 1971, 1986). According to dual-coding theory, we store concepts in secondary memory using more than one format. One is a verbal code or label. Another is a mental image. We can more easily retrieve concepts represented by both types of codes, explaining better memory of concrete concepts than of abstract concepts.

2.12 Inferring Structure, Process, and Control

In the preceding sections, I described early methods invented by cognitive psychologists to infer human information processing. The examples selected for Chapter 2 were important contributions to developing the *modal memory model* (Baddeley, 1990). That model is also known as the *multi-store memory model*, one of early cognitive psychology's crowning achievements (Shiffrin & Atkinson, 1969; Waugh & Norman, 1965). Figure 2-5 illustrates the modal memory model's general structure.

The modal memory model possesses several features typical of cognitive psychology. First, the model explains a very general phenomenon, memory, as an organized system of subsystems: sensory registers, primary memory, and secondary memory. Such an account illustrates cognitive psychology's core methodology, *functional analysis*. I explore functional analysis in Chapter 3.

Second, the model is functional in nature. The *physical* natures of the component memories are not described. "Our hypotheses about the various memory stores do not require any assumptions regarding the physiological locus of these stores" (Shiffrin & Atkinson, 1969, p. 179).

Third, the model's different components have different functions, and functions are organized in a particular fashion, with information being transferred (while being recoded) from one memory to another. For example, sensory registers such

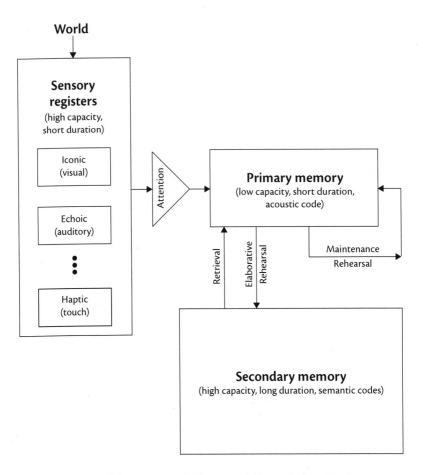

Figure 2-5 The modal memory model from cognitive psychology's early years.

as iconic memory briefly hold a large amount of information for a short duration so that some information can be transferred to primary memory. Primary memory holds a small number of chunks, encoded acoustically, representing our experience of the present. Information in primary memory can be transferred to large-capacity secondary memory to represent concept meanings for a long duration.

Fourth, each component in the modal memory model has different structural properties. Components differ in terms of capacity, information encoding, and memory duration.

Fifth, each component of the modal memory model is governed by a different kind of process. For instance, attention can be directed to different parts of a sensory register to transmit a small amount of its contents to be transferred to primary memory. The triangular shape of the attention process in Figure 2-5 illustrates that it transfers only a limited amount of information. Similarly, information can be preserved indefinitely in primary memory via maintenance rehearsal, or it can be transferred into secondary memory via elaborative rehearsal.

Sixth, though some processes for manipulating information in the model's stores are automatic (e.g., those causing information to be forgotten), others are under conscious control. For instance, we saw in Sperling's partial-report technique that participants can direct attention to different parts of iconic memory. Similarly, they can choose which contents of primary memory undergo elaborative rehearsal and the nature of this elaborative processing. Maintenance rehearsal is also under our explicit control.

Importantly, the properties of the modal memory model in Figure 2-5 are all architectural. As we saw in Chapter 1, an architectural account of a computer, which describes structures, processes, and control, explains how the computer processes information. The modal memory model also provides an architectural account by detailing the structures, processes, and control of different memory stores critical to human information processing. In Chapter 3, I explore why cognitive psychologists need to identify the architecture of cognition.

2.13 How to Remember π to 100 Digits

Section 2.11 described two intersections between associationism and imagery. First, associations between ideas are associations between images. Second, imagery has an important role in memory, as revealed by Paivio's research. We can illustrate a third intersection between associationism and mental imagery using the mnemonic technique called the *method of loci* (Yates, 1966), a method designed for remembering a sequence of ideas in a particular order. The method of loci stores an idea to remember in a location. The method uses familiar locations, spatially arranged in a particular order. For example, we could use the rooms of a familiar house as loci because we reach each room in a particular order by mentally "walking through the house."

To use the method of loci to remember a sequence, we create a mental image to represent the first item to remember and "place" that item in the mental image created for the first location. We then image the second item to remember and place it in the image of the second location and so on. Note the intersection of images and associations in the method. The method of loci requires mental images but associates a new image with a familiar one by mentally linking an item's image

Table 2-4 Phrases for using the major method to encode the first 100 digits of π

Phrase	Consonants	Number
motored loping lama	m-t-r-d l-p-n-g l-m	3.141592653
leaf pick poem name	l-f p-k p-m n-m	58979323
fur changer mom	f-r ch-n-g-r m-m	84626433
foam neck pails	f-m n-k p-l-s	8327950
navy frat picket	n-v f-r-t p-k-t	28841971
shabby map bomb	sh-b m-p b-m	693993
cold seal fins	k-l-d s-l f-n-s	75105820
packer bear earlobe	p-k-r b-r r-l-b	97494459
gnomes coffee	n-m-s k-f	23078
teachers shine fish nose	t-ch-r-s sh-n f-sh n-s	1640628620
hive o' pipe fish	v p-p f-sh	89986
knife swimmer fin	n-f s-m-r f-n	2803482
lemur wanted aches checkup	l-m-r n-t-d k-s ch-k-p	53421170679

with a place's image. The method also illustrates elaborative rehearsal because it links new information to already known information.

With the method of loci, recall involves mentally "walking" through the sequence of remembered locations; we perform the "walking" in a set order because locations have a particular spatial layout. At each location, we retrieve the image associated with the location earlier. As a result, we recall items in the correct order. Below I consider a concrete example of the method of loci, demonstrating use of the method to memorize long strings of digits: remembering the first 100 digits of π. We remember the 100 digits in order by combining the major method (Section 2.6) with the method of loci.

Memorizing the 100 digits begins by creating phrases for recoding and chunking the digits to remember. Table 2-4 provides one possible set of phrases. The table's first row provides a phrase representing the first digits to remember, the next row presents a phrase representing the next digits to remember, and so on to the end of the table. We must recall the phrases in their order in the table.

I can easily generate images for the phrases in Table 2-4. I imagine the first phrase as being like a coin-operated mechanical horse ride for a child, but in this case it is a mechanical lama whose legs lope when the machine activates. I imagine the second phrase as a person wearing a Toronto Maple Leafs jersey while picking the name of a poem from a book of poetry.

Given the phrases and images in Table 2-4, we next remember the (ordered) phrases. We use the method of loci, which explains our need to create an image for each phrase. Table 2-5 provides locations that I use to memorize the images for Table 2-4 in order. As noted earlier, we must use familiar, easily imagined, and sequentially arranged locations. Rooms in a well-known house serve that purpose well. Table 2-5 lists locations in my own house. I am very familiar with them, and I encounter them in a particular order as I move through them. For these locations, I start outside the house on the front sidewalk, go up the front stairs, into the front vestibule, and so on. Of course, readers must come up with their own loci to use as memory locations in order to be able to remember π.

The procedure used to memorize the digits is straightforward. I mentally link the image created for the first phrase in Table 2-4 to the image created for the first place in Table 2-5. For example, I imagine my coin-operated "motored loping lama"

Table 2-5 Images for using the method of loci to memorize the first 100 digits of π

Locus Image	Phrase Image
front sidewalk	motored loping lama
front step	leaf pick poem name
front vestibule	fur changer mom
front closet	foam neck pails
bathroom	navy frat picket
basement stairs	shabby map bomb
kitchen	cold seal fins
back entry	packer bear earlobe
pantry	gnomes coffee
dining room	teachers shine fish nose
living room	hive o' pipe fish
fireplace	knife swimmer fin
staircase	lemur wanted aches checkup

operating in the middle of my front sidewalk. Next I place the second image ("leaf pick poem name") on my front step. Then I place the third image ("fur changer mom") in the front vestibule. I continue until I place every phrase image in one of my locations. I need practice to ensure that I remember correct phrases in the correct order; I typically practise by moving through the loci a few times. I do not need a great deal of such practice.

With surprisingly little effort, we can learn, and recall, the images in order. Memorization and practice of the major method helps to convert phrases quickly into a sequence of digits. Most of the effort comes in the first step, generating phrases for recoding digits into imageable chunks.

The mnemonic technique described above illustrates many of the information processing properties inferred by cognitive psychologists from their memory experiments. For instance, rote learning or maintenance rehearsal commits the major method to memory. Elaborative rehearsal links the major method with existing knowledge using the memory aids of Table 2-2. The major method illustrates recoding and chunking. Converting images to phrases illustrates Paivio's dual-coding theory. Using images with the method of loci illustrates elaborative rehearsal as well as associating images together.

2.14 Chapter Summary

Cognitive psychologists hypothesize that cognition is information processing, an idea inspired by the digital computer. They assume that human thinking, like computers, is rule-governed symbol manipulation. Thus, cognitive psychologists must explain human cognition in the same way that computer scientists explain a computer's behaviour. In Chapter 1, I presented a general approach to explaining a computer by describing its architecture. Which symbols represent information? Which processes manipulate symbols? How does the computer control the order of applying processes?

Cognitive psychologists recognize that explanations of human cognition must answer similar questions. Such psychologists aim to identify human cognition's basic properties and do not worry about whether similarities exist between human cognition and computer information processing. Instead, cognitive psychologists *assume* that humans are a kind of computer and seek to determine *what kind* of computer humans are (Hunt, 1971).

However, cognitive psychologists face a formidable problem. Unlike computers, human participants do not permit cognitive psychologists to observe internal cognitive processes directly. As a result, these psychologists must invent new methods for collecting behavioural observations to support inferences about the properties of cognition.

In Chapter 2, I introduced many example methods: Sperling's partial report method, confusion matrices, Peterson and Peterson's delay of recall technique, the functional dissociation of the serial position curve, the sentence verification task, and the paired-associate learning task. All of these methods explored the properties of human memory in the early years of cognitive psychology and permitted cognitive psychologists to infer basic properties of human memory. Cognitive psychologists proposed a series of different memory stores, each defined by different properties (capacity, duration, kind of information represented, processes, and control). By the middle of the 1960s, experimental results supported one of cognitive psychology's most influential ideas, the modal memory model.

In Chapter 3, I will show that the modal memory model provides but one example of the philosophy of science adopted by cognitive psychologists: functional analysis. I now turn to describing functional analysis and how it converts cognitive descriptions into explanatory theories.

3

Using Functional Analysis to Explain Cognition

The first two chapters related cognitive psychology to computer science and to experimental psychology. This chapter relates cognitive psychology to philosophy by describing the explanations proposed by cognitive psychologists. Such explanations take the form of flow diagrams—a tool borrowed from computer science—to show how one function manipulates information, passing results to a different function for further processing. We create flow diagrams from basic operations built into an information processor. The basic operations used to create flow diagrams serve as the system's architecture, which provides the system's built-in programming language. The philosophy of science calls decomposing a system into organized sub-functions functional analysis. I begin Chapter 3 by describing functional analysis. I then turn to a consideration of four different kinds of evidence: relative complexity evidence, error evidence, intermediate state evidence, and the cognitive penetrability criterion. Cognitive psychologists collect such evidence to validate functional analyses, converting functional theories into scientific explanations.

3.1 Competing Notions of Explanation

Cognitive psychology's pioneers trained as behaviorists (Miller, 2003). In his first book, Miller (1951) adopted a behaviorist perspective that he would soon abandon. "In 1951, I apparently still hoped to gain scientific respectability by swearing allegiance to behaviorism. Five years later, inspired by such colleagues as Noam Chomsky and Jerry Bruner, I had stopped pretending to be a behaviorist" (Miller, 2003, p. 141). Pioneering cognitive psychologists discarded behaviorism because it limited what could be studied. Behaviorists argued that psychology must eliminate mental terms from its vocabulary (Watson, 1913). Cognitive psychologists fiercely rejected behaviorism's stance against mentalism (Bruner, 1990; Sperry, 1993).

Replacing behaviorism did not merely change the topics that psychologists could study. The cognitive revolution involved "discovering an alternative logic by which to refute the seemingly incontestable reasoning that heretofore required science to ostracize mind and consciousness" (Sperry, 1993, p. 881). Cognitive psychologists aimed to replace behaviorist theories with a new approach, an approach both mentalistic and scientific.

Chapter 1 introduced the inspiration for an alternative form of explanation, the computer. Computer scientists explain how computers work by appealing to the functional properties of computer programs. Chapter 2 illustrated how cognitive psychologists collect data to support similar accounts of human cognition. Like behaviorists, cognitive psychologists observe behaviour. Unlike behaviorists, cognitive psychologists use observations to infer information processes that cannot be observed directly.

Chapter 1 related cognitive psychology to computer science, and Chapter 2 related cognitive psychology to experimental psychology. Chapter 3 now relates cognitive psychology to the philosophy of science. Cognitive psychology uses explanations very different from those of behaviorism. Cognitive psychology's theories arise from a philosophical approach called *functional analysis*. In Chapter 3, I introduce functional analysis and explore how it shapes the practice of cognitive psychology.

3.2 Functionalism, Hierarchies, and Functional Decomposition

Cybernetics explained behaviour by appealing to the *feedback loop* (Ashby, 1956, 1960; Wiener, 1948, 1950). Feedback measures the distance between an agent's current state and a goal state that the agent desires. The agent acts on the world to decrease the distance between the current state and the desired state. A feedback loop cycles back and forth between an agent's actions and environmental changes, constantly measuring the distance from a desired goal to alter or guide the agent's future actions.

Cybernetics played an important role in founding cognitive psychology (Conway & Siegelman, 2005). For instance, one pioneering book on cognition, *Plans and the Structure of Behavior* (Miller et al., 1960), explored the relevance of cybernetics to psychology. Miller et al. proposed the feedback loop as behaviour's fundamental building block by introducing the *TOTE unit* (Figure 3-1). TOTE stood for "Test-Operate-Test-Exit." One component, "Test," provides feedback to the unit. "Test" compares the world's current state to a desired state. If the desired state is

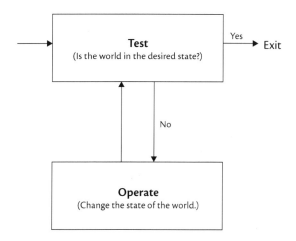

Figure 3-1 The basic structure of a TOTE unit.

true, then the unit "Exits," passing control elsewhere. However, if the desired state is false, then the TOTE unit passes control to the second component, "Operate."

"Operate" acts on the world to help achieve the desired state. "Operate" changes the world, making it more similar to the desired state. After "Operate" performs the action, control again returns to "Test" to determine whether the action achieved the goal. If not, then "Test" passes control back to "Operate." Thus, the TOTE unit repeatedly moves back and forth between testing and operating until achieving the desired state.

The TOTE unit illustrates one core assumption of cognitive psychology, *functionalism* (Polger, 2012). Functionalism explains how a system works by describing what its components do rather than by describing their physical properties. I describe TOTE units functionally, not physically, as detailed below.

Functionalism arises from a many-to-one relationship (introduced in Chapter 1). Functionalists realize that physically different components can serve the same function. For instance, the total artificial heart (Mollon, 1982) performs the same function as the human heart but is built from different physical materials. Miller et al. (1960) treat TOTE units functionally, not physically. First, they describe TOTE units as transmitting control, not as transmitting energy or neural pulses. Their proposal is deliberately abstract and non-mechanistic. Second, Miller et al. recognize that TOTE units can be studied with computer simulations, arguing that a valid simulation need only emulate a theory's functional characteristics. "A successful model does not have to *look* like the organism it simulates" (p. 48). Third,

Miller et al. spend 13 chapters developing their functional theory before mentioning the brain. A final chapter, entitled "Some Neuropsychological Speculations," has only fourteen pages. Cognitive psychologists typically develop a functional theory first and only later relate the theory to the brain.

The TOTE unit was but one of the pioneering ideas of Miller et al. (1960). They also proposed a *hierarchical organization* for TOTE units. The foundational concept of their book, the "Plan," appeals to hierarchy: "*A Plan is any hierarchical process in the organism that can control the order in which a sequence of operations is to be performed*" (p. 16). Importantly, they also treated hierarchical organization functionally.

Miller et al. (1960) hierarchically organize TOTE units by decomposing a TOTE unit's "Operate" component into organized sub-functions; each sub-function is

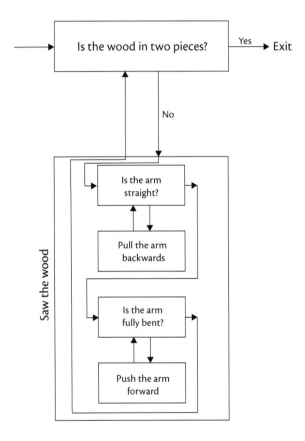

Figure 3-2 Hierarchical organization in a TOTE unit is accomplished by functionally decomposing "Operate" into sub-TOTE units.

another TOTE unit. We call recasting one function as an organized system of sub-functions *functional decomposition*. Figure 3-2 illustrates Miller et al.'s functional decomposition using a TOTE unit for sawing a wooden board into two. In Figure 3-2, the higher-level "Operate" component "Saw the Wood" is decomposed into two linked TOTE units, one for pulling a straight arm backward, the other for pushing a bent arm forward. Note that the second sub-component "Exit" passes control back to the upper-level "Test" "Is the Wood in Two Pieces?"

Figure 3-2 permits further functional decomposition. We could decompose both the "Pull Arm Backward" and "Push Arm Forward" operations into new TOTE units—sub-sub-functions—to ensure that "Saw the Wood" proceeds as desired.

Miller et al. (1960) use functional decomposition to explain how we perform operations. They realize that some operations (e.g., "Saw the Wood"), too complex to build directly into a device, must instead be created from simpler processes. Thus, they explain a complex operation by decomposing it into an organized system of simpler operations. However, such decomposition adds new TOTE units. Can we explain one functional component by decomposing it into other functions that also require explanation? Cognitive psychology must answer this question and does so using an approach outlined below.

3.3 Ryle's Regress

Behaviorists argued that mental terms did not carry any explanatory value. A theory including mental states could not explain because it incorporated unexplained components. "When we attribute behavior to a neural or mental event, real or conceptual, we are likely to forget that we still have the task of accounting for the neural or mental event" (Skinner, 1950, p. 194). Miller et al. (1960, p. 9) understood Skinner's concern: "The criticism is that the cognitive processes Tolman and others have postulated are not, in fact, sufficient to do the job they were supposed to do. Even if you admit these ghostly inner somethings, say the critics, you will not have explained anything about the animal's behavior."

Gilbert Ryle (1949) provided the philosophical foundations for Skinner's criticism. He opposed what he called the *intellectualist legend*, which requires intelligence to be produced by mental rules. Ryle argued that such accounts produce an infinite regress of mental state terms. To explain one cognitive process, cognitive psychologists decompose it into other cognitive processes. However, new cognitive processes themselves require explanation. If we use the intellectualist legend to explain new cognitive processes, then we perform further functional decomposition.

As a result, Ryle argued that functional decomposition creates an infinite regress of mental state terms. This infinite proliferation of unexplained functions is called *Ryle's regress*. If a cognitive psychologist is trapped in Ryle's regress, then her theories merely describe and do not explain.

Cognitive psychology's functionalism seems to lead into Ryle's regress. Consider the modal memory model (Figure 2-5). Cognitive psychologists began with the task of explaining human memory. However, they decomposed a general function—memory—into an organized system of sub-functions (e.g., sensory registers, primary memory, secondary memory, etc.). However, each new sub-function also requires explanation. But if we explain a new sub-function using functional decomposition, we produce new to-be-explained sub-sub-functions. Given Ryle's regress, how did cognitivism replace behaviorism? Cognitive psychologists adopted an explanatory approach to escape Ryle's infinite regress, which I consider in the next section.

3.4 Functional Analysis

In science, explanations typically appeal to *causal laws* or *transition laws* (Cummins, 1983). For instance, physicists explain the transition from one physical state to another by citing a law that "explains an effect by citing its cause" (Cummins, 1983, p. 4).

Behaviorists used physics to inspire their psychology (Köhler, 1947). As a result, in addition to focusing on observables (stimuli and responses), behaviorists appealed to transition laws. Behaviorist explanations cite causal laws: a stimulus causes a response. "In a system of psychology completely worked out, given the response the stimuli can be predicted; given the stimuli the response can be predicted" (Watson, 1913, p. 167). However, philosophy proposes other explanatory approaches. Scientists choose the approach that they prefer; their choice depends on beliefs about what constitutes good science (Osbeck, 2019).

When reacting to behaviorism, cognitive psychologists chose an alternative kind of explanation: *functional analysis* (Cummins, 1975, 1983). Functional analysis explains complicated systems by breaking them down into simpler subsystems and requires three general steps.

First, functional analysis specifies the function to be explained. This step is very general because it specifies only some regularity to convert stimuli into responses (Ashby, 1956), relating this step to the computational level of analysis (Section 1.7). At the computational level, a researcher specifies which information processing problem is being solved, equivalent to indicating the overall input-output mapping—the function—performed by the system.

Second, functional analysis performs the *analytic strategy*. With this step, a researcher analyzes the function into an organized set of sub-functions, a practice called *reverse engineering*. When a cognitive psychologist engages in functional decomposition, she adopts the analytic strategy. We conduct the analytic strategy iteratively; once we propose some sub-function, we might decompose it further into simpler sub-sub-functions. Analysis can continue again and again. We stay in Ryle's regress if we cannot stop applying the analytic strategy.

Importantly, any new sub-functions proposed during the analytic strategy must be simpler than the functions from which they were derived for cognitive psychologists to escape Ryle's regress. Functional analysis decomposes a system into functional components simple enough to be explained using causal laws.

Figure 3-3 illustrates the first two steps of functional analysis. The figure's top part defines some function to explain, a mapping between the input and the output indicated by the two arrows. The figure's middle part shows the first functional decomposition of the top function into two sub-functions. The figure's bottom part decomposes the two sub-functions into various sub-sub-functions.

Figure 3-3 portrays two additional characteristics of the analytic strategy. First, we decompose functions into *simpler* sub-functions, illustrated by making the boxes for sub-functions *smaller* than the boxes for functions. Second, we decompose a function into an *organized* set of sub-functions, reflecting the idea that information processing occurs in stages. First one sub-function manipulates symbols; then the sub-function passes results to another sub-function. The arrows in Figure 3-3 indicate how information moves from one function to another. These two ideas reflect a very powerful insight: when simple functions form an organized system, that system can perform a more complex function.

However, Figure 3-3 does not show how to escape Ryle's regress. We need to explain some simple function without further decomposing that function into further sub-functions. If (infinite) functional decomposition somehow stops, then we escape Ryle's regress. The final step in Cummins's (1983) functional analysis stops functional decomposition. The *subsumption strategy* describes how physical mechanisms *instantiate* functions. We explain an instantiated function by appealing to a causal law. Cummins calls such an appeal *causal subsumption*.

Causal subsumption explains some function's input-output regularity with a (physical) transition law. We subsume a function by explaining how we can replace the function with a physical device to perform the same input-output mapping.

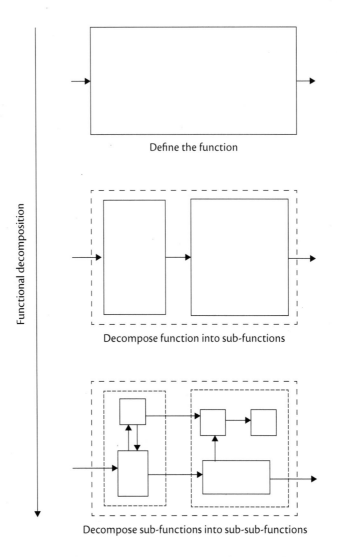

Define the function

Decompose function into sub-functions

Decompose sub-functions into sub-sub-functions

Figure 3-3 Illustrating the analytic strategy in which a function is decomposed into two sub-functions, and then these sub-functions are further decomposed.

We do not explain the device via further functional decomposition because of the physical nature of the device. Instead, we explain the device by appealing to causal law, ending Ryle's infinite regress.

Cummins's functional analysis provides an alternative scientific explanation. Unlike behaviorist explanations, functional analysis appeals to internal functions that we cannot observe directly. However, Cummins, sensitive to Ryle's regress, requires functional analysis to reach a set of final, instantiated, functions. Only then will a functional analysis explain. "Analysis of the disposition (or any other property) is only a first step; instantiation is the second" (Cummins, 1983, p. 31). Miller et al. (1960, p. 42) promoted testing theories with computer simulations by interpreting simulations as instantiations: "The reflex theorist is no longer the only psychologist who can summon up a tangible mechanism to make his claims sound more reasonable."

Cognitive psychologists assume that cognition is computation: rule-governed symbol manipulation. As a result, they must explain cognition by appealing to processes that they cannot observe directly. Cognitive psychologists must adopt a philosophy of science different from that of behaviorism. Behaviorists criticized the cognitive approach as being non-scientific because behaviorists believe that functional decompositions do not explain. In response, cognitive psychologists adopt a different approach to explanation, one no less scientific than the approach used by behaviorists.

Cognitive psychologists explain cognition by performing functional analysis, which proceeds in three basic steps: (1) defining a to-be-explained function; (2) iteratively decomposing this function into organized sub-functions; and (3) ending this decomposition by causally subsuming the final functions. The final step converts a functional analysis from a description into an explanation.

3.5 The Architecture of Cognition

We can explain a computer by describing its architecture: detailing the computer's basic symbols, rules, and control. When psychologists assume that cognition is information processing, they also claim that we can explain cognition in the same way, with an architectural account (Anderson, 1983; Newell, 1990; Pylyshyn, 1984).

Computers process information by executing a program, a sequence of processes for manipulating symbols to accomplish a goal. A program ultimately uses the computer's most basic operations. Basic operations are literally built into the machine and are called *primitives*. We explain a primitive function's operation by appealing to physical properties or to causal laws. A primitive is not explained by further decomposition into functional sub-components.

A computer's primitives define its *functional architecture*. "Specifying the functional architecture of a system is like providing a manual that defines some programming language" (Pylyshyn, 1984, p. 92). Functional analysis escapes Ryle's regress by causally subsuming basic functions, explaining functions via causal laws. The final stage of a functional analysis of human cognition must specify the primitives, the functional architecture of cognition. "Theories of human cognition are ultimately theories of physical, biological systems" (Newell, 1990, p. 42).

Cognitive psychologists must discover the architecture to convert functional descriptions into explanations. We sometimes call the cognitive architecture the *language of thought* (Fodor, 1975), realizing that language of thought refers to a *programming* language. How do we determine the language of thought? We do so with a complete functional analysis of human cognition. Higher-order functions in such an analysis describe the general information processing being carried out. Lowest-order functions are physically instantiated and therefore represent the cognitive architecture.

In short, then, determining the language of thought requires researchers to conduct a complete functional analysis, which includes collecting evidence for claiming that certain functions are primitive. The primitive functions define the language of thought. Therefore, cognitive psychologists aim to identify the architecture of cognition.

3.6 Functional Analysis of Colour Perception

To illustrate functional analysis, consider the *trichromatic theory* of colour perception (Wasserman, 1978), which begins with Sir Isaac Newton's 17th-century experiments using prisms. Newton found that a prism refracts sunlight into the rainbow's full spectrum. A second prism recombines the rainbow back into white light. Newton hypothesized that we can describe any perceived colour as a weighted combination of seven different primary colours (red, orange, yellow, green, blue, indigo, and violet).

Newton's theory inspired several competitors. The German poet Johann Wolfgang von Goethe proposed his own two-colour theory (based upon yellow and blue) in 1810. Thomas Young proposed a three-colour theory in 1801. Others proposed four-colour theories (Karl Hering in 1874 and Christine Ladd-Franklin in 1893). Physicist James Clerk Maxwell resolved the debate about the minimum number of primary colours for colour perception in 1856. He proved that we can express any perceived colour using no more than three primary colours.

Maxwell's proof provides the computational foundation for the trichromatic theory of human colour perception. That theory is also known as the Young-Helmholtz theory because physiologist Hermann von Helmholtz (1868/1968) popularized Young's theory in biological terms at the dawn of experimental psychology. Helmholtz hypothesized that colour vision uses three different "nerve fibres," each sensitive to a different colour (red, green, or blue). A perceived colour results from combining the different fibre activities. Equal (and maximum) stimulation of all three fibres causes us to experience the colour white. Otherwise, the three fibres produce the sensation of some other colour. Helmholtz refined Young's theory by proposing that the three fibres had overlapping colour sensitivities to explain why we might fail to match some spectral colour by mixing the three primary colours in the Young-Helmholtz theory.

How do we relate the trichromatic theory to functional analysis? Helmholtz's theory was functional, not physical: "It must be confessed that both in men and in quadrupeds we have at present no anatomical basis for this theory of colors" (Helmholtz, 1868/1968, p. 95). Given the functional nature of the theory, why was it so influential?

First, the trichromatic theory predicted many observations about colour perception. From the early 18th century on, artists knew that we could use trichromatic techniques to produce diverse colours (Mollon, 1982). More precise colour-mixing experiments performed by Helmholtz and Maxwell provided strong support for the theory and could explain colour blindness. In other words, the trichromatic theory's predictive power led to its wide acceptance without being causally subsumed. Even though the theory's red, blue, and green detectors were not linked to biology, there was no evidence to weaken the claim that the three detectors were primitives.

Causal subsumption of the Young-Helmholtz theory required 20th-century methodologies. We now know that Helmholtz's nerve fibres are instantiated as different retinal cone receptors. Different receptors contain different photo-pigments. Microspectrophotometry reveals that each photo-pigment generates maximum responses to different light wavelengths, the wavelengths required by Helmholtz's theory (Dartnall et al., 1983). Measures of action potentials from cone cells support Helmholtz's hypothesis that different channels have overlapping sensitivities (Schnapf et al., 1990). Mechanical principles explain how detected light generates an action potential. When a photo-pigment molecule absorbs light, the molecule's shape changes. The molecular shape change causes the receptor containing the photo-pigment to initiate a neural response (Nicholls et al., 1992). The trichromatic theory is a subsumed functional analysis.

3.7 The Cognitive Approach

Ulric Neisser (1967) tried to define cognitive psychology by the topics studied. He listed sensation, perception, imagery, retention, recall, problem solving, and thinking. But Neisser realized that his list did not separate cognitive psychology from other approaches: "It is apparent that cognition is involved in everything a human being might possibly do; that every psychological phenomenon is a cognitive phenomenon" (p. 4).

If we cannot define cognitive psychology via its topics, then perhaps we can define it via its research methods. However, we encounter problems. Modern textbooks show that cognitive psychologists use a staggering diversity of methods (Anderson, 2015; Goldstein, 2011; Sinnett et al., 2016). Many methods have long histories, and cognitive psychologists have borrowed and adapted them from other schools of experimental psychology. Hence, research methods do not uniquely define cognitive psychology.

Neisser (1967) finally adopted a broader perspective to define cognitive psychology. For him, cognitive psychology uniquely adopts the *cognitive approach*. That approach assumes a strong analogy between a computer program and human cognition. Neisser noted that a computer program is "a device for selecting, storing, recovering, combining, outputting and generally manipulating [information]" (p. 8). The cognitive approach aims to provide a similar account of human cognition. Importantly, functional analysis provides exactly the sort of theory required by Neisser's cognitive approach. Functional analyses can take the form of computer programs.

Consider one approach to computer programming, creating a *flow diagram*. A flow diagram illustrates a program's logical structure, defining what happens at different program stages. We can create a flow diagram without expressing how functions actually operate. Flow diagrams for computer programming appeared just after the Second World War (Goldstine & von Neumann, 1947). By the time of psychology's cognitive revolution, students learning to program first learned how to make flow diagrams (Farina, 1970; Schriber, 1969).

Crucially, we can represent both cognitive theories and computer programs as flow diagrams. Cognitive psychology's first flow diagram appeared in 1958 (Benjamin, 2019) to describe attentional filters (Broadbent, 1958). Using flow diagrams to represent cognitive theories rapidly grew in popularity. I discussed two examples earlier, the modal memory model (Figure 2-5) and hierarchical TOTE units (Figure 3-3). Modern cognitive psychology textbooks use many flow diagrams. Their use proliferated because cognitive psychologists employ functional analysis. When we explain some function by decomposing it into an organized system of sub-functions, we can easily express the explanation as a flow diagram (see Figure 3-3).

Although we can express cognitive theories as flow diagrams, and we can convert flow diagrams into computer programs, we need not *always* frame cognitive theories as working computer simulations. Neisser himself counselled against using simulations, arguing that "none of them does even remote justice to the complexity of human mental processes" (1967, p. 9). He believed instead that the cognitive approach generates testable hypotheses about whether computer programming ideas also apply to human cognition.

The usefulness of functional analysis comes from producing information processing accounts to generate testable hypotheses about human cognition. We need not convert a functional analysis into a working simulation to generate hypotheses. Instead, we can think through the flow diagram to make predictions (Braitenberg, 1984). Nevertheless, cognitive psychology has a long history of converting theories into working computer models (Dutton & Starbuck, 1971; Feigenbaum & Feldman, 1963; Lewandowsky, 1993; Newell, 1990; Newell & Simon, 1961; Simon, 1979). Creating such models offers many benefits (Lewandowsky, 1993). For instance, the computer simulation's behaviour provides testable predictions about human behaviour.

Cognitive psychology works to validate functional analyses by comparing behaviour predicted by functional analyses to behaviour observed in human participants. Have we decomposed the system into the correct set of sub-functions? Have the sub-functions been organized correctly? Do we have evidence of the causal subsumption of any sub-function? I now relate such questions to methods used by cognitive psychologists.

3.8 Seeking Strong Equivalence

Cognitive psychologists perform functional analysis to develop theories analogous to computer programs, theories for generating testable hypotheses about human cognition. Cognitive psychologists conduct experiments either to support or to reject a particular functional analysis by comparing the behaviour predicted by the theory to the behaviour observed in human participants. How do cognitive psychologists compare theories to data? Let us start by relating the comparison to a task from computer science: deciding about a computer program's intelligence.

Alan Turing (1950) proposed a method, now known as the *Turing test*, to determine whether a machine had achieved intelligence. He believed that we require intelligence to carry on meaningful conversations. In the Turing test, a human judge converses with different agents, some human, others computer programs. Turing argued that, if the judge cannot correctly distinguish humans from a program, then the computer program must be intelligent.

For example, consider testing a computer simulation of paranoid schizophrenia, PARRY, which participated in conversations, but its contributions became more paranoid over time. Colby et al. (1972) evaluated PARRY by having psychiatrists compare its conversations with conversations with human paranoids. The psychiatrists could not reliably determine whether a conversation was generated by a human or by PARRY. PARRY had passed the Turing test.

Unfortunately, the Turing test can be passed for the wrong reasons, as shown by another conversation-making program called ELIZA (Weizenbaum, 1966, 1976). ELIZA mimicked a humanistic psychologist's conversational style and generated extremely compelling conversations. "Some subjects have been very hard to convince that ELIZA is not human. This is a striking form of Turing's test" (Weizenbaum, 1966, p. 42). However, Weizenbaum did not create ELIZA to model natural language understanding. Instead, ELIZA used some programming tricks to parse incoming sentences into templates for creating convincing responses. "A large part of whatever elegance may be credited to ELIZA lies in the fact that ELIZA maintains the illusion of understanding with so little machinery" (Weizenbaum, 1966, p. 43).

ELIZA is simply a procedure—a flow diagram—for converting stimuli into responses. Let us consider the human with whom ELIZA converses as another flow diagram. When ELIZA and a human produce a convincing conversation, both flow diagrams generate appropriate outputs to inputs. We call two different systems generating the same input-output behaviour *weakly equivalent* systems (Pylyshyn, 1984).

We call input-output equivalence weak equivalence because two very different procedures can produce the same input-output mapping. Weak equivalence therefore illustrates another many-to-one relationship. For example, ELIZA uses the programming tricks invented by Weizenbaum, who intended ELIZA not to understand language. In contrast, humans use very different methods, methods for actually understanding sentences.

Weak equivalence affects our validation of functional analyses. A cognitive psychologist wants to claim that her functional analysis correctly explains some cognitive phenomenon. But weak equivalence means that methods only examining input-output mappings—like the Turing test—cannot validate a cognitive theory.

Cognitive psychologists do not want to propose weakly equivalent theories about human cognition. Instead, they want to propose strongly equivalent theories about cognition. *Strong equivalence* exists when two systems use the same procedures to generate the same input-output mapping (Pylyshyn, 1984). Strongly equivalent systems (1) generate the same input-output mapping, (2) use the same program or algorithm to produce the mapping, and (3) use the same architecture or programming language to bring the algorithm to life. In other words, both systems use the same flow diagram, which in turn uses the same primitive functions.

To establish the strong equivalence of a functional analysis to human cognition, cognitive psychologists must go beyond the Turing test and examine additional evidence. They must observe behaviours, produced as unintended consequences of information processing, that reveal the nature of internal processing. We call such unintended behaviours *second-order effects* (Newell & Simon, 1972). Pylyshyn (1984) argues that we can study second-order effects using three different measures: relative complexity evidence, error evidence, and intermediate state evidence. In the next sections, I consider second-order effects in more detail.

3.9 Relative Complexity Evidence

In the 19th century, Dutch physiologist Franciscus Donders (1869/1969) launched *mental chronometry* to measure the duration of mental processes. Prior to Donders, researchers used the *simple reaction time task* to measure nerve impulse latency. Researchers presented a stimulus (e.g., a mild shock to the foot) to a participant, who pressed a response key as soon as he felt the shock, and measured the time elapsed between presenting the stimulus and pressing the key.

Donders added a condition that required participants to decide before responding; we call his method the *choice reaction time task*. For instance, Donders could deliver a shock to either foot; the participant would then press one key if he felt a shock in the left foot or a different key if he felt a shock in the right foot. Participants decided which key to press. Donders reasoned that participants would take longer to respond by having to decide (about shock location) in addition to performing the other actions required by the simple reaction time task. Figure 3-4 illustrates the differences that he assumed to exist between the two reaction time tasks.

Donders believed that the differences between the two tasks permitted him to measure the duration of mental processes. He argued that we can measure the

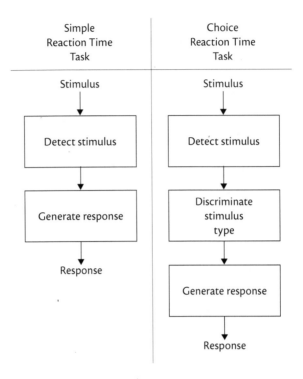

| Simple
Reaction Time
Task | Choice
Reaction Time
Task |

Figure 3-4 Two types of reaction time tasks to be compared to determine the amount of time required for the "Discriminate Stimulus Type" stage of processing.

time required to decide by subtracting the response time for the simple reaction task from the response time for the choice reaction time task, because the only difference between the two tasks is the decision-making stage. We call his technique the *subtractive method*.

The subtractive method requires two assumptions. First, a processing stage must start only after the preceding stage finishes. Second, adding a new processing stage must not affect the other stages—the *assumption of pure insertion* (Sternberg, 1969b). The subtractive method fell out of favour in the 19th century when some researchers questioned these two assumptions (Külpe & Titchener, 1895). However, by the 1960s, cognitive psychologists altered the method established by Donders to address such concerns.

One variation was the *additive factors method* (Sternberg, 1969a, 1969b). This method holds the number of processing stages constant across conditions but manipulates processing steps *within* a processing stage. For instance, consider

Sternberg's (1969b) landmark *memory scanning task*. In that task, participants remember a list of items (in primary memory). When presented with a probe item, they decide as quickly and accurately as possible whether the probe item belongs to the remembered list.

The additive factors method manipulates processing within a particular stage. For instance, Sternberg (1969b) varied the number of items remembered in the list. By increasing the length of a list, Sternberg influenced processing times within the stage in which memorized items compared with the probe. Sternberg generated different hypotheses about how manipulating list length would affect reaction time; different hypotheses assumed that memory scanning uses different search processes.

For instance, Sternberg hypothesized that an *exhaustive search* scans the memory. An exhaustive search scans every item (in order) before responding. If scanning each item requires constant time, then speed in responding to the presence of the probe will increase as the list increases. Furthermore, an exhaustive search should produce no differences in response time for trials in which the probe belongs to the list versus trials in which the probe does not belong to it (Figure 3-5, left panel).

Sternberg made different predictions if a *serial self-terminating search* scanned memory. This search moves from the first item to the last item on the list but stops when it discovers the probe item. The serial self-terminating search hypothesis predicts the same reaction time function as that predicted by an exhaustive search for trials in which the probe does not belong to the list, because both processes scan

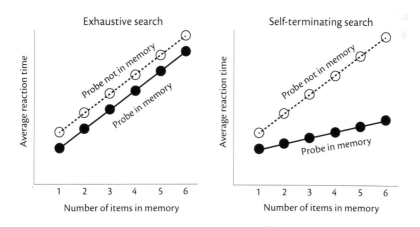

Figure 3-5 Predicted reaction time functions for an exhaustive search and for a serial self-terminating search in Sternberg's memory scanning task.

all items. However, when the probe belongs to the list, the reaction time function will have a shallower slope (in fact, half of the slope found when the probe does not belong to the list; Figure 3-5, right panel). When the probe belongs to the list, the scan will only process, on average, half of the items before finding the probe. "Yes" responses with a serial self-terminating search require half of the scanning compared with "No" responses, halving the slope of the reaction time function.

Sternberg (1969b) found that human participants in the memory scanning experiment produced reaction time functions consistent with the exhaustive search hypothesis and proposed a memory scanning model for which an exhaustive search provided more efficiency than a serial self-terminating search.

Sternberg's use of reaction time to evaluate memory scanning illustrates what Pylyshyn (1980, 1984) calls *relative complexity evidence*, which recognizes that some problems are more challenging, and require more processing, than others. A valid cognitive theory will produce relative complexity rankings of problems identical to rankings based upon human performance. Both the model and the participant will find the same problems "easy"; both the model and the participant will find the same problems "hard."

Reaction time provides relative complexity evidence, because harder problems presumably require more processing time than do easier problems. Sternberg's predicted reaction time functions (Figure 3-5) illustrate the relative complexity of different memory scan techniques. The number of items in memory, and whether the probe belongs to the list, affect Sternberg's techniques differently. Sternberg supported exhaustive search over serial self-terminating search by comparing modelled reaction time functions to functions obtained from human participants.

Relative complexity evidence informs functional analysis. Researchers frequently use *visual search tasks* to study visual cognition. In a visual search task, a participant sees several displayed objects and must decide whether one object (the target) is unique compared with the others (the distractors). The dependent measure is reaction time, and the independent variables include the number of distractors and the features used to define objects.

Visual search tasks reveal the *pop-out effect*. Some targets immediately "pop out" from the display, so the number of distractors does not influence the time to detect the presence of the target (Treisman & Gelade, 1980). A target that pops out possesses a unique visual feature (e.g., a unique colour, orientation, contrast, or motion). For example, a red object pops out from a display in which all distractors are green.

However, other unique targets do not pop out from a display. These targets are unique feature *combinations*, such as a red circle among distractors that are either red squares or green circles. The time to detect unique feature combinations increases with an increase in the number of distractors.

Visual search results inspired Treisman's *feature integration theory* (Treisman, 1985, 1986, 1988; Treisman & Gelade, 1980; Treisman & Gormican, 1988; Treisman et al., 1977). In feature integration theory's early processing stages, different detectors register the locations of different, basic, visual features. Unique basic features produce pop out. A different feature map represents locations of different features (different colours, orientations, movements, etc.). A target possessing a unique feature will be the only active location in one feature map and will pop out.

However, targets created from unique feature combinations do not produce unique activity in a single feature map and therefore do not pop out. Instead, detecting such targets requires additional processing. The additional processing aligns different feature maps using a master map of locations. The master map indicates which feature combinations exist at each location. An attentional spotlight performs a serial self-terminating scan of the master map. Attention scans from one location to the next until discovering a unique target. With such a serial search from location to location, the reaction time for detecting a unique combination of features increases as the number of distractors increases.

Feature integration theory explained why some unique targets pop out, but others do not. Reaction time data motivated a particular functional decomposition. However, reaction times can provide relative complexity evidence for evaluating competing functional analyses. For instance, *guided search theory* arose from concerns about feature integration theory (Wolfe, 1994; Wolfe et al., 1989; Wolfe et al., 1988). Wolfe worried that feature integration theory did not use results from early feature processing stages to direct the attentional spotlight. In contrast, guided search theory informs the search with both early feature processing and attentional processing. Early feature processing directs attention to visual objects that differ from their neighbours; higher-order processes direct attention to objects possessing target features. Thus, the two processes produce an efficient search by directing attention to locations likely to hold the target.

3.10 Error Evidence

Relative complexity evidence uses problem difficulty to rank order problems for comparing two systems (e.g., a functional analysis and a human participant). A valid functional analysis should match a human participant when we order problems from the easiest to the hardest. Section 3.9 related relative complexity evidence to measuring reaction time, because more challenging tasks should take longer to perform than less challenging tasks. However, relative complexity evidence can come from other sources, such as measuring performance accuracy. Harder problems cause more errors than easier problems.

A recent study gives an example of using errors to provide relative complexity evidence (Dawson, 2022). In this study, cue combinations signalled reward probability. The logical structure of cue combinations was manipulated; the interaction was either the AND of two cues (signalling a reward if both cues were present) or the XOR of two cues (signalling a reward if only one cue was present). The reward probability signalled by the cue interactions was also manipulated (high versus low probability) to alter the interaction's size as measured by a probabilistic value called conditional dependence.

Dawson (2022) trained very simple artificial neural networks called perceptrons (Rosenblatt, 1958) to predict the reward probability signalled by cues. He found an interaction between the manipulations of the logical structure and of reward size associated with the cue interaction. As a result, the networks were very poor at estimating reward probability for the XOR/low-probability condition compared with the other conditions.

Dawson (2022) then ran an experiment in which human participants learned to estimate probabilities signalled by stimuli defined by different cue patterns. He discovered higher accuracy for participants in conditions for which the perceptrons also performed well and lower accuracy for participants in conditions for which the perceptrons also performed less well. Dawson proposed the perceptron as a plausible model of human probability learning.

The example provided by Dawson (2022) illustrates how accuracy measures can provide relative complexity evidence. However, the errors made by models or by participants can also provide additional information. A system's mistakes can reveal information about internal processing, information called *error evidence* (Pylyshyn, 1984).

Cognitive psychology frequently examines error evidence. We saw in Chapter 2 that Conrad's (1964) analysis of letter confusion provided evidence for acoustic, not visual, representations in primary memory. Similar results emerge when using words as stimuli (Baddeley, 1966). Baddeley found more confusion between memories of similar-sounding words, even when he presented words visually. The semantic similarity between words held in primary memory interferes far less with recall.

In contrast, semantic similarity produces more recall errors from secondary memory (Baddeley & Dale, 1966). For instance, for two semantically similar word lists, learning the second list of words interfered with memory of the first list. However, primary memory did not produce the same effect. Such error evidence indicates that secondary memory encodes concept meanings. Encoding meanings causes other memory errors. For instance, human participants will mistakenly recognize a sentence as having been seen before provided that the sentence conveys the same meaning as that provided by previously presented material (Bransford et al., 1972).

Error evidence also provides insight into finer details. One study used multivariate statistics to explore letter confusion in iconic memory (Dawson & Harshman, 1986). The study found more likely confusion between letters with many features and letters built from a subset of the features than vice versa. For example, confusion between *E* and *F* or between *E* and *L* occurred more frequently than confusion between *F* and *E* or between *L* and *E*. Dawson and Harshman argued that such error evidence supports a letter recognition model involving feature accumulation. For instance, such a model would accumulate a vertical line and three horizontal lines as the features of *E*. Mistakes occur when not all features are correctly detected. For instance, a failure to detect one of the horizontal lines in *E* could incorrectly register *F*, and a failure to register two of these lines could incorrectly register *L*. Confusion asymmetries—*E* is more likely to be confused with *L* than *L* is with *E*—emerge naturally from feature accumulation failures.

3.11 Intermediate State Evidence

Cognitive psychologists also use *intermediate state evidence* to validate a functional analysis (Pylyshyn, 1984). Such evidence concerns the intermediate knowledge states that a system passes through during information processing. If a functional analysis is strongly equivalent to a modelled system, then both proceed through identical intermediate states.

Intermediate state evidence plays a central role in studying human problem solving. Newell and Simon's classic 1972 book *Human Problem Solving* summarized 20 years of studying how humans solved problems. Their explanations took the form of working computer simulations; they evaluated simulations by comparing their intermediate states to those of human problem solvers.

Newell and Simon (1972) used a core methodology called *protocol analysis* (Ericsson & Simon, 1984). Protocol analysis begins by collecting verbal protocols from participants solving problems. A verbal protocol records what participants say as they "think out loud" while solving a problem. The problems that Newell and Simon studied—problems in cryptarithmetic, logic, and chess—were difficult enough to ensure that participants engaged in problem-solving behaviour but not so difficult that the problem could not be solved in a reasonable time, or the problem would produce a verbal protocol too long for later analysis.

Protocol analysis proceeds in several steps. First, a single participant solves a problem, speaking aloud at all times. Participants have been trained to think out loud and are encouraged to think out loud by the experimenter if they stop talking during a session. The session is tape-recorded, providing the raw data for the analysis.

Second, the recorded protocol is transcribed, breaking the transcription into short phrases labelled for later reference. The labelling is a form of data preprocessing because each labelled phrase is assumed to represent a single problem-solving state. However, there is very little additional editing of the protocol.

Third, the transcribed problem is used to infer the participant's *problem space*. A problem space defines the different knowledge states used to represent a problem during its solution. A particular knowledge state can be thought of as a set of symbols that represents a problem's current condition. To move from one state to the next is to apply some rule to manipulate symbols in order to change the knowledge state. A participant was presumed to "encode these problem components—defining goals, rules, and other aspects of the situation—in some kind of space that represents the initial situation presented to him, the desired goal situation, various intermediate states, imagined or experienced, as well as any concepts he uses to describe these situations to himself" (Newell & Simon, 1972, p. 59). The problem space makes explicit such encoded properties.

Fourth, a participant's problem space is converted into a *problem behaviour graph*. This graph is a set of connected nodes. Each node represents a knowledge state about the problem. Each link represents a rule in the problem space that, when applied to a knowledge state, produces the next knowledge state in the graph. Typically, nodes are linked from left to right to illustrate the process of solving a problem.

However, a problem behaviour graph can also represent a participant's changing approach to a problem. Sometimes in pursuing a train of thought a participant reaches a dead end and backtracks to some earlier point in her reasoning. A problem behaviour graph represents such backtracking by going back to the knowledge state to which the participant has returned, drawing a link downward, and duplicating the returned-to knowledge state. Thus, the problem behaviour graph illustrates both progress on a problem (by growing outward from left to right) and backtracking to previous knowledge states (by growing downward from top to bottom).

Fifth, a *production system* is used to create a working computer simulation to solve the problem. A production system's basic operations are derived from the problem behaviour graph by inferring potential rules that describe the links between states. Intermediate state evidence evaluates how well the production system emulates human performance by comparing the production system's problem behaviour graph to the participant's.

Newell and Simon (1972) proposed the production system as the cognitive architecture. A production system consists of a set of operators. Each operator is a condition-action rule. A simulation begins with each operator scanning memory simultaneously, searching for its condition (i.e., a particular string of symbols). When one operator finds its condition, it temporarily inhibits the other operators and performs its action. A production's action involves manipulating the symbols in memory. Once symbol manipulation finishes symbols, the production releases control, and the system returns to the state in which all operators scan memory in search of their conditions.

Note that a production system like the one described above generates all of the information required to create a problem behaviour graph for the simulation. At any moment in time, the current knowledge state for the production system is the set of symbols being held in memory. To move from this state to the next, a particular production captures control and manipulates the symbols in memory. Thus, a link between knowledge states indicates which production was used. The fact that a production system can generate its own problem behaviour graph means that we can compare the production system graph to the problem behaviour graph created from a participant's example.

For instance, Newell and Simon (1972) studied the cryptarithmetic problem DONALD + GERALD = ROBERT. A participant is presented with this statement and told that D = 5. The task is to determine the integer represented by each remaining letter. Newell and Simon's protocol analysis of one participant's work on this problem generated a problem behaviour graph consisting of 238 nodes. Newell and Simon used this graph to find evidence for 14 separate productions and used them to create a working production system. They found that the production system accounted for approximately 80% of the subject's problem behaviour graph. This is a striking correspondence between the intermediate states measured for a human participant and those created by a computer simulation of his thought processes.

3.12 The Cognitive Impenetrability Criterion

Cognitive psychology seeks strong equivalence between systems. Strongly equivalent systems generate the same input-output mapping by using the same information processing steps. Three different sources of information can establish whether two systems use the same algorithm: relative complexity evidence, error evidence, and intermediate state evidence.

However, strong equivalence requires that two systems not only run the same program but also use the same programming language, the same information processing primitives, and the same functional architecture (Section 3.5). "Devices with different functional architectures cannot, in general, directly execute identical algorithms" (Pylyshyn, 1984, p. 96).

In many cases, supporting the claim that a function is a primitive involves appealing to findings collected from outside cognitive psychology, such as evidence from neuroscience. For instance, discovering that the surgical removal of part of the human brain disrupted primary memory, but not secondary memory (Scoville & Milner, 1957), provided anatomical evidence for the modal memory model (Squire, 2009). Similarly, evidence from visual neuroscience (Livingstone & Hubel, 1988) supports the existence of the various feature maps proposed as the early stages of feature integration theory (Treisman, 1986; Treisman & Gelade, 1980).

In other cases, a functional theory becomes widely accepted by explaining experimental results. Such success permits the theory to flourish while awaiting its subsumption, as illustrated earlier by the trichromatic theory, which provided the dominant account of colour perception, a century before being subsumed.

Given the importance of discovering primitive functions, can cognitive psychologists do so by collecting data from *within* their own discipline? Can the results of a cognitive psychology experiment help to subsume causally a functional analysis? Pylyshyn (1980, 1981b, 1984) proposes the *cognitive penetrability criterion* as one approach that cognitive psychologists can use to examine whether a function is primitive. If we can change a function's behaviour by altering a participant's beliefs, then we call the function *cognitively penetrable*. Cognitively penetrable functions are not primitive.

In contrast, if a wide variety of relevant belief changes do not affect the function, then we call the function *cognitively impenetrable*. Primitive functions must be cognitively impenetrable. The cognitive penetrability criterion "allows us to drive a wedge between cognitive processes and the part of the cognitive system fixed with respect to cognitive or semantic influences" (Pylyshyn, 1984, p. 139).

The cognitive penetrability criterion's logic begins by assuming that human information processing is instantiated by brain function. As we learn about the world, our brain structure changes (Doidge, 2007; Kolb, 1995). Knowledge must be stored by modifying neural connections. However, some brain features must be less modifiable than others (Newell, 1990). Newell argued that the brain has some structures, called *fixed structures*, that change relatively slowly. Fixed structures provide the architecture of cognition and differ from other structures that change much more rapidly because they store information.

An architecture associated with fixed brain structures will not change as new information is acquired. Adding new mental contents will not change the mechanisms for manipulating information. "An architecture provides a boundary that separates structure from content. Behavior is determined by variable content being processed according to the fixed processing structure, which is the architecture" (Newell, 1990, p. 82). Therefore, we can test whether a particular function belongs to the architecture by changing mental contents. If changes in contents *alter* the function's operation, then the function is not part of the architecture. If the function belongs to the architecture, then it is fixed and should not be affected by content manipulations.

Pylyshyn's cognitive penetrability criterion follows directly from this logic. Pylyshyn's method proceeds by first measuring some function of interest. Then a participant's beliefs are changed in a fashion related meaningfully to the function. Finally, the function is measured again after manipulating mental content. If the function changes in a way related to the changed belief, then it is cognitively penetrable and does not belong to the architecture. The cognitive penetrability criterion plays an important role in the debate about whether the spatial properties of mental images belong to the architecture.

We experience mental images as "pictures in the head" when we solve spatial problems. Many experiments study the properties of mental images (Kosslyn, 1980; Shepard & Cooper, 1982). These experiments reveal that mental images have spatial properties. Mental images have a spatial layout, so we require time to scan from one image location to another. Similarly, the time to rotate mental images to a new orientation increases with the amount of rotation required. The imagery debate examines whether the spatial properties of mental images belong to the cognitive architecture (Block, 1981; Pylyshyn, 1973). Some evidence in the imagery debate shows cognitive penetrability of spatial properties of mental images; such properties do not belong to the architecture.

To illustrate using such evidence, consider the *image scanning task* (e.g., Kosslyn, 1980, pp. 36–52). In a typical scanning experiment, participants create a mental image of a memorized map. Then they use the image to answer questions. For instance, Kosslyn asked participants to focus their attention on one location, and then Kosslyn named another location. Participants scanned the image from the first location to the second one. Kosslyn manipulated the distance between the two locations and found that a participant's response time increases with increases in the distance between the two locations.

Kosslyn (1980) presumed that the linear relation between distance and response time arose because a mental image's spatial extent belonged to the architecture. If so, then changing a participant's beliefs about the task should not alter the relationship between distance and scanning time. However, some evidence indicates that belief changes alter scanning times, meaning that image scanning is cognitively penetrable.

For instance, Liam Bannon first replicated the linear relationship between image distance and reaction time (Pylyshyn, 1981b, pp. 242–243). However, Bannon hypothesized that task instructions led participants to believe that scanning should take time, because they were told to press a response button "when they arrived" at the second location. To test his possibility, Bannon altered the instructions to change participants' beliefs about the task. "The instructions specified merely that subjects give the compass bearing of the second place—that is, to state whether the second place was north, northeast, east, southeast, and so on of the first" (Pylyshyn, 1981b, p. 243). With these instructions, Bannon discovered that there was no relation between distance and reaction time; this result has been replicated by other researchers (e.g., Finke & Pinker, 1982). Thus, the map-scanning results are not caused by a primitive property of imagery, because results change when participants change beliefs about the task.

Cognitive psychologists must causally subsume their functional analyses and usually do so by appealing to evidence from other disciplines, such as neuroscience (Dawson, 2013). However, some results from experimental psychology can determine whether functional properties are primitives. The cognitive penetrability criterion, as illustrated in the imagery debate, shows how cognitive psychologists can explore architectural issues.

3.13 Cognitive Psychology in Principle and in Practice

In principle, cognitive psychology proceeds by conducting functional analysis, an approach inspired by the computer metaphor. In general, cognitive psychologists analyze cognition into components that we can describe as information processing functions. Such functions use rules to manipulate symbols. Furthermore, strong similarities exist between functional analyses and programs or algorithms. Explaining human cognition with functional analysis uses techniques similar to the methods used to explain a computer's behaviour. A functional analysis rests on the results of psychological experiments. Experimental observations of human behaviour motivate carving a complex process into an organized system of simpler sub-processes (see Chapter 2).

If, in principle, cognitive psychologists conduct functional analysis, then we expect, over time, that they will produce theories that include organized systems of larger numbers of sub-functions. For example, by the mid-1960s, cognitive psychology's crowning achievement was the modal memory model (Figure 2-5). Since then, both primary memory and secondary memory have been further analyzed into sub-components.

For instance, cognitive psychologists have decomposed primary memory into a more complex system known as *working memory* (Baddeley, 1986, 1990). Working memory consists of three sub-functions. The *central executive* operates on symbols stored in buffers and determines how attention is allocated across simultaneously ongoing tasks. The *visuospatial buffer* stores visual information. The *phonological loop* stores verbal information and itself has been further analyzed into sub-functions that include a phonological store for holding symbols and a rehearsal process for preserving items in the phonological store. Similarly, cognitive psychologists have decomposed secondary memory into distinct functional sub-components, including declarative versus non-declarative memory (Squire, 1992), semantic versus episodic memory (Tulving, 1983), and memory for words versus memory for images (Paivio, 1971, 1986).

Cognitive psychologists do not only use experimental results to decompose functions into sub-functions. They also use special observations—relative complexity evidence, error evidence, and intermediate state evidence—to validate a particular functional analysis. Furthermore, the cognitive penetrability criterion can determine if a function is primitive.

In practice, when cognitive psychologists conduct functional analysis, they do not produce unified accounts of human cognition. Instead, they generate diverse, competing theories. Validating a functional analysis not only establishes strong equivalence but also finds support to counter competing theories. For example, in Chapter 2 I briefly reviewed experimental results from studying human memory and used these results to motivate the modal memory model. Chapter 2 implies that all cognitive psychologists accepted the modal memory model. However, other theories offer very different explanations of the same results.

The *levels of processing* theory provides one example (Cermak & Craik, 1979; Craik & Lockhart, 1972). This theory emphasizes different kinds of processing instead of different kinds of memory stores. According to levels of processing, we retain items receiving deeper or more semantic processing better and longer than we retain items receiving shallower or less semantic processing. Levels of processing deliberately opposed the multi-store approach introduced in Chapter 2. "While multistore models have played a useful role, we suggest that they are often taken too literally, and that more fruitful questions are generated by the [levels of processing] formulation" (Craik & Lockhart, 1972, p. 681).

Because competing memory theories exist, cognitive psychologists who study memory must design experiments to determine whether to prefer one account (e.g., levels of processing) over another (e.g., multi-store models). The kinds of evidence introduced in Chapter 3 can evaluate competing functional analyses of the same cognitive phenomenon. Such evaluation is not limited to studying memory. For instance, earlier we saw different functional analyses exist for a visual search (i.e., feature integration theory versus guided search). Most topics in cognitive psychology have inspired competing theories.

Cognitive psychology's diversity arises from an evolving notion of what "information processing" means. In the mid-20th century, the digital computer provided the only notion of information processing available to cognitive psychology. Since then, new ideas about information processing have inspired competing cognitivist positions (Dawson, 1998, 2013). *Connectionism* arose from the belief that biological brains do not process information in the same way that digital computers do, leading to theories that abandon the explicit distinction between symbols and rules (Bechtel & Abrahamsen, 2002; Clark, 1989, 1993; Horgan & Tienson, 1996; McClelland & Rumelhart, 1986; Rumelhart & McClelland, 1986b). *Embodied cognition* arose from a rekindling of cyberneticists' interest in the interactions between agents and environments (Shapiro, 2011, 2014). Embodied theories propose that complex behaviours emerge from the interactions between simple agents and complicated environments (Braitenberg, 1984; Clark, 1997, 2003, 2008, 2016; Dawson et al., 2010; Noë, 2004, 2009). Many embodied cognitivists believe that the mind extends from inside the skull to include the surrounding environment (Clark & Chalmers, 1998).

Different ideas about information processing also inspire a diversity of proposed cognitive architectures. For instance, Dawson (1998, Table 6-1) lists 24 different proposals for the language of thought. We should not be surprised that many competing theories, and many competing architectures, exist in cognitive psychology. All psychological schools of thought have exhibited similar diversity (Heidbreder, 1933). Earlier schools began not by organizing pre-existing facts but by investigating general notions of the mind, collecting new facts along the way. A school's general ideas about the mind "can best be understood not as statements of scientific fact, not as summaries of existing knowledge, but as ways and means of arriving at knowledge, as temporary but necessary stages in the development of a science" (Heidbreder, 1933, pp. 16–17).

Cognitive psychology provides a modern illustration of Heidbreder's point. Cognitive psychology begins by asserting that cognition is computation and then develops new methodologies to collect evidence to permit cognitive psychologists to explain human cognition in the same way that computer scientists explain the operations of a computer.

Neisser's cognitive approach requires evaluating competing functional theories and competing architectural proposals. We cannot define cognitive psychology by which facts it collects or by which theories it considers. Instead, we must define it by using its primary method, functional analysis, as well as the directions in which functional analysis leads cognitive psychologists. "Science does not proceed in the light of reason alone, but like other human enterprises is a muddled adventure working itself out" (Heidbreder, 1933, p. 17). Cognitive psychology's diversity illustrates its unique "muddled adventure."

3.14 Chapter Summary

Chapter 1 related cognitive psychology to computer science, arguing that cognitive psychologists assume that human cognition is similar to the processing used by digital computers. Chapter 2 related cognitive psychology to general experimental psychology by illustrating how cognitive psychologists infer human information processing because we cannot directly observe it. Chapter 3 related cognitive psychology to the philosophy of science by arguing that cognitive psychologists analyze complex phenomena into organized systems of simpler sub-functions, an approach called functional analysis.

However, cognitive psychologists appear to explain one function by decomposing it into further, unexplained, sub-functions, leading to Ryle's regress. Cognitive psychologists must escape Ryle's regress if their functional descriptions are to achieve the status of scientific explanations. They escape Ryle's regress by discovering sub-functions simple enough to be explained by physical causes: causally subsumed functions. We do not explain a causally subsumed function by decomposing it into further functions.

Cognitive psychology aims to show strong equivalence between a functional analysis and human cognition. Chapter 3 introduced three kinds of evidence for establishing strong equivalence: relative complexity evidence, error evidence, and intermediate state evidence. The chapter also introduced the cognitive penetrability criterion for testing whether a function belongs to the architecture.

Cognitive Architectures

The information processing hypothesis leads cognitive psychologists to conduct functional analysis and face Ryle's regress. To escape Ryle's regress, they must discover a cognitive architecture. However, not all cognitive psychologists propose the same architecture, and many different architectures appear in cognitive psychology. In Chapter 4, I explore architectural variety and its causes by examining different architectural properties. Each property can take on different forms. Cognitive psychologists generate competing architectures when they make different decisions about the forms that these properties take.

4.1 The Variety of Cognitive Psychology

Cognitive psychologists hypothesize that cognition emerges from the rule-governed manipulation of mental representations. Cognitive psychology aims to explain such processing by conducting functional analysis. Cognitive psychologists collect data to infer processes that they cannot observe directly. They intend to make functional analysis explanatory by discovering primitive functions, the cognitive architecture.

One might expect that, if all cognitive psychologists perform functional analysis, then they must all discover the same architecture. However, cognitive psychology hosts many competing theories and rival architectures. How can such variety arise if cognitive psychologists embrace the same general research strategy? At least three answers exist.

First, we can infer different information processes from the same results. For example, consider memory scanning experiments (Sternberg, 1969b). Earlier we saw graphs of a linearly increasing relationship between reaction time and list length (Figure 3-5). Sternberg predicted such functions by assuming that we scan list items in serial fashion (i.e., one at a time). However, such graphs also conform to theories based upon parallel scanning of memory (i.e., scanning all items at once)

(Townsend, 1971, 1990). Consider a parallel scanning process that slows down as the list length increases. Such a process also predicts the Figure 3-5 graphs. Thus, completely opposite proposals—serial versus parallel processing—can produce identical predictions.

Second, the ideas explored by cognitive psychology's general approach do not arise in a theoretical vacuum. Cognitive psychologists explore predictions emerging from interesting hypotheses. But contrasting hypotheses about the same phenomenon lead different researchers in different directions, producing results supporting different theories. Consider the visual search (Treisman, 1986, 1988; Treisman & Gelade, 1980) introduced in Section 3.9. Treisman motivated her research by hypothesizing a single attentional spotlight that shifts from one location to another. As a result, she studied a visual search in tasks requiring participants to locate an individual target, discovering results to support feature integration theory.

However, different hypotheses about attention lead to very different studies. Pylyshyn (2001, 2003a, 2007) rejects the attentional spotlight hypothesis and instead proposes multiple attentional tags that attach themselves to different targets at the same time. As a result, in Pylyshyn's studies, participants track *multiple* targets simultaneously (Pylyshyn et al., 2008). Pylyshyn's results support a theory quite different from feature integration theory. In short, different hypotheses inspire different investigations. In turn, different investigations produce results supporting different theories of the same phenomenon.

Third, cognitive psychology does not restrict ideas, because it permits deliberate rebellions against established theories, rebellions that produce new ideas. Cognitive psychologists explain many well-studied topics by using widely accepted theories. We can move research in new directions by *rejecting* the established theory's assumptions. Roboticist Rodney Brooks promoted such scientific rebellion,

> During my earlier years as a postdoc at MIT, and as a junior faculty member at Stanford, I had developed a heuristic in carrying out research. I would look at how everyone else was tackling a certain problem and find the core central thing that they all agreed on so much that they never even talked about it. I would negate the central implicit belief and see where it led. This often turned out to be quite useful. (2002, p. 37)

Cognitive psychology provides many examples of rebelling against established theory. Established theories assume that memory involves different storage systems

(Shiffrin & Atkinson, 1969; Waugh & Norman, 1965). Very different theories arise if we abandon the assumption and instead assume that different memories reflect differences in control (Baddeley, 1986) or differences in processing (Craik & Lockhart, 1972). Established theories assume that explicit symbols and processes exist (Newell & Simon, 1972). Very different theories arise when we rebel by assuming that cognition does not require symbols or rules (McClelland & Rumelhart, 1986; Rumelhart & McClelland, 1986b). Established theories assume that the skull completely contains the mind (Adams & Aizawa, 2008; Fodor, 1968). Very different ideas emerge when we assume that the mind extends into the world, making the world part of cognition (Brooks, 2002; Shapiro, 2011).

Thus, cognitive psychologists can share a general research strategy but still produce widely varying theories. Chapter 4 describes how different models arise when researchers make different assumptions about the cognitive architecture. Some propose serial processing, whereas others propose parallel processing. Some propose data-driven processing, yet others propose theory-driven processing. Some propose automatic processing, but others propose controlled processing. Some propose innate processes, whereas others focus on learning. Some propose isotropic processing, yet others propose modular processing. Different cognitive psychologists propose different structure-process pairings or different kinds of control. Chapter 4 shows how different assumptions produce radically different cognitive theories.

4.2 Serial and Parallel Processing

Chapter 4 illustrates that theoretical variety emerges in cognitive psychology when different cognitive psychologists make different assumptions about the cognitive architecture. To begin, I explore one architectural property: does the architecture execute one rule at a time (serial processing) or several rules at a time (parallel processing)? Many different theories begin when cognitive psychologists make different assumptions about serial versus parallel processing.

Mental chronometry, pioneered by the subtractive method (Donders, 1869/1969) (see Section 3.9), measures the time taken by mental processes (Luce, 1986; Posner, 1978). If Task B requires one more processing stage than Task A does, then we measure the additional stage's processing duration by subtracting the time required to perform Task A from the time required to perform Task B.

The subtractive method assumes that mental operations involve *serial processing*, which only executes one process at any given moment (Figure 4-1). Figure 4-2 illustrates four different processes carried out in serial fashion. Process 1 occurs first, then Process 2, and so on. However, results like the famous Stroop effect indicate that cognitive processing is not always serial.

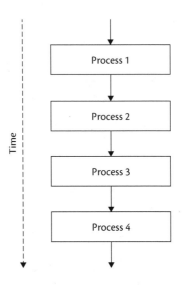

Figure 4-1 Serial processing.

Stroop (1935) studied the interference between information available at the same time. He presented participants with a list of colour names. In one condition, the ink colour for each word differed from the colour named by the word. For instance, Stroop printed the word *red* in blue, green, brown, or purple ink but never in red ink. He asked some participants to read the printed words out loud (ignoring the colour of the ink) and found that ink colour did not interfere with performance. Stroop found no difference between the time to read coloured words and the time to read the same words printed in black ink. However, he found a very different result when participants named each word's ink colour (ignoring the colour named by the word). Colour words interfered with naming ink colour; participants required 50 seconds more to name the ink colour of colour words than required when naming the ink colours of squares.

Stroop's result illustrates *parallel processing*, which occurs when more than one process occurs at the same time. If words slow down naming ink colour, then two different processes operate simultaneously: processing the word and processing the ink colour. Researchers have proposed numerous explanations for the Stroop effect (Dyer, 1973; Jensen & Rohwer, 1966; Macleod, 1991, 2015). All explanations share the idea that we process words and ink colours in parallel.

For example, consider the "horse race model" (Posner & Snyder, 1975) illustrated in Figure 4-2. That model has two processing streams—one for words, the other for ink colours—operating in parallel, as illustrated by the vertical overlap of the boxes in the figure. For example, Process 1 and Process A start at the same time, because the tops of their boxes align vertically in Figure 4-1.

The horse race model proposes that we process words faster than we process colours. Figure 4-2 illustrates faster word processing by shortening the height of word process boxes compared with the height of colour process boxes. Because the model processes words faster, the word stream will finish first. Therefore, word processing will finish before colour processing interferes. But, by finishing first, the word stream can interfere with naming ink colour by delivering a competing colour word participants must ignore to name ink colour.

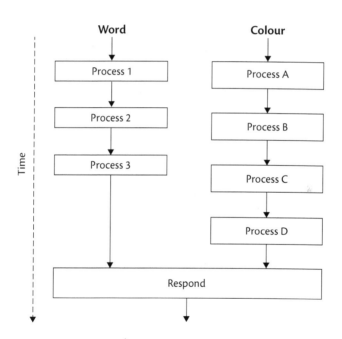

Figure 4-2 The Stroop effect indicates that different processes can operate in parallel. The "Word" processing stream finishes before the "Colour" processing stream: Process 3 finishes before Processes C or D.

Figure 4-2 combines parallel and serial processing. The two different processing streams run in parallel. However, each stream operates in serial. Feature integration theory provides another example of combining both serial and parallel processing in the same theory (Treisman, 1986, 1988; Treisman & Gelade, 1980). Feature integration theory (Figure 4-3) begins when specialized processors detect different features such as colour, motion, and so on. Feature detection occurs in parallel; Figure 4-3 illustrates parallel processing by vertically aligning feature detection processors.

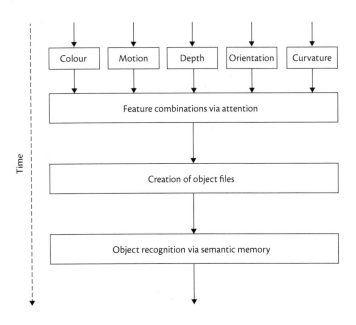

Figure 4-3 Feature integration begins with parallel processing. This is then followed by processing stages operating in serial.

Once parallel processes detect various features, serial processing begins. First, attention combines different features together to create object representations called *object files* (Kahneman et al., 1992). Next, object recognition (object classification or object naming) occurs by linking object files to semantic memory. Note that the final three stages in Figure 4-3—combining features, building object files, and accessing semantic memory—operate in serial. Figure 4-3 illustrates serial processing by placing the three final stages at different vertical positions.

Researchers can propose other combinations of parallel and serial processing. *Cascaded processing* provides one example (McClelland, 1979). In cascaded processing, a second (serial) process begins before the preceding (serial) process finishes. Cascaded processing (Figure 4-4) permits incomplete information to be passed from one process to the next, giving the second process a head start before the first process ends. Figure 4-4 illustrates mostly serial processing: Process 1 occurs first, Process 2 second, and so on. However, the vertical overlap between Process 1 and Process 2 in the figure indicates that Process 2 begins before Process 1 finishes. Similarly, Process 2 is cascaded with Process 3, and Process 3 is cascaded with Process 4. The *dual route cascaded model* of reading uses cascaded processing (Coltheart et al., 2001).

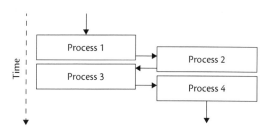

Figure 4-4 Four processes in cascaded processing.

Still other theories use only parallel processing. Figure 4-5 illustrates four processes running at the same time, continually sending information to each other, in a system called an *auto-associative network* (Ackley et al., 1985; Hopfield, 1982; Kohonen, 1977). Auto-associative networks can model many cognitive phenomena, such as tracking moving objects (Dawson, 1991), paired-associate learning (Rizzuto & Kahana, 2001), visual search (Fukushima, 1986; Gerrissen, 1991), and concept categorization (Anderson et al., 1977).

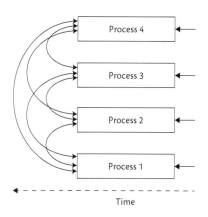

Figure 4-5 A system in which all processing is parallel.

Auto-associative networks illustrate *connectionism* (Bechtel & Abrahamsen, 2002; Churchland et al., 1990; Dawson, 2004; McClelland & Rumelhart, 1986; Rumelhart & McClelland, 1986b). Connectionists believe in dramatic differences between information processing in brains and information processing in digital computers. We can treat each process in Figure 4-5 as a model neuron, each operating in parallel, continually sending signals back and forth to one another.

Importantly, many connectionist models combine parallel and serial processing. Figure 4-6 illustrates one network, the multi-layer perceptron. Processors in the multi-layer perceptron represent neurons, and therefore connectionists describe such networks as using parallel processing. However, multi-layer perceptrons also include serial processing: input units must first send signals to hidden units before the hidden units activate. Similarly, output units cannot activate until they receive signals from the hidden units.

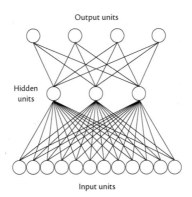

Figure 4-6 The multi-layer perceptron is a typical connectionist network. Circles represent neuron-like processors.

Connectionism arises from adopting a rebellious counter-assumption to conventional theory: what if cognition differs from the serial digital computer? Connectionists produce theories quite different from other approaches (Bechtel & Abrahamsen, 2002; Dawson, 1998, 2013). We will encounter connectionism again in Chapter 5. In Chapter 4, I only need to emphasize connectionism's preference for parallel processing over serial processing.

By making different assumptions about serial versus parallel processing, or by combining both serial and parallel processing in the same theory, cognitive psychologists can create diverse theories. Such diversity emerges from making different assumptions about one architectural property (temporal relations between processes). Other architectural properties also permit different assumptions, generating theoretical diversity. The next section explores a second architectural property, whether a theory proposes data-driven or theory-driven processing.

4.3 Data-Driven and Theory-Driven Processing

Researchers produce different theories by proposing different combinations of parallel and serial processing (Section 4.2). The direction in which information flows in a system provides another architectural property to vary to create diverse cognitive theories.

We define the direction in which information flows by distinguishing between *peripheral processing* and *central processing*. Peripheral processing occurs early (at cognition's start), has direct contact with the world, and involves detecting information. In contrast, central processing occurs later (after we detect and represent information), has no direct contact with the world, and manipulates information already represented. Information can flow from peripheral to central processes, or in the opposite direction, from central to peripheral processes.

Data-driven processing, or *bottom-up processing*, occurs when information flows from peripheral to central processing (Figure 4-7). In Figure 4-7, sensation is the most peripheral processing and involves detecting information from the world. Awareness is more central and involves being consciously aware of some detected information. Thought is most central and involves reasoning about detected information (e.g., classifying conscious information as an object, such as "scruffy brown dog"). Figure 4-7 illustrates data-driven processing because the arrows between the boxes point in the direction from peripheral processes toward central processes.

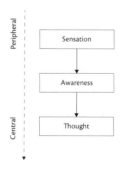

Figure 4-7 In data-driven processing, information flows from peripheral processes toward central processes.

The multi-layer perceptron presented in Figure 4-6 illustrates data-driven processing because input units first detect environmental information. Input units send signals to hidden units, which detect more complex features. Finally, hidden units send activity to output units, which generate a complex response. We describe the network's processing as data-driven processing because information always flows from input units (peripheral) toward output units (central).

Theory-driven processing, or *top-down processing*, occurs when information flows from central processes toward peripheral processes (Figure 4-8). Note that the arrows between boxes in Figure 4-8 point in the opposite direction when compared with the arrows in Figure 4-7. In theory-driven processing, results from central processes influence or guide more peripheral processing.

We find theory-driven processes in many cognitive theories of perception (Bruner, 1957, 1992; Bruner et al., 1951; Gregory, 1970, 1978; Rock, 1983). Most perceptual theories recognize that data-driven processing does not deliver all of the information that we need to experience the world (Marr, 1982). Theory-driven processes use our beliefs, knowledge, or expectations to fill in missing information. "We not only believe what we see: to some extent we see what we believe" (Gregory, 1970, p. 15). For example, my data-driven processes provide me with information indicating that I see a small black-and-white animal. Top-down processing permits a more sophisticated experience. When I am in my house, my expectations lead me to recognize my cat Phoebe. In contrast, when I am in the ravine, my expectations

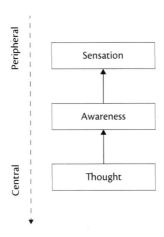

Figure 4-8 In theory-driven processing, information flows from central processes toward peripheral processes.

lead me to recognize, and avoid, a skunk. Top-down processing enables different expectations to add different information to the same representation delivered by data-driven processes.

Figures 4-7 and 4-8 illustrate models involving only data-driven or only theory-driven processing. However, information can flow in both directions in the same theory, as illustrated in Figure 4-9.

Treisman's feature integration theory combines both data-driven and theory-driven processing (Treisman, 1986, 1988; Treisman & Gelade, 1980). The first stage, feature detection, uses data-driven processing. Different feature maps represent locations of different features. We recognize objects by combining features at the same location in different maps. However, data-driven processes do not combine features. In feature integration theory, an attentional spotlight provides the "glue" to hold different feature maps together. Higher-level processes position the attentional spotlight: we deliberately direct our attention to a location of interest. Thus, theory-driven processing moves the attentional spotlight from location to location.

Feature integration theory combines not only data-driven with theory-driven processing but also serial processing with parallel processing. Thus, feature integration theory illustrates that making different assumptions about architectural properties permits diversity within cognitive theory. Other architectural properties also support theoretical diversity. Section 4.4 introduces another example,

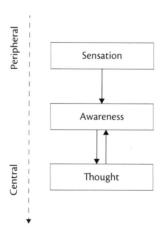

Figure 4-9 Many modern theories, such as Treisman's feature integration theory, include both data-driven and theory-driven processing.

when cognitive psychologists hypothesize whether processing is automatic or controlled.

4.4 Automatic and Controlled Processing

In Sternberg's (1969b) memory scanning task (see Section 3.9), participants determine whether a probe belongs to a memorized list. To study how we search primary memory, Sternberg varied list size and measured participants' response time. Sternberg argued that we scan memory with an exhaustive serial search. Later researchers varied Sternberg's task to discover additional properties of search processes (Schneider & Shiffrin, 1977; Shiffrin & Schneider, 1977). Schneider and Shiffrin varied not only how many items were memorized but also how many probes participants searched for in memory.

Schneider and Shiffrin also manipulated the number of elements used to create memory sets and stimulus sets. A target belongs both to the stimulus set and to the memory set. A distractor belongs to the stimulus set but not to the memory set. In Schneider and Shiffrin's *varied mapping condition*, items served as targets in some trials but as distractors in others. The varied mapping conditions increase task difficulty because participants must constantly attend to which items are targets since targets change from trial to trial. In contrast, in Schneider and Shiffrin's *consistent matching condition*, one set of items always served as targets, and a different set of items always served as distractors. In the consistent matching condition, targets never served as distractors.

Schneider and Shiffrin discovered that the two conditions produced strikingly different results. Participants found the varied mapping condition much more difficult than the consistent mapping condition. In the former condition, performance became poorer (slower, less accurate) with increases in the size of the memorized lists or in the number of probes. Performance did not improve with training. In contrast, participants performed faster in the consistent mapping condition, and varying the number of memorized items or the number of probes did not affect performance. Performance in the consistent matching condition improved with training: participants reported that early trials demanded effort but experienced less effort after performing several trials (Shiffrin & Schneider, 1977).

Schneider and Shiffrin used their results to argue for two qualitatively different types of processes. *Automatic processes* are fast, automatically activated by stimuli, place few demands on cognitive resources such as attention, and do not require top-down control. In contrast, *controlled processes* are slow, initiated by higher-order processes, place high demands on attentional resources, and require top-down control. Although the architectural distinction between automatic and controlled processing differs from the architectural proposals introduced earlier in this chapter strong relationships do exist. Automatic processing is more likely to be data driven and parallel, whereas controlled processing is more likely to be theory driven and serial.

Feature integration theory, which contains both parallel and serial processing, and both data-driven and top-down processing, also contains both automatic and controlled processing. For instance, pop out results from automatic processing, whereas searching for unique feature combinations is controlled processing. We could create variations of feature integration theory by changing how all of the different processing types combine in the model. We could make attentional scanning parallel instead of serial but slow down the processing with increases in how many objects are scanned. We could make parallel scanning of objects data driven. Such changes involve modifying architectural properties, and each modification produces a different theory.

We have seen three architectural properties in Chapter 4 (serial versus parallel processing, data-driven versus theory-driven processing, and automatic versus controlled processing). Varieties of cognitive theories emerge when researchers assign different values to any of these processes. I now turn to another important architectural property that permits different design decisions, the format of symbols and the nature of rules to manipulate them.

4.5 Structures and Processes

Cognitive psychologists believe that a *physical symbol system* produces cognition (Newell, 1980; Newell & Simon, 1976). The physical symbol system describes a class of devices "capable of having and manipulating symbols, yet is also realizable within our physical universe" (Newell, 1980, p. 136). Digital computers belong to the class of physical symbol systems. Cognitive psychologists believe that the brain also belongs to the same class. However, we must do more than merely claim that a physical symbol system causes cognition. Cognitive psychologists must also provide many architectural details. If cognition emerges from a physical symbol system, then which symbols does the system manipulate, and which processes perform the manipulating?

The many-to-one relationship between physical and functional properties (Section 1.2) means that any physical entity is a possible symbol. Because of the many-to-one relationship, we can construct universal machines (Section 1.5) from gears (Swade, 1993), LEGO (Agullo et al., 2003), electric train sets (Stewart, 1994), hydraulic valves, or silicon chips (Hillis, 1998). As a result, cognitive psychologists can consider many options for the nature of mental symbols and processes. Fortunately, the relationship between symbols and the processes for manipulating them is not arbitrary. Symbol properties—a symbol's format or *structure*—determine which processes can manipulate them. Symbols of one format can be manipulated only by certain processes, making some problems easier to solve than others. Changing the format means that symbols can be manipulated only by different processes, making different problems easier to solve. The close relationship between symbols and processes helps cognitive psychologists to define a cognitive architecture.

Let me illustrate how different structure-process pairings affect performance. Consider using a roadmap to represent spatial locations of places. A roadmap's format—its spatial layout—permits us to execute specific operations easily, such as visual scanning. We scan a roadmap to determine quickly which city will be encountered next along a route. However, a roadmap's spatial layout makes other operations more difficult to execute, making some questions more difficult to answer. For instance, we cannot determine the precise distance between two cities simply by scanning the roadmap. Instead, we must measure the distance on the map and then use a scale to convert the measured distance into kilometres.

If we represent the same information in a different format, then we can more easily execute different operations and therefore answer different questions more quickly. For instance, we can use a table of distances as a different format for representing the spatial relationships between cities. Each row or column of the table corresponds to a particular city. Each table number represents the distance between the row city and the column city. A table easily permits one operation called *table lookup*. We perform table lookup when we quickly read a table to retrieve information from the intersection between a row and a column. Table lookup permits us to use the table to quickly find the distance between two cities, a question more difficult to answer with the roadmap. However, table lookup does not permit us to easily determine the next city along our route, a question that we can answer quickly using a roadmap.

The roadmap versus distance table example illustrates the *structure-process relationship* (Dawson, 1998, 2013). Structure refers to the symbols' format (e.g., spatial map versus distance table). Process refers to the operations for manipulating structure (e.g., scanning versus table lookup). According to the structure-process relationship, when one chooses a particular structure, one also chooses which operations can easily manipulate that structure. The structure-process relationship determines the questions that we can easily answer because of a particular pairing between structure and process. Roadmaps permit scanning, making questions about routes easy but questions about distances difficult. In contrast, a different structure-process pairing—distance tables and table lookup—makes questions about distance easy but questions about routes difficult.

The practice of cognitive psychology depends on the structure-process relationship, which indicates that we can easily answer certain questions but cannot easily answer others. Thus, choosing a particular architecture for a theory, or choosing a particular combination of structure and process, generates hypotheses to test by collecting relative complexity evidence, error evidence, or intermediate state evidence (Sections 3.9–3.11). To illustrate, let us consider one theory about mental imagery.

We experience mental imagery as mental pictures, which we often use to solve spatial problems (Kosslyn, 1980). For instance, to remember how many windows a building has, we might create a mental image of the building, scan the image, and count how many windows we see with our "mind's eye."

Which mental structure produces mental imagery? Which format do mental images take in the cognitive architecture? Cognitive psychologist Stephen Kosslyn answers such questions with his *depictive theory* of mental imagery (Kosslyn, 1980, 1994; Kosslyn et al., 2006). According to the depictive theory, mental images literally depict spatial information with a picture-like format: mental images have a picture-like spatial layout.

According to the depictive theory, the picture-like characteristics of mental images result from a small number of *privileged properties* (Kosslyn, 1980). First, images occur in a spatial medium functionally equivalent to a coordinate space: images are analog representations possessing spatial extent. Second, images visually resemble the things that they represent: there is an "abstract spatial isomorphism" between mental images and the world (Kosslyn, 1980, p. 33). Mental images represent visible properties such as colour and texture.

The privileged, architectural, properties of mental imagery define its structure. In turn, the structure permits certain visual processes to manipulate images easily. We can scan mental images, inspect images at different apparent sizes, or rotate images to new orientations. By coupling visual processing with the depictive structure of images, we can easily solve visuospatial problems. Furthermore, the privileged properties generate strong predictions about the time required to use mental images to answer specific questions.

For example, in the *mental rotation task*, Roger Shepard presented participants with two side-by-side images, each rotated to a different orientation (Cooper & Shepard, 1973a, 1973b; Shepard & Metzler, 1971). Participants decided whether both images represented the same object. Shepard measured the angular disparity between the two images (the difference between the images' orientations) and how long it took participants to decide.

The depictive theory proposes that participants perform the mental rotation task by creating a mental image of one stimulus and then rotating the image to a new orientation. In the new orientation, participants can compare the rotated image to the other stimulus and decide whether the two represent the same object. The mental rotation task reveals that response time increases with increases in the amount of required mental rotation (angular disparity between stimuli). The result supports the depictive theory, which proposes that we rotate mental images holistically (as whole pictures), through intermediate orientations, because images have a picture-like format. The greater the angular disparity, the greater the time we need to rotate an image from the starting orientation to the ending orientation.

The *image scanning task* provides another example of testing the privileged properties of the depictive theory (Kosslyn, 1980; Kosslyn et al., 1978). In the image scanning task, participants create a mental image of a map. Kosslyn asked participants to scan the image from one location to another and to press a button when they arrived at the second location. Researchers manipulate the distance between the two locations and measure the time required for participants to respond. The image scanning task produces a linear relationship between response time and distance between locations (Kosslyn et al., 1978). Increasing the distance produces a corresponding increase in reaction time. The result supports the depictive theory, which claims that we scan the spatial extent of mental images at a constant rate. The distance-time relationship arises from an image being extended in space.

Researchers have also used computer simulations to study the depictive theory's privileged properties (Kosslyn, 1980, 1987, 1994; Kosslyn et al., 1984; Kosslyn et al., 1985; Kosslyn & Shwartz, 1977). The simulations demonstrate that the hypothesized properties of mental images produce many regularities observed in experimental studies of mental imagery.

The mental imagery example shows that detailed proposals about the structure-process relationship generate hypotheses for cognitive psychologists to test. Importantly, results obtained from mental imagery experiments do not restrict the variety of architectures that cognitive psychologists can explore. They can create alternative theories by proposing alternative structure-process relationships or by taking issue with one proposed by others.

For instance, some researchers challenged the depictive theory in a decades-long *imagery debate* (Block, 1981; Tye, 1991). The imagery debate (Section 3.12) examines one basic question: do Kosslyn's privileged properties belong to the architecture? Pylyshyn (1973, 1981a, 1981b, 1984, 2003a, 2003b, 2003c, 2007) argues that the depictive properties of mental images do not belong to the architecture; instead, primitive, non-spatial elements give rise to our spatial experience of mental images. Pylyshyn's argument led to variations of the image scanning task that produce results against the depictive theory. Cognitive psychology uses experimental evidence to resolve debates about the architecture.

4.6 Structure, Process, and Control

The preceding sections described many possible architectural choices, which in turn produce a variety of cognitive theories. I now explore how cognitive psychologists can create radically different accounts of the same phenomena by making different architectural decisions.

Many examples in Chapter 2 involved the modal memory model (Shiffrin & Atkinson, 1969; Waugh & Norman, 1965). That model depicts memory as a sequence of different stores (iconic memory, primary memory, and secondary memory) with different architectural properties (symbols, processes, durations, and capacities). The architectural differences between stores in the modal memory model emphasize different assumptions about structure and process (Section 4.5).

However, we do not define information processing using only structure and process. Information processors must also incorporate control (Section 1.1). Control determines which process manipulates a data structure at any given time. Cognitive psychologists who emphasize control over structure and process produce very different theories from the ones produced by cognitive psychologists who emphasize structure and process over control.

The *levels of processing* theory of memory provides one example of a control-based memory theory (Cermak & Craik, 1979; Craik, 2002; Craik & Lockhart, 1972; Lockhart & Craik, 1990). That theory replaces a structural account of memory with a procedural account. Lockhart and Craik (1990, p. 88) sought to displace "the idea (a) that memory could be understood in terms of elements ('items') held in structural entities called *memory stores*, (b) that the fate of an item so stored was determined by the properties of this store."

Craik and Lockhart used *depth of processing* to displace structural accounts of memory. Depth of processing reflects the degree to which we analyze a stimulus. Deep processing involves a semantic analysis of an item. For example, participants might determine whether each word in a list belongs to the category *flower*. Shallower processing involves analyzing non-semantic properties. For instance, participants might determine whether each word in a list rhymes with *train*.

Participants who perform deeper processing of a list also perform better in a surprise memory test, supporting levels of processing as an alternative account of the memory phenomena introduced in Chapter 2. Many view Craik and Lockhart's theory as attacking the distinctions between memory stores in the modal memory model. Craik and Lockhart believe that this view is overstated (Craik, 2002; Lockhart & Craik, 1990).

Importantly, depth of processing is under conscious control. We can deliberately decide to pay attention to stimulus meanings and therefore determine how well we remember items. Improving memory by performing deeper analysis offers another perspective on the mnemonic techniques introduced in Chapter 2.

4.7 Nativism and Empiricism

Chapter 4 demonstrates that various cognitive theories emerge when cognitive psychologists make different assumptions about the cognitive architecture. We have considered many different assumptions, ranging from serial versus parallel processing to emphasizing structure and process over control. Section 4.7 introduces yet another architectural property, whether information is innate or learned, by briefly considering the psychology of language.

Symbols make particular information explicit. For example, a grammatical sentence contains words in a linear order. In addition, a sentence's words belong to various parts of speech, and parts of speech are hierarchically organized. A sentence's representation must make explicit linear order, parts of speech, and hierarchical organization.

One representation, *phrase marker*, makes the three properties explicit (Figure 4-10). The words at the bottom of a phrase marker are in linear order. The nodes of a phrase marker represent different parts of speech: determinant ("Det"), adjective ("Adj"), noun ("N"), and verb ("V"). Links between nodes show the hierarchical organization of parts of speech. For instance, a noun phrase ("NP") can combine a determinant, an adjective, and a noun in a particular order.

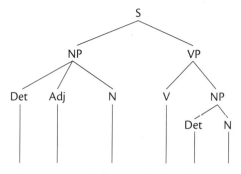

The cognitive psychologist seeks the architecture

Figure 4-10 An example phrase marker.

To define an architecture, we must also specify the rules for manipulating symbols and not just specify the symbols themselves. Two different kinds of rules manipulate phrase markers. A *context-free grammar* consists of rewrite rules for creating a phrase marker. For Figure 4-10, one rule, "S → NP VP," creates the figure's top two branches. The rule "NP → Det Adj N" and the rule "VP → V NP" create the figure's next level of branches. Other rules, called *transformations*, belong to a different grammar called a *transformational grammar*. Such a grammar converts one phrase marker into a different one. For instance, one transformation could convert the phrase marker for the Figure 4-10 sentence "The cognitive psychologist seeks the architecture" into a different phrase marker to represent the question "Does the cognitive psychologist seek the architecture?"

Phrase markers, and the rules for creating and manipulating them, belong to *generative grammar* (Chomsky, 1957, 1965, 1966, 1995; Chomsky et al., 2000). A generative grammar consists of explicit, well-defined rules for assigning structural descriptions (e.g., phrase markers) to sentences or for manipulating such descriptions (e.g., converting one phrase marker into another). We achieve language competence when we master and internalize a generative grammar. How do we do that? Obviously, we learn languages: children learn to speak the languages of the households in which they are raised. However, though we learn some aspects of language, researchers believe in the innateness of other important aspects of generative grammars.

Consider *Gold's paradox* (Gold, 1967; Pinker, 1979). Gold proved that generative grammars are too complex to learn under the conditions that children experience during typical language learning. Paradoxically, children clearly learn a language under these conditions! How do children avoid Gold's paradox? We can avoid it if much of a generative grammar is innate and therefore does not require learning.

We find one example of language innateness in a transformational grammar theory called *principles and parameters* (Chomsky, 1995). That theory includes phrase markers and rules for manipulating them but allows certain properties to vary from language to language. For instance, languages such as English are *head-initial* (noun phrases precede verb phrases), whereas others such as Japanese are *head-final* (verb phrases precede noun phrases). The head-directional property is an example of a *parameter*, a property that can adopt different values. A parameter's value determines certain phrase marker properties (e.g., head-initial versus head-final).

Linguistic experience determines parameter values. For instance, the head-directional property will adopt one value for children raised in an English-speaking household but adopt a different value for children raised in a Japanese-speaking household. However, a grammar's other properties (i.e., phrase markers and rules for manipulating them) are innate. We avoid Gold's paradox because we can learn parameter settings but cannot learn an entire transformational grammar. A grammar's partial innateness permits mastery of the whole grammar.

A transformational grammar's innate components define what Chomsky calls the *universal grammar*: "The study of innate mechanisms leads us to universal grammar" (1980, p. 206). Proposing an innate universal grammar illustrates *nativism*. We often associate nativism with the 17th-century philosophy of Rene Descartes. Cartesian philosophy (sometimes called *rationalism*) asserted that we derive new knowledge from the logic-like manipulation of innate ideas. When cognitive psychologists hypothesize that cognition is the rule-governed manipulation of symbols, and relate rules and symbols to a biological architecture, they adopt a modern version of Cartesian rationalism (Dawson, 2013). Indeed, Chomsky (1966) titled one of his books *Cartesian Linguistics*.

Cartesian psychology did not go unchallenged. The 17th-century philosopher John Locke (1706/1977) rejected the Cartesian claim of innate knowledge. For Locke, we acquire all of our ideas through experience: "Let us then suppose the mind to be, as we say, white paper, void of all characters, without any *idea*, how comes it to be furnished? . . . To this I answer, in one word, from *experience*" (p. 54). Locke's philosophy is known as *empiricism*.

Like nativism, empiricism also provides the philosophical foundation for many cognitive theories (Dawson, 2013), such as connectionist networks like the multilayer perceptron in Figure 4-6. Such a network's connection weights usually begin as small, randomly selected values, making the weights analogous to "white paper, void of all characters." Networks learn by responding to stimuli; mistakes cause connection weight changes to make response errors smaller. Networks illustrate empiricism, learning to solve problems from experienced mistakes.

Many modern cognitive theories combine nativism and empiricism. For instance, though principle and parameters theory (Chomsky, 1995) is nativist in its appeals to an innate transformational grammar, it is empiricist in its appeals to experience-based parameter setting. Competing theories weight empiricism and nativism differently. For instance, connectionist networks play an important role in another theory of language development emphasizing empiricism (Elman et al., 1996). However, Elman et al. also invoke nativism by assuming that the biology of neural development constrains connectionist learning mechanisms.

Our understanding of the architecture is affected by cognitive psychology's tendency to combine nativism and empiricism. The architecture consists of primitive information processing capabilities (Chapter 3). Since primitives are built into the system, and cognitively impenetrable, we cannot functionally decompose them. The brain must instantiate the architecture, suggesting that the architecture is innate. However, this suggestion need not be true.

Cognitive psychologists believe that brains cause cognition. But the brain brings other, non-architectural, cognitive characteristics to life. For instance, when we change our beliefs, or when we learn new information, our brains change: learning and experience modify neural connections (Dudai, 1989; Eichenbaum, 2002; Gluck & Myers, 2001; Lynch, 1986; Squire, 1987). The brain must bring such non-architectural properties to life.

If the brain causes the architecture, but also stores (non-innate) information, then how can we distinguish the architecture from information? Importantly, brain structures change over time but not at the same rate (Newell, 1990). For Newell, the architecture is a relatively fixed structure and changes very slowly. In contrast, other structures change much more rapidly, such as the memories holding the information for the architecture to manipulate. Newell does not say *why* the architecture might (slowly) change. Architectural changes could be innate (e.g., neural development), or they could be caused by experience (e.g., when practice makes object recognition automatic). Explaining the architecture might require appealing to both nativism and empiricism. Appealing to both nativism and empiricism arises in another varying architectural property, isotropic processing versus modular processing.

4.8 Isotropic and Modular Processing

Karl Duncker (1945) pioneered the experimental study of problem solving and profoundly influenced the development of cognitive psychology (Simon, 2007). Duncker famously studied the *radiation problem*: "Given a human being with an inoperable stomach tumor, and rays which destroy organic tissue at sufficient intensity, by what procedure can we free him of the tumor by these rays and at the same time avoid destroying the healthy tissue which surrounds it?" (1945, p. 1). Duncker discovered fundamental characteristics of problem solving by having participants think out loud when solving the radiation problem.

Modern researchers studied whether participants find the radiation problem easier to solve after reading seemingly unrelated stories (Gick & Holyoak, 1980). Gick and Holyoak presented some participants with the Attack-Dispersion story, in which a general wants to capture a fortress. Many different roads lead to the fortress, all protected by explosive mines. A small squad of soldiers, because of their light weight, can cross the mines, but the weight of a large army causes the mines to explode. The general captures the fortress by dividing her army into many small groups, each taking a different road and safely reaching the fortress at the same time.

We can relate, via analogy, the general's solution in the Attack-Dispersion story to the solution for the radiation problem. We can destroy the tumor, but preserve the surrounding tissue, if we aim lower-intensity rays at the tumor from many different directions. As a result, the tumor receives a massive dose of radiation not received by the surrounding tissue. Gick and Holyoak (1980) found that the Attack-Dispersion story helped participants to solve the radiation problem faster than participants who did not read the story.

Results like Gick and Holyoak's (1980) inform cognitive psychologists who believe in the centrality of analogical thinking to problem solving (Gentner et al., 2001; Holyoak & Thagard, 1995). Analogical thinking finds insightful relationships between very different domains. Famous scientific analogies include Kepler's comparison of the motion of the planets to the motion of a clock and Huygens's hypothesization that light is wavelike by considering waves on water.

Analogical thinking requires cognition to relate disparate domains, to access information about clocks and planets, or about military strategy and cancer treatment, at the same time. We call the wide-ranging access to very different kinds of information *isotropic processing* (Fodor, 1983). As Fodor notes, isotropic scientific reasoning occurs when "everything that the scientist knows is, in principle, relevant to determining what else he ought to believe. In principle, our botany constrains our astronomy, if only we could think of ways to make them connect" (p. 105). For Fodor, central processes—thinking and problem solving—are necessarily isotropic.

However, Fodor (1983) also argues that many cognitive processes are neither central nor isotropic, processes that Fodor calls *modules*, specialized devices for solving specific information processing problems. A module receives information from sensors, manipulates information to solve a problem, and sends the solution on to central processes. A module uses parallel processing, is data driven, and is automatic. These characteristics arise because localized neural functions instantiate a module.

Being associated with localized neural functions makes modules domain specific or *informationally encapsulated*. We achieve modular processing by "wiring" modules only to necessary information. "The intimate association of modular systems with neural hardwiring is pretty much what you would expect given the assumption that the key to modularity is informational encapsulation" (Fodor, 1983, p. 98). Modules are not isotropic; they cannot access information *irrelevant* to their specialized function.

Neuroscience provides evidence for the existence of modules. Results from anatomy, physiology, and clinical neuroscience reveal the modularity of visual perception. Two distinct pathways exist in the human visual system (Livingstone & Hubel, 1988; Maunsell & Newsome, 1987; Ungerleider & Mishkin, 1982). We process the appearances of objects, while the other processes object locations. We can describe the two pathways as modules because we do not process the information (features versus location) processed by the other. Furthermore, each pathway consists of smaller modules. Researchers have identified over 30 distinct visual processing modules, each responsible for detecting a very specific kind of information (van Essen et al., 1992).

For Fodor (1983), modules are informationally encapsulated, domain specific, fast, and automatic because localized neural processes implement each module. Fodor also argues that the same properties cannot be true of central or isotropic processing and concludes that cognitive psychologists cannot explain isotropic processes: "The more global (e.g., the more isotropic) a cognitive process is, the less anybody understands it" (p. 107).

We can treat that pessimistic conclusion skeptically. For instance, the memory systems introduced in earlier chapters are isotropic because they can store many different kinds of information. Nevertheless, cognitive psychologists have acquired a deep understanding of these systems.

4.9 An Example Architecture

In this chapter, I have introduced several different architectural properties for cognitive psychology. Cognitive psychologists create different theories by choosing different values for different architectural properties. I now take a different approach to considering architectural questions by describing one important candidate for the cognitive architecture, the production system. I then consider the example architecture in the context of the various properties that we have considered.

A *production system* is a computer simulation used to model problem solving (Anderson, 1983; Newell, 1973; Newell & Simon, 1972). The simplest production system (Figure 4-11) has a working memory for holding strings of symbols and a set of rules, called *productions*, for manipulating memory contents.

In a production system, each rule or production is a condition-action pair. A production searches memory for symbols matching its condition. When a production finds a match, the production performs its action, which manipulates memory contents. A production system starts with a to-be-solved problem in memory. All productions simultaneously search memory for conditions. When one production finds its condition, it first disables the other productions, and then it performs its action. After performing the action, all of the productions scan memory in parallel again.

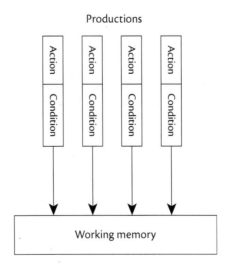

Figure 4-11 A simple production system consisting of four different productions.

We can represent a production system's behaviour over time using a *problem behaviour graph* (Newell & Simon, 1972). Such a graph (Figure 4-12) consists of a set of linked nodes. Each node represents the current memory contents. One production's action links two nodes together. For instance, the top left of Figure 4-12 shows that, when production P1 acts on memory State 1, the memory changes into State 2.

Problem behaviour graphs also depict changes in knowledge states not directly related to productions. In some instances, a participant might recall a previous state of knowledge during problem solving. A problem behaviour graph depicts such backtracking by copying the recalled state and placing the copy below the original in the graph. Figure 4-12 illustrates two examples of backtracking, one for State 1, the other for State 2. The examples indicate that time proceeds both horizontally and vertically in a problem behaviour graph.

Production systems can model human problem solving. How do we create such a model? Production systems emerge from a methodology called *protocol analysis* (Ericsson & Simon, 1993), which involves a detailed analysis of what participants say when they think aloud during problem solving (Section 3.11). Protocol

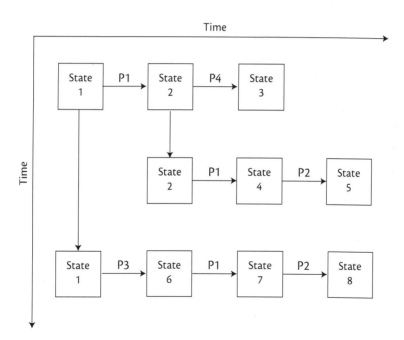

Figure 4-12 An example problem behaviour graph. States are different memory contents, and links are created by a production's action.

analysis produces a problem space for representing a participant's knowledge at each moment during problem solving. Researchers use a problem space to create a problem behaviour graph. The graph represents the rule-governed transition from one knowledge state to the next. The graph also helps researchers to create a production system to simulate the participant's problem solving.

Newell and Simon (1972) used their method's utility for a variety of problems. They found a high degree of correspondence between the problem behaviour graph created using protocol analysis and the problem behaviour graph generated by the production system. In general, production systems can generate a very accurate step-by-step account of a participant's problem-solving operations. Because production systems can successfully simulate many psychological phenomena (Anderson, 1983; Anderson et al., 2004; Anderson & Matessa, 1997; Meyer et al., 2001; Meyer & Kieras, 1997a, 1997b; Newell, 1990; Newell & Simon, 1972), numerous researchers treat the production system as a plausible cognitive architecture for providing a unified theory of cognition (Anderson, 1983; Anderson et al., 2004; Newell, 1990).

The simple production system presented in Figure 4-11 has evolved into more complex models (Anderson, 1983; Anderson, 1990; Meyer & Kieras, 1997a, 1997b). Different production systems emerge from different combinations of the architectural properties discussed in this chapter.

Simple production systems scan memory in parallel, but act on memory in serial, because only one production operates at any time. However, other production systems permit productions to act in parallel (Meyer & Kieras, 1997a, 1997b).

Simple production systems model problem solving using data-driven, automatic processing, because patterns held in working memory trigger productions. However, other production systems permit theory-driven, controlled processing. For instance, the adaptive control of thought-rational (ACT-R) architecture includes components for directing the system to accomplish a desired goal (Anderson et al., 2004).

Memory contents do not perfectly control simple production systems. Sometimes multiple productions discover their conditions at the same time, or one production discovers its condition at more than one memory location. Additional control mechanisms can resolve conflicts between productions or conditions. Production systems can differ from one another in terms of the control mechanisms used to deal with such conflicts.

When Newell and Simon (1972) described modelling problem solving with production systems, they said little about nativism and empiricism. Although not claiming innateness, their simple production systems did not learn. Later production systems included learning mechanisms. For example, ACT-R uses learning mechanisms to modify existing productions and uses learning mechanisms to add new knowledge to memory (Anderson et al., 2004).

We can describe simple production systems as modules because such systems accomplish particular tasks, such as solving a specific cryptarithmetic problem (Newell & Simon, 1972). However, later production systems seem to be more isotropic (Anderson, 1983; Anderson et al., 2004; Newell, 1990). These systems include general knowledge of the world and goal-directed problem solving, which make them general purpose problem solvers.

In short, even when researchers view production systems as a plausible cognitive architecture, they need not agree on various specific details. Many different production systems emerge when researchers make different decisions about architectural properties.

4.10 Chapter Summary

To overcome Ryle's regress, cognitive psychologists must discover a cognitive architecture. However, not all cognitive psychologists will converge on the same architecture. Many different architectures appear in cognitive psychology because the same results can support different models, because different researchers explore different ideas, and because researchers can negate the architectural assumptions held by others. Cognitive psychologists frequently explore competing architectures.

Furthermore, potential cognitive architectures exhibit many possible properties. Are processes serial or parallel? Are they data driven, or theory driven? Are they automatic or controlled? Which particular combination of structure and process is involved? How are processes controlled? Are they innate or learned? Are they isotropic or modular? Different cognitive psychologists generate different answers to such questions, producing architectural variety. In addition, we can answer some questions in many different ways. For instance, we can propose many different combinations of symbolic structures and manipulated rules (Dawson, 1998, Table 6.1). Again, different answers to architectural questions produce architectural variety.

Thus, cognitive psychology hosts a number of competing models. Is language embedded in the innate structure of a universal grammar (Cook & Newson, 1996), or are its regularities learned by connectionist networks (Joanisse & McClelland, 2015)? Is memory a set of different stores (Shiffrin & Atkinson, 1969), or do different memories reflect different levels of processing (Craik & Lockhart, 1972)? Is attention a serial spotlight (Treisman & Gelade, 1980), or is it a set of indices deployed in parallel (Pylyshyn, 2003a)? Radically different theories arise when researchers adopt radically different hypotheses about the architecture.

Further variety emerges because different answers to the same architectural question exist in a single theory. For instance, feature integration theory includes feature detectors operating in parallel but then uses serial processing to combine features into objects (Treisman & Gelade, 1980). One model exhibiting multiple architectural properties (e.g., both parallel and serial processing) illustrates another source of theoretical variety.

Theoretical variety also arises when models differ in their emphasis on architectural properties. For example, where does data-driven processing stop? In feature integration theory, it ends early, delivering fairly simple visual features (Treisman & Gelade, 1980). In natural computation theories, data-driven processing ends later, delivering more complex representations of surfaces and objects (Biederman, 1987; Marr, 1982). It is little wonder that cognitive psychology hosts so many different models.

In short, even when cognitive psychologists share foundational assumptions, they can still propose and explore different architectures. Cognitive psychology possesses notable theoretical diversity. Nevertheless, its diversity faces a common fate: empirical testing. Cognitive psychologists must collect data to support architectural proposals.

Of course, finding a single, unifying cognitive architecture requires that such an architecture exists, which many researchers assume. Allen Newell defines a unified theory of cognition as "a single set of mechanisms for all of cognitive behavior" (1990, p. 15), and an elaborate production system called SOAR ('state, operator and result') can provide a unifying theory (Laird et al., 1987). However, not everyone agrees that a unifying cognitive architecture exists. Instead, some believe that diverse arrays of processes carry out cognition, each possessing distinct architectural properties. The *society of mind* provides one example, producing cognition with a large number of simple, distinct processes called agents (Minsky, 1985, 2006). A related idea is *massive modularity*, which proposes that many specialized modules produce human cognition (Carruthers, 2006; Pinker, 1997).

The architecture of one agent or of one module need not be identical to the architecture of another. When two cognitive psychologists propose different architectures, both can be correct, because different architectures can exist in different agents or modules. Questioning the existence of a unifying cognitive architecture illustrates a foundational debate. Cognitive psychology requires such debates to develop. In the next and final chapter, I explore some example debates. Different positions in such debates produce radically different theories. Ultimately, different theories reflect different ideas about the fundamental nature of cognition.

Questioning Foundations

The first four chapters introduced cognitive psychology's foundations. The first chapter presented the computer metaphor adopted by cognitive psychologists. The second chapter discussed how cognitive psychologists use experimental methods to infer human information processes. The third chapter defined cognitive psychology's philosophy of science, functional analysis. The fourth chapter demonstrated how cognitive psychology's hypotheses, methods, and philosophy allow cognitive psychologists to propose many competing theories. Competing theories lead to many debates about the nature of human cognition, debates that I explore in Chapter 5. Each debate challenges cognitive psychology's foundations. By understanding these debates, we can sharpen our understanding of—and concerns about—the discipline's foundations.

5.1 Questioning Foundational Assumptions

What are cognitive psychology's foundations? Cognitive psychologists often debate cognitive psychology's foundational assumptions (Dawson, 2013). The rise of connectionism in the mid-1980s challenged the digital computer metaphor. Embodied cognition challenged cognitive psychology's dismissal of the environment and the body. Cognitive neuroscience challenged cognitive psychology's functionalism. We can express such challenges as questions about foundations. Does cognitive psychology need the computer metaphor? Does cognition require rules? Do people think? Can we reduce cognition to brain operations?

Chapter 5 explores such challenges. Each section poses a different question, a different challenge to a foundational assumption. I begin by considering a different notion of information processing, connectionism. Next, I discuss a different challenge, embodied cognition. Then I explore cognitive neuroscience's role in cognitive psychology and address more general questions about the "textbook" presentation of cognitive psychology. I end the chapter by considering the question in the book's title: what is cognitive psychology?

5.2 Do We Need the Computer Metaphor?

Chapter 1 launched our discussion of cognitive psychology by introducing the computer metaphor: the assumption that cognition involves symbol manipulation like the information processing operations used by digital computers. The computer metaphor leads directly to cognitive psychology's experimental methodologies (Chapter 2) and explanatory practices (Chapter 3). Chapter 4 revealed that the computer metaphor permits cognitive psychologists to develop diverse cognitive theories by making different architectural assumptions. Most examples in Chapter 4 involved specific assumptions (replacing parallel processing with serial processing or proposing new formats for symbols).

Importantly, radically different cognitive theories arise when cognitive psychologists propose more consequential architectural challenges. Not all cognitive psychologists endorse the computer metaphor. Connectionists abandon the metaphor, propose alternative brain-like theories, and move cognitive psychology in very different directions. I briefly mentioned connectionism earlier (Sections 3.13, 4.2, 4.7), but now I consider connectionism in more detail as a challenge to traditional cognitivism. Sections 5.2 through 5.4 explore connectionism's challenges to the computer metaphor and which evidence connectionists need to support radically different theories.

Our discussion of connectionism begins with a core question: why did cognitive psychology adopt the digital computer metaphor? When cognitive psychology arose in the 1950s, the digital computer offered the best example of information processing. However, other information processing examples also existed.

For instance, analog computers appeared decades before digital computers. Analog computers do not use rules to manipulate symbols. Instead, they vary continuously changeable physical properties (e.g., a mechanical or electrical value) to model variables for solving problems. Some researchers suggested that neurons were a kind of analog computer (von Neumann, 1958). Thus, even in the beginning, the digital computer metaphor had plausible alternatives.

Connectionism arose from exploring alternatives to the digital computer metaphor. Connectionists hypothesize that networks of simpler processors, operating in parallel, process information. We often describe connectionist models as *neuronally inspired* or *biologically plausible*. Analogous to neurons, connectionist processors send signals to one another through weighted connections. Processors receive signals sent from other processors; we call the total signal received the *net input*. Processors convert net input into internal activity ranging in value between 0 and 1.

A connectionist network, a system of such processors, converts a stimulus into a response. Processors called *input units* represent stimuli, and processors called *output units* represent responses (see Figure 5-1). The network distributes the knowledge for converting a stimulus into a response among all of the weighted connections, a *distributed representation*. Connectionists replace the digital computer metaphor with the idea that *parallel distributed processing* (PDP) networks carry out human cognition.

Using networks to model human cognition has a long history. Warren McCulloch and Walter Pitts (1943) proposed the first artificial neural networks, using mathematical logic to describe neural processing. When the net input for a McCulloch-Pitts neuron exceeds a threshold, the neuron generates an activity of 1. Otherwise, the neuron generates an activity of 0. McCulloch and Pitts mapped the binary activity of their neurons onto the logical notions of "true" or "false." McCulloch and Pitts then established the power of networks by creating a universal Turing machine (Section 1.5) from a network of McCulloch-Pitts neurons: "To psychology, however defined, specification of the net would contribute all that could be achieved in that field" (p. 37).

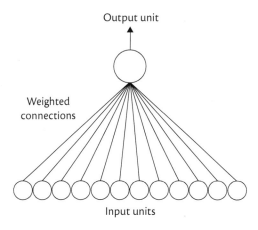

Output unit

Weighted
connections

Input units

Figure 5-1 A perceptron consisting of 12 input units connected to one output unit via weighted connections.

Networks of McCulloch-Pitts neurons can solve difficult problems but have one drawback: such neurons do not learn. Instead, the network's designer must predetermine a neuron's connection weights and threshold. Experience neither creates nor modifies thresholds or connection weights. Frank Rosenblatt (1958, 1962) introduced learning to networks with his *perceptron*. A perceptron has multiple input units and a single output unit. Perceptrons have weighted connections from each input unit to the output unit (Figure 5-1). The activity of a perceptron's output unit, like a McCulloch-Pitts neuron, is either 0 or 1.

Perceptrons differ from a McCulloch-Pitts neuron because perceptrons learn. When the perceptron receives a stimulus, the output unit determines its net input and then responds. A learning rule computes response error by comparing the output unit's response to the desired response. Rosenblatt's learning rule then alters connection weights to decrease response error. His *perceptron convergence theorem* guaranteed that his learning rule could teach a perceptron to solve a problem—if the perceptron could represent a solution (Rosenblatt, 1962). We will see below that perceptrons cannot learn to solve every problem.

One example perceptron generates the logical operator AND. Using two input units, we present two stimuli to the perceptron; each stimulus has a value of either 0 or 1. The AND perceptron outputs a value of 1 if both stimuli equal 1. Otherwise, the perceptron responds with 0. The top of Figure 5-2 plots the *pattern space* for the AND perceptron. Each circle represents one of the four possible stimuli (pairs of input values). The input unit values give the coordinates of each circle: that is, 0,0, 0,1, 1,0, and 1,1. The colour of each circle represents the perceptron's response to each pattern. A white circle indicates a response of 0, and a black circle indicates a response of 1. The bottom part of Figure 5-2 shows a perceptron trained to generate correct AND responses. Each connection weight has a value of 1, and the threshold of the output unit has a value of 1.5.

How does the perceptron's structure generate AND? Each input unit sends activity to the output unit, but the perceptron first multiplies the activity by the input unit's connection weight. To compute net input, the perceptron's output unit sums up the two weighted signals. When we activate both input units with 1, the perceptron receives a net input of 2. A net input of 2 causes the output unit to respond with 1, because the net input exceeds the threshold of 1.5. For the three other possible patterns, the net input equals either 0 or 1, does note the threshold (either 0 or 1), and causes the output unit to respond with 0.

Rosenblatt's perceptron led to growing interest in training networks and motivated a formal analysis of what perceptrons could and could not learn to do

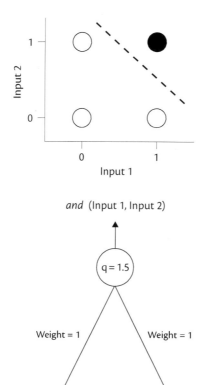

and (Input 1, Input 2)

Figure 5-2 The top part of the figure provides the pattern space for AND. The bottom part of the figure illustrates the structure of a perceptron trained to generate the correct responses for AND.

(Minsky & Papert, 1969). Minsky and Papert proved that perceptrons cannot learn to solve many problems that people can learn to solve. Perceptrons cannot model human cognition.

Minsky and Papert (1969) established the negative assessment of perceptrons by proving that they can only learn *linearly separable problems*. We call a problem linearly separable if a single, straight cut through a pattern space separates all patterns associated with a response of 1 from all patterns associated with a response of 0. The pattern space for AND (Figure 5-2) is linearly separable because the figure's one dashed line separates the "on" pattern from the three "off" patterns.

Perceptrons cannot solve *linearly non-separable problems*. Figure 5-3 provides the pattern space for another logical operator, exclusive or (called XOR). Like AND, XOR performs a logical judgment about two stimuli, generating a response of 1 when the two stimuli (each input unit value) differ from one another. XOR returns a value of 1 when one stimulus is 1 and the other is 0. If both stimuli are 1, or if both are 0, then XOR returns a 0.

Figure 5-3 illustrates that XOR is a non-linearly separable problem because one single straight cut cannot separate both black circles from both white circles. XOR's pattern space requires *two* cuts. A perceptron can never solve XOR, because the output unit can make one cut, or the other, but not both. How can we increase the power of a perceptron? We could include intermediate processors between input and output units, called *hidden units*. The multi-layer perceptron presented earlier (Figure 4-6) possesses one layer of hidden units.

Hidden units add power by detecting more complex features, such as correlations between different input unit activities. Each hidden unit makes its own straight cut through a pattern space (Lippmann, 1989). To solve XOR, we require two such cuts; we can solve XOR using a multi-layer perceptron with two hidden units; each hidden unit provides one required cut (Rumelhart et al., 1986).

By the late 1960s, researchers realized that replacing the computer metaphor with connectionist processing required more powerful networks such as multi-layer perceptrons. However, connectionists did not yet know how to train networks with hidden units. As a result, connectionist research languished (Medler, 1998; Papert, 1988). Connectionist research lay largely dormant until the mid-1980s, when a learning rule for training multi-layer perceptrons, called

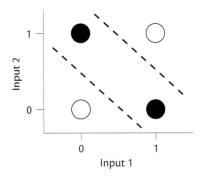

Figure 5-3 The pattern space for the linearly non-separable logical operator XOR (Input 1, Input 2).

backpropagation of error, appeared in the journal *Nature* (Rumelhart et al., 1986). Backpropagation of error led to an explosion of connectionist models of cognitive phenomena.

Some famous examples of connectionist models included networks for converting present tense verbs into past tense verbs (Rumelhart & McClelland, 1986a), for simulating recognition memory (Ratcliff, 1990), for learning categories (Kruschke, 1992), and for generating the Stroop effect (Cohen et al., 1991). We often see connectionist networks in the modern cognitive literature. Backpropagation of error launched a connectionist revolution.

Although the connectionist revolution arose directly from the ability to train multi-layer perceptrons, broader issues made cognitive psychology eager for change (Bechtel & Abrahamsen, 2002; Dreyfus, 1972; Dreyfus & Dreyfus, 1988; Fodor & Pylyshyn, 1988; Medler, 1998; Rumelhart & McClelland, 1986b). Researchers argued that fatal flaws existed in models inspired by the computer metaphor, which used slow serial processing and failed to recognize that brains differed from digital computers. The connectionist revolution offered new ideas to researchers dissatisfied by slow progress in developing sophisticated simulations of cognition. "Almost everyone who is discontent with current cognitive psychology and current 'information processing' models of the mind has rushed to embrace 'the Connectionist alternative'" (Fodor & Pylyshyn, 1988, p. 3). Connectionism offered a paradigm shift for cognitive psychology (Schneider, 1987).

The rise of connectionism shows that the computer metaphor does not provide the only view of information processing for cognitive psychology. However, replacing that metaphor with connectionism does not abandon the information processing hypothesis. Connectionists still treat cognition as information processing (Churchland et al., 1990). But they also believe that cognitive information processing differs from the information processing performed by computers. "These dissimilarities do not imply that brains are not computers, but only that *brains are not serial digital computers*" (Churchland et al., 1990, p. 48, their italics).

How can we make sense of a discipline possessing two views that appeal to paradigmatically different notions of information processing? Computer metaphor models and connectionist networks do have many similarities (Dawson, 1998, 2013). Both perspectives agree that cognition is information processing but disagree about its basic information processing properties. Thus, the two views provide different proposals about the cognitive architecture.

In the next section, I explore greater similarities between the two views of information processing than we might expect. I will examine the connectionist claim that cognition does not require the rule-governed manipulation of symbols, a claim surprisingly hard to defend.

5.3 Does Cognition Require Rules?

In Section 5.2, I considered the connectionist claim that human information processing differs from computer information processing. I described connectionism as exploring brain-like processing in which simple, neuron-like processors send signals to other processors. However, in challenging the computer metaphor, the connectionist revolution encouraged more focused reactions to traditional cognitive architectures. In Section 5.3, I explore one example, claiming that cognition not only is not rule-governed symbol manipulation but also requires neither rules nor symbols. I also note that connectionists often fail to use appropriate evidence—interpretations of network structures—to support cognitive theories with no rules or symbols. I end by showing that, when we collect appropriate evidence, we blur the differences between traditional and connectionist cognitive psychology.

Multi-layer perceptrons offered cognitive psychology a paradigm shift (Schneider, 1987). Why might we describe connectionism as a paradigm shift? When we examine a production system (Figure 4-11), we see a set of explicit rules (the productions) and explicit symbols (in working memory). In contrast, when we examine a connectionist network (Figure 4-6), we see neither rules nor symbols. "One thing that connectionist networks have in common with brains is that if you open them up and peer inside, all you can see is a big pile of goo" (Mozer & Smolensky, 1989, p. 3). We describe connectionist networks as offering a paradigm shift for traditional cognitive psychology because networks process information *without* apparent rules or symbols.

To criticize the computer metaphor, connectionists trained networks to solve problems that other (traditional) researchers believed required rules and symbols. If connectionist networks solved such problems, then connectionists would claim that the networks offered alternative, rule-less and symbol-less, accounts. For example, Rumelhart and McClelland (1986a) trained one network to convert present tense verbs into past tense verbs. We saw in Section 4.7 that Chomsky proposed that mastering a language involves acquiring grammatical rules. Rumelhart and McClelland proposed an alternative: "We suggest that lawful behavior and judgments may be produced by a mechanism in which there is no explicit representation of the rule" (p. 217).

Rumelhart and McClelland's (1986a) network learned the past tense task, and its changes in performance during learning mirrored the development of handling verb tenses by children. As a result, the model became very influential by providing a radically different account of language learning. Rumelhart and McClelland could *describe* the network as if it used rules, but no rules were actually *represented*. "The child need not figure out what the rules are, nor even that there are rules" (p. 267).

However, we can see problems with that conclusion (Pinker & Prince, 1988). Rumelhart and McClelland (1986a) claim that the network does not use rules, but they do not supply evidence about how the network operates to support that claim. Instead, the claim emerges from an uncritical assumption of qualitative differences between networks and rule-governed systems. Rumelhart and McClelland do not actually report the network structure to reveal the alternative (rule-less) nature of its processing. Without such evidence, we cannot establish a qualitative difference between the network and other rule-based models.

Rumelhart and McClelland's (1986a) failure to examine the internal structure of the past tense verb network should not surprise us. We encounter great difficulties when we attempt to understand the internal workings of connectionist networks (Hecht-Nielsen, 1987; Mozer & Smolensky, 1989). Some researchers argue that failing to understand network structure limits networks' ability to contribute new cognitive theories (McCloskey, 1991; Seidenberg, 1993). However, various techniques do exist for understanding how networks operate (Berkeley et al., 1995; Dawson, 2018; Dawson et al. 2020; Hanson & Burr, 1990). Importantly, when we use such techniques to interpret networks, the distinction between networks and rule-based models becomes less clear.

Consider a network trained to perform logical judgments. Propositional logic is a system of rules for manipulating symbols. Therefore, logical reasoning provides a prototypical example of rule-governed thinking (Johnson-Laird, 1983; Leighton & Sternberg, 2004; Wason, 1966; Wason & Johnson-Laird, 1972), a position challenged by connectionist networks. Bechtel and Abrahamsen (1991) trained a multi-layer perceptron to classify logical arguments and to indicate argument validity. They hypothesized that "connectionist networks encode knowledge without explicitly employing propositions" (p. 147). Thus, if a network could solve the logic problem, then logical reasoning need not require using rules to manipulate symbols. After successfully training the network, Bechtel and Abrahamsen claimed, "propositionally encoded knowledge might not be the most basic form of knowledge"

(p. 174). However, similar to the study by Rumelhart and McClelland (1986a), Bechtel and Abrahamsen did not examine their network's internal structure.

Other researchers interpreted a different network trained on the Bechtel and Abrahamsen (1991) logic problem (Berkeley et al., 1995). The interpretation discovered the features detected by each hidden unit and determined how the network combined detected features to solve the logic problem. The analysis revealed standard rules of logic represented by network structure. Berkeley et al.'s network solved the logic problem by discovering, and using, rules.

Other examples also show that network interpretations reveal striking similarities between connectionist models and more traditional information processing. For instance, cognitive neuroscientists use *dissociations* as evidence to relate psychological processes to brain structure. A dissociation occurs when damage to a brain area produces a specific cognitive or behavioural deficit. Researchers combine such evidence with the *locality assumption* that the brain consists of functionally localized areas (Farah, 1994). Under the locality assumption, cognitive neuroscientists use dissociations to infer that specific brain areas bring to life specific cognitive or behavioural processes.

Farah (1994) used connectionist networks to challenge the locality assumption. She demonstrated that lesions to networks produce dissociations and used her evidence *against* the locality assumption. Farah argued that networks are distributed systems, not local systems. Therefore, networks do not conform to the locality assumption. If lesions to (non-local) networks produce dissociations, then we cannot claim that dissociations must be caused by damaging localized brain functions.

However, Farah (1994) did not examine the internal structure of her networks to support her argument. She did not confirm that her lesions did not remove a localized structure. A different study lesioned connectionist networks but also interpreted the structure of ablated processors (Medler et al., 2005). When the lesioned networks produced dissociations, the interpretation revealed that local network structure had been removed.

Musical cognition provides another example. Many researchers train connectionist networks to perform various musical tasks (Griffith & Todd, 1999; Todd & Loy, 1991). Most researchers who conduct such research assume that networks capture musical properties that we cannot express using formal rules (Bharucha, 1999). However, when we interpret the internal structures of musical networks, we discover many formal musical properties (Dawson, 2018; Dawson et al., 2020).

A final example concerns a benchmark problem in the machine learning literature. Schlimmer's (1987) mushroom problem requires a system to learn to classify over 8,000 mushrooms as being edible or poisonous. We describe each mushroom as a set of 21 different features. One study trained a connectionist network with 10 hidden units to classify Schlimmer's mushrooms (Dawson et al., 2000). Dawson et al. analyzed the network's internal structure and related it to alternative rule-based models of mushroom classification.

A production system provided one rule-based model for comparison. Dawson et al. (2000) created a set of nine different productions for correctly classifying mushrooms. A set of mushroom features defined each production's condition. A classification (poisonous versus edible) defined a production's action. For instance, one production was "if (odour = anise) OR (odour = almond) → edible." Another production was "if (odour ≠ anise) AND (odour ≠ almond) AND (odour ≠ none) → poisonous."

What relationship holds between the production system and the network? Dawson et al. (2000) analyzed their network in two different ways. The first analysis determined the features detected by each hidden unit. The second analysis assigned similar mushrooms to groups, defining similarity in terms of the activity produced by a mushroom in the hidden units. If two different mushrooms produced similar activity patterns, then Dawson et al. assigned the mushrooms to the same group. Otherwise, they assigned them to different groups. Dawson et al. required only 12 different groups to summarize the entire stimulus set.

Dawson et al. (2000) combined their two analyses to translate the network into the production system. They summarized each group of mushrooms in terms of the average activity produced in each hidden unit by group members. Furthermore, on the basis of the first analysis, they translated each average activity into a set of mushroom features. Dawson et al. translated each set of mushroom features into one of the production's conditions. For instance, when the hidden units produced activities associated with one group of mushrooms, the hidden units detected the features representing the condition for a particular production. Furthermore, the hidden unit activities caused an output unit to generate the production's action (e.g., to classify a mushroom as edible). In other words, we can describe the Dawson et al. model as a connectionist network, but we can also describe it as a production system, blurring the distinction between connectionist and rule-based processing.

The two accounts of the mushroom network introduce the notion of *sub-symbolic networks* (Smolensky, 1988). Smolensky called networks sub-symbolic because we can explain them by appealing to finely detailed properties: the signals that processors send through weighted connections. Furthermore, the finely detailed properties of sub-symbolic networks (e.g., processor activities) need not represent rules or symbols. If we view networks as being sub-symbolic, then we also believe that higher-level symbolic explanations of networks (e.g., appealing to rules) serve only as approximations. From Smolensky's perspective, when Dawson et al. (2000) analyzed the details of hidden unit responses, they revealed the mushroom network's sub-symbolic properties. In contrast, when they translated hidden unit activities into productions, they provided a symbolic approximation of network processing. We can interpret the network "as if" it represents a production system, but in so doing we ignore the fine details of network operations.

However, we need not adopt Smolensky's (1988) perspective. We have no reason to believe that one of the accounts offered by Dawson et al. (2000) is more accurate, or more informative, than another. Each account depends on the other, and both accounts provide insight into the network. "The picture that emerges is of a symbiosis between the symbolic and subsymbolic paradigms" (Smolensky, 1988, p. 19). To understand a network completely, we require both sub-symbolic and symbolic accounts, implying that connectionism does not eliminate rules from cognitive explanations.

5.4 Can Connectionist Networks Provide Cognitive Theories?

In Sections 5.2 and 5.3, I explored two architectural challenges by connectionists to rule-based cognitivism. I now examine connectionism's explanatory role in cognitive psychology. Connectionist researchers almost always develop computer simulations of cognitive phenomena because connectionism studies trained networks. In Chapter 3, I detailed rule-based cognitivism's explanatory mission: subsumed functional analyses. In Section 5.4, I explore connectionism's philosophy of science by asking whether connectionist networks can serve as theories or explanations.

Simulations as theories. Cognitive psychology aims to explain cognition. Psychological theories take many forms and have many purposes. Some researchers express theories mathematically (Bock & Jones, 1968; Estes, 1975; Restle & Greeno, 1970). Other researchers express theories as interactions between mechanistic components, interactions for producing predictable behaviour (Eichenbaum, 2002; Martinez & Kesner, 1998). Mechanistic components can also belong to an information processing architecture (Anderson, 1983; Carruthers, 2006; VanLehn, 1991). Researchers often express architectural theories as computer simulations

(Dutton & Briggs, 1971; Dutton & Starbuck, 1971; Feigenbaum & Feldman, 1963; Simon & Newell, 1958).

Expressing theories as computer programs provides many advantages (Lewandowsky, 1993). Simon and Newell (1958, pp. 7–8) boldly predicted "that within ten years most theories in psychology will take the form of computer programs, or of qualitative statements about the characteristics of computer programs." Simon and Newell (1958) based their prediction upon their own experience with the computer metaphor. A different kind of simulation, the artificial neural network, also arose at the same time (Rosenblatt, 1958, 1962; Widrow & Hoff, 1960). We saw in Section 5.3 that psychology's interest in networks exploded when researchers discovered how to train multi-layer perceptrons (McClelland & Rumelhart, 1986; Rumelhart & McClelland, 1986b).

However, multi-layer perceptrons have many practical limitations. The brain has many layers of intermediate neurons, layers that can deliver the brain's enormous computational power (Bengio, 2009). However, when we add many layers of hidden units to multi-layer perceptrons, the networks become very difficult to train with backpropagation of error. Recently, connectionists have discovered new rules to train networks with many hidden layers, called *deep belief networks* (Bengio et al., 2013; Hinton, 2007; Hinton et al., 2006; Hinton & Salakhutdinov, 2006; Larochelle et al., 2012; LeCun et al., 2015). *Deep learning* rules train deep belief networks to accomplish tasks far more complex than we can teach multi-layer perceptrons when we use traditional learning rules.

For instance, deep belief networks learn to solve complex classification problems related to language, image, and sound (Hinton, 2007; Hinton et al., 2006; Mohamed et al., 2012; Sarikaya et al., 2014). Deep belief networks have applications in agriculture, biology, chemistry, and medicine (Ching et al., 2018; Gawehn et al., 2016; Goh et al., 2017; Kamilaris & Prenafeta-Boldu, 2018; Shen et al., 2017). "Deep learning is making major advances in solving problems that have resisted the best attempts of the artificial intelligence community for many years" (LeCun et al., 2015, p. 436).

Yet, as deep belief networks revolutionize machine learning, we rarely see them used by cognitive psychologists. In Section 5.4, I discuss why researchers have difficulty converting deep learning networks into cognitive theories.

Bonini's paradox. Although computer simulations offer many advantages, they also face disadvantages (Lewandowsky, 1993). We call one important disadvantage Bonini's paradox (Dutton & Briggs, 1971). A computer simulation encounters Bonini's paradox when we have at least as much difficulty explaining the simulation as we do explaining the phenomenon that we want to model. Researchers "can easily construct a computer model more complicated than the real thing. Since science is to make things simpler, such results can be demoralizing as well as self-defeating" (Dutton and Briggs, 1971, p. 103).

Bonini's paradox applies to any computer simulation but frequently plagues connectionist networks. I noted in Section 5.3 our difficulties understanding the internal structures of trained networks (Hecht-Nielsen, 1987; Mozer & Smolensky, 1989). As a result, connectionists rarely interpret or report network structure. Connectionism replaces one unknown (human performance on a cognitive task) with two unknowns (human and network performance on a cognitive task).

Bonini's paradox causes connectionists problems because a network can provide a cognitive theory only if researchers can describe precisely how the network converts stimuli into responses. We cannot merely claim that networks offer new theories because we believe that networks differ qualitatively from rule-based models. We must provide details about the alternative theory that a network provides. Otherwise, we merely practise "gee whiz connectionism" (Dawson, 2009).

When connectionists fail to interpret network structure, connectionist networks fail to provide cognitive theories. McCloskey (1991) argues that networks serve as neither theories nor simulations of theories. Seidenberg (1993, p. 229) admits that "connectionist models do not clarify theoretical ideas, they obscure them." To address such criticisms, connectionists must develop techniques for understanding exactly how networks convert stimuli into responses. We saw earlier (Section 5.3) that such techniques do exist, and when we interpret networks, they can provide theoretical contributions.

Consider one recent example in which networks learn to solve musical problems (Dawson, 2018). After training, Dawson interprets network structure by inspecting connection weights, by plotting distributions of hidden unit activities, and by performing multivariate analyses of processor activities. He provides a detailed account of each musical network. His interpretations reveal that networks represent formal musical properties, but the properties differ from those used in traditional music theory. For example, music theory assumes that we create Western music from a set of 12 different pitch classes (C, C#, D, etc.) (Forte, 1973). However, the hidden units of Dawson's networks use smaller sets of pitch classes. His networks treat pitch classes differentiated in traditional music theory as being identical.

Dawson (2018) shows that interpreted connectionist networks can inform cognitive theory. His networks inform music theory by introducing different notions of pitch class. In turn, his results raise questions for experimentally studying musical cognition. Does human cognition use musical representations similar to the representations found in the networks? Importantly, not all types of networks can produce cognitive theory. Bonini's paradox causes Dawson deliberately to avoid deep belief networks (Turner et al., 2018). Deep belief networks have not yet penetrated cognitive psychology because few methods exist for interpreting deep networks (Erhan et al., 2010).

Deep belief networks accomplish incredible feats but do so as black boxes. Researchers cannot explain how complex networks make decisions. However, growing legal pressure might motivate researchers to develop methods for interpreting deep belief networks (Deeks, 2019). When courts challenge decisions made by networks (e.g., rejecting a bank loan), judges demand that banks explain exactly how the networks made those decisions. Uninterpretable networks lose companies money! Interest in explainable artificial intelligence, or XAI, has grown in response to such concerns (Arrieta et al., 2020). XAI researchers aim to develop more easily understood new systems or to develop new approaches for understanding existing technologies such as deep belief networks. Perhaps, once researchers achieve the goals of XAI, we will see deep belief networks playing a larger role in cognitive psychology.

5.5 Do People Think?

In Sections 5.2 through 5.4, I explored architectural debates about cognitive psychology's foundations related to connectionism's challenge to the computer metaphor. Connectionism's challenges arose from claiming that human information processing differs significantly from the processing carried out by digital computers. However, connectionists did not propose the only alternative to the computer metaphor. An alternative position, called *embodied cognition*, critiques both traditional and connectionist cognitive psychology. We encountered embodied cognition briefly in Section 3.13, and I now explore it in more detail.

Embodied cognitive psychologists argue that both rule-based and network-based theories pay too little attention to the roles of the world and of agents' bodies in human cognition. These psychologists note that both traditional and connectionist theories appeal to sense-think-act processing. Embodied cognitive psychologists intend to replace sense-think-act theories with theories based upon sense-act processing.

To replace sense-think-act processing with sense-act processing is to propose an alternative architecture for cognition. As was the case with connectionism, the alternative architecture for embodied cognition leads to new debates about cognitive foundations. I now consider some debates arising from embodied cognition's alternative architecture. In Section 5.5, I explore one immediate consequence of removing "thinking" from the sense-think-act cycle: when we assume that only human cognition involves sense-act processing, do we claim that people do not think? In Section 5.6, I consider a radical implication of embodied cognition's emphasis on the environment: the mind extends outside the skull and into the world, a world that becomes part of cognition. In Section 5.7, I study one question raised in Chapter 1: can machines think? However, in Chapter 5, I reconsider that question by recognizing that embodied cognition defines "thinking" quite differently from traditional cognitive psychology. To begin our exploration of debates arising from embodied cognition, let us ask why embodied cognitive psychologists prefer sense-act processing over sense-think-act processing.

During a baseball game, a batter hits a fly ball to the outfield. Seeing the hit, an outfielder runs across the field to catch the ball. How does she know where to go? Perhaps the outfielder solves this problem by *thinking*. She mentally models the ball's trajectory, using some initial variables, and uses the model to predict where to run to catch the ball (Saxberg, 1987a, 1987b). Alternatively, perhaps when the outfielder starts to run, she simply *watches* the ball. She runs in the direction that makes the ball's trajectory look like a straight line (McBeath et al., 1995). If the trajectory does not look straight, then the outfielder changes direction, eventually reaching the location where the ball can be caught.

The two approaches differ dramatically from one another. The first appeals to thinking and mental representation, whereas the second does not. Instead, the second approach involves only *sensing* (watching the ball) and *acting* (running across the field). If the second answer works, then we might be able to solve some complex problems *without* thinking. We might then ask which other problems can we solve without thinking? Do people need to think at all? I now explore such questions by considering sense-act theories in cognitive psychology.

Experimental psychology arose in the 19th century to study consciousness scientifically. Psychology changed when behaviorism arrived; behaviorists argued that scientific psychology could study observable phenomena only (Watson, 1913). Behaviorism provided a stimulus-response psychology. Cognitive psychology reacted to behaviorism by adopting a competing view, the *sense-think-act cycle*. According to that cycle, organisms first sense information from the environment. Then they think by manipulating sensed (and represented) information. The purpose of thinking is to *plan*—to hypothesize actions that might achieve desirable outcomes and reject actions that do not. Finally, sense-think-act processing converts a chosen plan into action on the world. We call the sense-think-act cycle the *classical sandwich*, because thinking is necessarily sandwiched between sensing and acting (Hurley, 2001). In that cycle, direct connections do not exist between sensing and acting. We must think before we act.

In reacting to behaviorism, cognitive psychology appealed to information processing concepts as intervening variables (Bruner, 1990; Sperry, 1993). However, the "sense" and "act" components of the classical sandwich seemed to be too behaviorist by being too strongly linked to "stimulus" and "response." As a result, cognitive psychologists *overemphasized* thinking and *underemphasized* both sensing and acting. "One problem with psychology's attempt at cognitive theory has been our persistence in thinking about cognition without bringing in perceptual and motor processes" (Newell, 1990, p. 15). Which problems arise when cognitive psychologists overemphasize thinking?

A first problem is that, when we overemphasize thinking, our theories become overly complex (Braitenberg, 1984). Researchers who emphasize thinking assume that complicated actions result from intricate thought processes. Thus, cognitive psychologists explain complex behaviour by proposing complex thought processes. However, complex behaviour might arise from much simpler processes.

Consider the parable of the ant (Simon, 1969). Imagine explaining the winding path that an ant takes along a beach. If we focus exclusively on thinking, then we explain the path's shape via complex internal processes. However, we can adopt a simpler sense-act theory: the complex path emerges from the ant's simple reactions to obstacles. As Simon noted, "Viewed as a geometric figure, the ant's path is irregular, complex, hard to describe. But its complexity is really a complexity in the surface of the beach, not a complexity in the ant" (p. 24).

A second problem emerges when our theories overemphasize thinking and planning. Information processing creates plans by constructing and updating a mental model of the world. We plan our actions by manipulating our mental models. However, modelling and planning require excessive time and resources (Ford & Pylyshyn, 1996; Pylyshyn, 1987). Consider the famous robot Shakey, which navigated through an environment, pushing objects to new locations to accomplish assigned tasks (Nilsson, 1984). Shakey sent sensor readings to a computer, which created a model of the robot's world. The computer used the model to plan actions and sent the plan back to Shakey's robot body for execution. Shakey exemplified the sense-think-act cycle. Unfortunately, the robot performed behaviours extremely slowly. Shakey required several hours to complete tasks (Moravec, 1999), spending much time idling in place while the computer modelled and planned. Shakey's "thinking" required a great deal of time, making Shakey's actions uselessly slow.

This slow performance inspired an alternative, *behaviour-based robotics*, to speed up behaviour by removing thinking (Brooks, 1991, 1999). "Models of the world simply get in the way. It turns out to be better to use the world as its own model" (Brooks, 1991, p. 139). Behaviour-based robotics replaced the sense-think-act cycle with a *sense-act cycle*. By removing thinking, behaviour-based robotics resembles behaviorism, and behaviour-based roboticists only consider stimuli and responses, using "highly reactive architectures with no reasoning systems, no manipulable representations, no symbols, and totally decentralized computation" (Brooks, 1999, p. 170). Behaviour-based robots sense and react; they do not think and plan.

In cognitive psychology, ideas from behaviour-based robotics appear to inspire an approach called *embodied cognition* (Calvo & Gomila, 2008; Chemero, 2009; Clark, 1997, 1999, 2008; Dawson et al., 2010; Lakoff & Johnson, 1999; Rowlands, 2010; Shapiro, 2014, 2019; Varela et al., 1991; Wilson, 2002).

Shapiro (2019) identifies three characteristics of embodied theories. The first characteristic is *conceptualization*. The concepts that an organism uses to interact with the environment depend on the form of the organism's body. If different agents possess different bodies, then their understanding of or engagement with the world also differs. We find conceptualization in biology's notion of the *umwelt* (Uexküll, 1957, 2001) and in psychology's related idea of *affordance* (Gibson, 1979). Gibson called a possible action offered by the world to an organism an affordance, which depends on the shape of the world and the nature of the organism's body. A smooth, vertical wall does not afford "climbing" to a human, but the same wall affords "climbing" to a housefly.

The second characteristic is *replacement* (Shapiro 2019). The environment can aid or replace cognitive resources. For instance, a student who takes lecture notes replaces her internal memory with an environmental record. When we use the environment to support cognition, the environment provides *cognitive scaffolding* (Clark, 1997).

And the third characteristic is *constitution* (Shapiro 2019). An organism's body and environment have more than causal *effects* on cognition. Instead, the body and the world *belong* to cognition. The constitution hypothesis leads to a radical proposal, the extended mind hypothesis, which I consider in Section 5.6.

Shapiro (2019) observes that his three characteristics appear to different degrees in different embodied theories. For example, when theories exhibit different degrees of replacement, some are more comfortable than others with the existence of mental representations. Some embodied theories are hybrid because they explain some cognition with the sense-think-act cycle and other cognition with sense-act processing. If the world scaffolds cognition, then *some* thinking moves from inside the head to outside in the world—but not *all* thinking can move to the world.

Many embodied theories of language, social cognition, and mathematical reasoning propose that we use our own bodies to scaffold cognition (Dove, 2014; Fischer & Zwaan, 2008; Gallese & Goldman, 1998; Gallese et al., 2004; Gallese & Sinigaglia, 2011; Lakoff & Johnson, 1999; Lakoff & Núñez, 2000). For example, children often develop number concepts by counting with their fingers (Dehaene, 2011). Fingers offer the affordance of "countable" (Chrisomalis, 2013). Finger-based representations provide prototypical examples of replacing symbols with bodily representations (Bender & Beller, 2012; Fischer & Brugger, 2011; Tschentscher et al., 2012; Wasner et al., 2014).

However, not all theories in embodied cognition propose representations. *Radical embodied cognitive scientists* propose explicitly anti-representational theories (Anderson et al., 2012; Chemero, 2000, 2009; de Oliveira et al., 2019). Radical embodied cognitivists believe that cognitive psychologists err when appealing to representations. Radical embodied cognitive science avoids making such a mistake by eliminating representation and by explaining all of cognition using sense-act theories.

We can find many sense-act accounts of diverse cognitive phenomena (Shapiro, 2014). By understanding the parable of the ant, and by paying more attention to the roles of the environment and bodies in cognition, embodied cognitive psychologists can propose new and important theories. However, radical embodied cognition might not succeed in eliminating mental representations. Focusing only on sensing and acting moves embodied cognition closer to behaviorism and to the challenges that it failed to meet.

Gestalt psychologists challenged behaviorism by discovering *insight*—the sudden and unexpected experience of a solution to a problem (Köhler, 1925/2018; Wertheimer & Asch, 1945). Can sense-act theories explain insight? The stimulus-response theories of behaviorism provided inadequate accounts of human language (Chomsky, 1959). Do the sense-act theories of radically embodied cognition offer more explanatory power? Do people think? We have no compelling evidence to throw away the representations proposed by cognitive psychologists. However, we also have no reason to believe that every cognitive phenomenon has a representational explanation.

Embodied cognition reveals that we can explain many interesting phenomena via rich interactions between bodies and environments. Embodied cognitive researchers "get to work providing non-representational explanations of cognitive phenomena both convincing and sufficiently rich in their implications to guide further research" (Chemero, 2000, p. 646). Embodied cognition adopts a fruitful strategy likely to show how much cognition requires thinking—and how much does not.

5.6 Where Is the Mind?

Where is the mind? According to modern, materialist psychology, the mind resides inside the skull, because brains cause minds, and skulls contain brains (Searle, 1980, 1984). However, embodied cognition challenges this answer. Embodied cognition uses feedback to link or couple organisms to their environments (Ashby, 1956, 1960; Grey Walter, 1963; Wiener, 1948). Organisms act to change the world, and changes in the world influence future actions. Feedback means that we can use the world for cognitive scaffolding (Clark, 1997, 2008; Scribner & Tobach, 1997).

We can easily propose many concrete examples of cognitive scaffolding. When we write a reminder to ourselves, we use the environment to scaffold memory. Children gain insight into calculating the areas of irregular figures by cutting cardboard models with scissors (Wertheimer & Asch, 1945). When a player rearranges her tiles while playing Scrabble, the rearranged tiles scaffold word retrieval (Kirsh, 1995).

We can find more abstract examples of scaffolding. In education, Vygotsky (1986) called *the zone of proximal development* the difference between a child's ability to solve problems without aid and his ability to solve problems when provided with support or assistance. Vygotsky championed educational techniques for bridging the gap using scaffolding, which involves social and cultural factors and includes language.

Cognitive scaffolding typifies an important characteristic of embodied cognition, replacement, which occurs when environmental scaffolds replace internal cognitive resources (Shapiro, 2019). Replacement frees cognitive resources, reducing "the loads on individual brains by locating those brains in complex webs of linguistic, social, political, and institutional constraints" (Clark, 1997, p. 180).

Replacement, however, also leads to questions about the mind's location. If I scaffold my memory with written notes, then do they make up part of my memory? If I find rules to calculate area by manipulating cardboard models, then do the cardboard models make up part of my mathematical reasoning? "If, as we confront some task, a part of the world functions as a process which, *were it done in the head*, we would have no hesitation in recognizing as part of the cognitive process, then that part of the world *is* (so we claim) part of the cognitive process" (Clark & Chalmers, 1998, p. 8).

Questions about the mind's location intensify after realizing that scaffolding consists of more than using the environment to store information. The organism's body—its embodiment—determines the rich interaction between an organism and its world (Gibson, 1979). Embodiment defines possible actions; Gibson claims that "it is often neglected that the words *animal* and *environment* make an inseparable pair" (p. 8). The rich interactions involved in scaffolding lead to a controversial property of embodied cognition, constitution (Shapiro, 2019). If the environment can replace cognitive resources, and if embodiment and environment determine how we experience the world, then the environment does more than supply information. Constitution claims that the world *belongs* to cognition and does not merely provide information to cognition.

Constitution alters the definition of "mind" or "self" and questions the mind's location (Bateson, 1972). If the environment belongs to cognition, then the mind extends into the world. What does the extended mind imply? "But what about 'me'? Suppose I am a blind man, and I use a stick. I go tap, tap, tap. Where do *I* start? Is my mental system bounded at the handle of the stick? Is it bounded by my skin?" (Bateson, 1972, p. 465). Embodied cognition takes Bateson's questions seriously by proposing the *extended mind hypothesis* (Clark, 1997, 1999, 2003, 2008; Clark & Chalmers, 1998; Menary, 2008, 2010; Noë, 2009; Rupert, 2009; Wilson, 2004, 2005). According to this hypothesis, no boundary exists between the mind and the world. "It is the human brain *plus* these chunks of external scaffolding that finally constitutes the smart, rational inference engine we call mind" (Clark, 1997, p. 180).

The extended mind hypothesis also permits more elaborate notions of mind, such as cooperative cognition, which occurs when several agents share an environment (Hutchins, 1995). More than one cognitive agent can manipulate the world, which also scaffolds the information processing of other group members. As a result, "organized groups may have cognitive properties that differ from those of the individuals who constitute the group" (Hutchins, 1995, p. 228).

Hutchins (1995) uses his idea to extend the parable of the ant (Simon, 1969). Hutchins proposes watching generations of ants at work at a beach after a storm. Later generations will appear to be smarter because they behave more efficiently. But, as Hutchins notes, "the environment is not the same. Generations of ants have left their marks on the beach, and now a dumb ant has been made to appear smart through its simple interaction with the residua of the history of its ancestor's actions" (p. 169).

Collective cognition appears to be outside cognitive psychology, such as in entomology's concept of the *superorganism*, which imparts intelligence to the colony instead of the individual (Wheeler, 1911). The superorganism describes how colonies create elaborate structures, such as nests; we cannot predict such achievements from the capabilities of individual colony members.

Furthermore, the superorganism's intelligence emerges from cognitive scaffolding called *stigmergy* (Grasse, 1959; Theraulaz & Bonabeau, 1999). Stigmergy proposes that members of insect colonies do not themselves coordinate nest-building behaviour. Instead, the nest controls its own construction by stimulating insect behaviour. The nest-as-stimulus elicits particular insect actions for changing the nest in particular ways. Once changed, the nest becomes a different stimulus and elicits different nest-building actions.

The success of exploring the extended mind or collective cognition in other fields fuels new interest in these ideas within cognitive psychology. Such interest flourishes in embodied cognition, which has very different ideas about the mind and the role of the environment. However, the extended mind hypothesis faces intense criticism (Adams & Aizawa, 2008; Menary, 2010; Robbins & Aydede, 2009). Adams and Aizawa argue that embodied cognitivists do not define principled differences between cognitive and non-cognitive processing: "What the advocates of extended cognition need, but, we argue, do not have, is a plausible theory of the difference between the cognitive and the non-cognitive that does justice to the subject matter of cognitive psychology" (p. 11). They worry that the extended mind means that *anything* is cognitive.

Where is the mind? A psychology more open to cognitive contributions from the world, contributions also depending on the body, raises important questions about where cognition occurs. Such questions mean that researchers must reconsider how we need to study cognition. "We need a greater understanding of the ways in which the institutional setting, norms and values of the work group and, more broadly, cultural understandings of labor contribute to the reorganization of work tasks in a given community" (Scribner & Tobach, 1997, p. 373).

5.7 Can Machines Think?

Can machines think? The answer depends on our definition of "thinking." For instance, if we believe the information processing hypothesis—if cognition is rule-governed symbol manipulation—then other symbol-manipulating devices, such as digital computers, can think (Section 1.6). However, the answer also depends on our definition of "machine." Traditional cognitive psychologists, connectionists, and embodied cognitive psychologists propose different notions of "machine."

The possibility of thinking machines begins with the mechanical view of human bodies. In the 17th century, philosophers described humans as machines (Descartes, 1637/1960; Hobbes, 1651/1967). Philosophers described 18th-century clockwork automata as "living machines" offering support to mechanistic philosophies (Grenville, 2001; Wood, 2002). Some 18th-century philosophers claimed that thought itself is mechanical (La Mettrie, 1750). In the 19th century, elaborations of the mechanical view heralded modern notions of machine intelligence. George Boole (1854/2003) invented mathematical logic because he wanted to study thought mathematically. He equated thinking with performing logical operations and introduced his mathematical ideas in a book titled *The Laws of Thought*.

Researchers soon realized that machines could perform Boole's logical operations and invented various devices for solving problems of logic. The first such device, called the logical piano (Jevons, 1870), inspired more powerful logic machines (Marquand, 1885). Marquand even designed an electromagnetic logic machine (Mays, 1953). Boole's logic also set the stage for the 20th century's information age. Alan Turing's (1936) universal machine had far more power than did the 19th-century logic machines. Claude Shannon (1938) represented electric circuits as Boolean operators. The digital computer's invention depended on Turing's and Shannon's insights (Goldstine, 1993).

Digital computers appeared to be capable of thinking (Section 1.6). Early computers performed intelligent tasks, such as playing games, generating logical proofs, or solving problems (Feigenbaum & Feldman, 1963; Newell et al., 1958; Newell & Simon, 1956; Samuel, 1959; Simon & Newell, 1958). Turing (1950), convinced of the inevitability of machine intelligence, developed a test of computer intelligence. Books, aimed at the general public, described computers as thinking machines (Adler, 1961; Bell, 1962; Berkeley, 1949; Wiener, 1950). Advances in artificial intelligence strengthened the widespread belief in thinking machines. The age of intelligent machines spanned the late 1960s to the late 1980s (Kurzweil, 1990). During the age of intelligent machines, researchers developed numerous expert systems (Feigenbaum & McCorduck, 1983; Kurzweil, 1990). An expert system, a computer program, solves problems with an ability equal to, if not greater than, a human expert. Expert systems appeared in diverse domains, such as finance, manufacturing control, and medical diagnosis.

However, expert systems could only solve very narrowly defined problems and did not deliver general intelligence. "An overall pattern had begun to take shape . . . : an early, dramatic success based on the easy performance of simple tasks, or low-quality work on complex tasks, and then diminishing returns, disenchantment, and, in some cases, pessimism" (Dreyfus, 1992, p. 99). The pattern noted by Dreyfus produced harsh criticisms of the computer metaphor (Dreyfus, 1972, 1992; Winograd & Flores, 1987). AI researcher Terry Winograd (1972, 1983) pioneered computer programs for understanding language. However, by the late 1980s, he held little hope for his enterprise: "Our position . . . is that computers cannot understand language" (Winograd & Flores, 1987, p. 107).

Rising pessimism led many to argue that the computer metaphor does not provide an adequate account of human thinking. The Chinese room argument provides one influential example (Searle, 1980, 1984, 1990). In Searle's thought experiment, we write a question in Mandarin symbols, pass the question into a room through a slot, and then receive an answer, again written in Mandarin symbols. Clearly, the room understands the symbols because the room provides intelligible answers to written questions. But concerns arise when we look inside to see the mechanisms in the room. We see boxes of Mandarin symbols and instructions for converting sequences of symbols passed into the room into new sequences (answers). Inside we also see a native English speaker who does not understand Mandarin symbols, but she can follow the room's instructions and answer the questions even though she does not understand what the symbols mean.

The Chinese room contains the core elements of an information processing theory: the rule-governed manipulation of symbols. However, the room's components possess no true understanding of Mandarin. Therefore, Searle uses the Chinese room to argue that the computer metaphor cannot explain intelligent acts, such as understanding language. "Understanding a language, or indeed, having mental states at all, involves more than just having a bunch of formal symbols" (Searle, 1984, p. 33). If computers cannot produce intelligence, then what kind of machine can? Searle answers "the brain" because brains cause minds and—given the Chinese room argument—must do so by doing more than running a computer program. Thus, "anything else that caused minds would have to have causal powers at least equivalent to those of the brain" (p. 40). In other words, the possibility of machine intelligence depends on the nature of the machine itself.

Concerns about the computer metaphor produced alternative approaches to information processing, including a growing interest in neural accounts of cognitive processes. I have already discussed one related topic, the rise of connectionism, in Section 5.2. Unsurprisingly, connectionism arose at the same time that serious criticisms of the computer metaphor appeared. Figure 5-4 illustrates such a trend by plotting the number of times that four different terms ("expert systems," "neuroscience," "connectionism," and "cognitive neuroscience") appear in books curated by Google in the period from 1970 to 2008. I obtained the plotted results using the Google nGram viewer. The graph shows the dramatic rise, and the equally dramatic fall, of the term "expert system." When its usage decreases, we also see increases in using the other three terms, reflecting more brain-based approaches to mental phenomena.

Searle (1990) modified the Chinese room argument to challenge connectionism by proposing a Chinese gym filled with many native English speakers, each performing the same function as a neuron or a network processor. No one inside the gym understands Chinese. The gym can answer the same questions answered by the room. Searle concluded that, because no understanding of Chinese exists inside the gym, the gym refutes connectionism just as the room refutes the computer metaphor.

Searle's Chinese gym provoked a connectionist rebuttal (Churchland & Churchland, 1990). The Churchlands noted that "no neuron in my brain understands

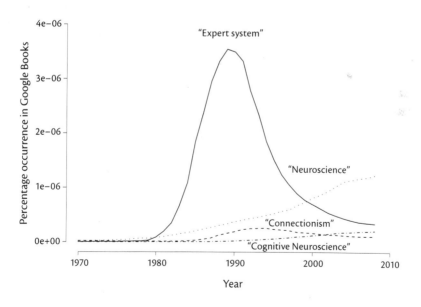

Figure 5-4 The results from Google's nGram viewer for the term "expert system" and for three other brain-based terms for the period from 1970 to 2008.

English, although my whole brain does" (p. 37). They provided an example of the *whole system reply* to the Chinese room argument. According to that reply, the whole room (or the whole gym), not its components, understands Chinese. The whole system reply also encourages us to consider which kinds of whole systems can understand. For instance, some could argue that an intelligent Chinese room must take the form not of a room but of a humanoid. To understand a language, computers might require bodies similar to those of humans, because our physical interactions with our world define our semantics (Dreyfus, 1967).

We frequently see roboticists claiming that humanoid intelligence depends on humanoid embodiment. The early successes in behaviour-based robotics involved machines with insect-like embodiment (Brooks, 1999, 2002). However, robots with such embodiment can achieve at best insect-level intelligence (Moravec, 1999). We must develop alternative embodiments if we want to emulate human intelligence. Such criticisms have driven recent advances in behaviour-based robotics.

For example, Brooks developed a humanoid robot called Cog (Brooks, 1997; Brooks et al., 1999; Brooks & Stein, 1994). Cog began as a torso with a single jointed arm and a head. Brooks aimed to make Cog's interaction with the world as human-like as possible. For instance, its visual system consisted of cameras to emulate human saccadic eye movements. Brooks developed Cog to explore ideas central to embodied cognition: "All human representations are ultimately grounded in sensory motor patterns. Thus to build an artificial system with similar grounding to a human system it is necessary to build a robot with human form" (1997, p. 968).

Social robotics provides another example of emphasizing human embodiment. The embodiment of a social robot facilitates and modulates social interactions with humans (Breazeal, 2002, 2003, 2004; Breazeal et al., 2009). Social robots typically have human or animal embodiments to permit dynamic interactions with humans via verbal or non-verbal behaviours (Breazeal et al., 2016). For instance, one robot uses variations of head position, mouth shape, direction of gaze, opening of eyelids, or raising of eyebrows to influence social interactions or to communicate internal states. The robot's behaviours influence people because humans have high sensitivity to such social signals (Breazeal et al., 2016). Socially intelligent robots require appropriate embodiment.

Can machines think? Early adopters of the computer metaphor answered affirmatively. However, the failure of expert systems to produce general intelligence produced new ideas. Some argue that machines can think if their inner workings resemble those of the brain. Others argue that, for machines to think like humans, they must have humanoid embodiment. Ideas about intelligent machines have evolved as different approaches to human information processing have emerged.

Interestingly, Searle dismisses such approaches. His Chinese gym argument attacks connectionists (Searle, 1990). As for humanoid embodiment, Searle (1984) argues that a robot cannot understand language using a computer "brain." Searle believes that only biological brains can think. We will see in Section 5.8 that many other researchers share Searle's belief.

5.8 What Is the "Cognitive" in Cognitive Neuroscience?

Sections 5.2 through 5.7 explored debates arising from challenges to the computer metaphor. Both connectionism and embodied cognition reject similarities between human and computer information processing. The new views of information processing provided by connectionism and embodied cognition represent architectural challenges to traditional cognitive psychology. However, the new views also lead to philosophical challenges. Both connectionism's appeal to brain-like processing and embodied cognition's appeal to physical embodiment react to cognitive psychology's functionalism because the new views place particular emphasis on physical substrates or mechanisms.

I now explore a particular rejection of functionalism, cognitive neuroscience. Since the 1990s, the so-called decade of the brain, researchers have increasingly proposed cognitive theories related to brain areas or neural functions. Such theories reject functionalism. How might non-functionalist theories contribute to cognitive psychology? In Section 5.8, I argue that cognitive neuroscientists should contribute to cognitive psychology by supporting functional analyses and not by reducing cognition to brain operations. In Section 5.9, I elaborate the argument in Section 5.8 by considering recent philosophical criticisms of cognitive neuroscience. I begin by relating cognitive psychology and cognitive neuroscience using many-to-one relationships.

Theories in cognitive psychology reveal many-to-one relationships. Different algorithms can produce the same behaviour. Different architectures can perform the same algorithm. Different physical systems can create the same architecture. We call the last relationship, from the physical to the architectural, *multiple realization* (Polger & Shapiro, 2016). Multiple realization recognizes that different physical substrates can produce identical functions (Putnam, 1975a, 1975b). "We could be made of Swiss cheese and it wouldn't matter" (Putnam, 1975b, p. 291). Cognitive psychologists endorse multiple realization by appealing to functions instead of physical states (Polger, 2012). Multiple realization permits computer simulations of cognitive theories. Provided that we use the correct functions, we need not concern ourselves with the physical differences between computers and brains.

Although early cognitive psychology adopted functionalism, modern cognitive psychology appeals more and more to cognitive neuroscience. The rise of cognitive neuroscience began in the 1990s with the so-called neuro-turn in the social sciences (Cooter, 2014; Pedersen, 2011; Vidal & Ortega, 2017). The neuro-turn grew with increased funding for brain research during the "decade of the brain" (Jones & Mendell, 1999). Cognitive psychology's neuro-turn appears in many textbooks, which display brain imaging pictures and include chapters about cognitive neuroscience (Section 5.10). Modern texts also include cognitive neuroscience in definitions of cognitive psychology (Section 5.11). Given the functionalism of cognitive psychology, how can cognitive psychology include cognitive neuroscience? What is the "cognitive" in cognitive neuroscience (Figdor, 2013)?

Cognitive neuroscientists assume that brains cause minds and explore their assumption scientifically. "Cognitive neuroscience is an experimental investigation that aims to discover empirical truths concerning the neural foundations of human faculties and the neural processes that accompany their exercise" (Bennett & Hacker, 2013, p. 238). Cognitive neuroscientists adopt three additional assumptions to guide their investigations (Frisch, 2014). The first is *localizationism*: assuming an association between mental functions and localized brain areas. The second is *internalism*: assuming that neural mechanisms produce localized mental functions. And the third is *isolationism*: assuming that we can use biological causes to explain how mental functions are generated by local brain regions.

The history of the three assumptions dates back to the early 18th-century hypothesis associating specific mental functions with specific, local brain regions. Gall's now discredited phrenology popularized localizationism (Simpson, 2005). Proper scientific support for localized brain functions arose in the middle of the 19th century. Paul Broca and Carl Wernicke discovered that damage to different regions of the brain produced different types of aphasia (Bennett & Hacker, 2013). Thus, we find historical links between cognitive neuroscience and the study of the relationships between brain injuries and mental deficits.

We can also link cognitive neuroscience to more recent invasive studies of animal brains. David Hubel and Torsten Wiesel (1959, 1962) recorded the responses of visual neurons in cats and pioneered techniques used to provide a modern, detailed, functional map of the primate visual system (van Essen et al., 1992). The modern map has 32 different cortical areas, each understood as detecting different visual features. Thus, invasive explorations of the visual system also provide evidence to associate local brain areas with particular psychological processes.

Modern cognitive neuroscience distinguishes itself from older traditions by using *non-invasive* techniques to study the *normal* brain (Kok, 2020). Cognitive neuroscience's older techniques measured the brain's electrical activity and included the electroencephalogram (EEG), a technique developed in the 1920s (Stone & Hughes, 2013). An EEG measures electrical activity in different parts of the brain via electrodes attached to the scalp. A related technique, the event-related potential (ERP), uses the EEG to measure brain responses to specific sensory, cognitive, or motor events. We measure ERPs by combining multiple EEG recordings (Cox & Evarts, 1961; Dawson, 1954). More modern techniques create brain images from magnetic fields. Researchers invented magnetic resonance imaging (MRI) in the early 1970s (Lauterbur, 1973). Functional MRI (fMRI), developed in the early 1990s (Bandettini, 2012), measures brain activity by detecting changes associated with cerebral blood flow. fMRI's key metric is BOLD: blood-oxygen level-dependent.

How do cognitive neuroscientists use such modern methods? We can describe one common approach as a new version of the subtractive method established by Donders (Sections 3.9 and 4.2). The modern subtractive method measures brain activity during a "reference" task as well as during a "target" task (Cabeza & Nyberg, 1997, 2000). Researchers presume that the target task differs from the reference task by a single cognitive process of interest. By subtracting reference task brain activity from target task brain activity, cognitive neuroscientists can correlate the cognitive process of interest with brain regions exhibiting higher activity ("activations") or lower activity ("deactivations").

One imaging study of the Stroop effect provides an example of cognitive neuroscience's subtractive method (Langenecker et al., 2004). The study compared the neural processing of older adults with that of younger adults. Older adults tended to produce larger Stroop effects. Langenecker et al. hypothesized an association between the brain's frontal lobes and age-related differences in Stroop effects, and they used three different Stroop task conditions. The first, the congruent condition, had the names of colours printed in correct ink colours. The second, the incongruent condition, had the names of colours printed in incorrect ink colours. The third, the neutral condition, had non-colour words printed in various ink colours. Langenecker et al. examined brain activations using variations of the subtraction method. In the first variation, they treated the incongruent condition as the target condition and the neutral condition as the reference condition. In the second, they treated the incongruent condition as the target condition and the congruent condition as the reference condition. And in the third, they treated the congruent condition as the target condition and the neutral condition as the reference condition.

Langenecker et al. (2004) found results to support the hypothesis that older adults needed to recruit more inhibitory mechanisms in order to perform the task. For instance, the incongruent-congruent comparisons revealed higher activations in frontal lobes for older adults compared with younger adults. Langenecker et al. obtained similar results for the congruent-incongruent comparison. They concluded that frontal lobes (in particular, the left inferior frontal gyrus) control inhibition.

Brain imaging studies like the one conducted by Langenecker et al. (2004) provide insights into the relationship between the brain and cognition. One paper reviewed the results of 275 different imaging studies conducted between 1988 and 1998 (Cabeza & Nyberg, 2000). The review covered many cognitive domains (attention, perception, imagery, language, and several different aspects of memory). Cabeza and Nyberg found that specific regions of the brain demonstrate consistent activation patterns for each cognitive domain.

In spite of cognitive neuroscience's apparent success, researchers express persistent and growing concerns about its utility. Some concerns focus on brain imaging methodology. Others question the inferences that we can make about relations between the brain and cognition. Let us briefly consider some criticisms of cognitive neuroscience.

One extensive literature review challenges cognitive neuroscience's localizationism (Uttal, 2011). Uttal argues that brain imaging results fail to demonstrate functional localization. Instead, the results provide overwhelming evidence of *distributed* representations and processing. As Uttal notes, "Brain imaging meta-studies show that when the results of a number of experiments are pooled, the typical result is to show activations over most of the brain rather than convergence on a single location" (p. 365).

Uttal (2011) also questions the subtractive method. When it reveals no activation differences between tasks, different microscopic processes can still occur. Different processes might produce the same activity. Worries about the subtractive method, coupled with concerns about localizationism, lead Uttal to promote a new approach emphasizing distribution, interconnectedness, poly-functionality, and microscopic processing.

Uttal (2011) also charges that cognitive neuroscientists appeal to poorly defined cognitive terms: "The reference of such terms as learning, emotion, perception, and so on [is] . . . not precisely defined by either these words or the experimental context in which they arise. There is a major disconnect between our understanding of what cognitive processes are and the brain measures we try to connect to them" (pp. 367–368). Similar concerns underlie criticisms of how cognitive neuroscientists present their work to the public (Figdor, 2013). Other scholars question whether cognitive neuroscience adds any understanding to pre-existing cognitive concepts (Vidal & Ortega, 2017). The public sees cognitive neuroscience as offering a naive reductionism. When relating some cognitive function X and some brain area Y, cognitive neuroscientists imply that we can explain X with Y or that we can reduce X to Y: a false implication. Knowing (from brain imaging studies) that the medial temporal lobe relates to consolidating memories (Squire & Wixted, 2011) is quite different from knowing how the brain performs consolidation. Knowing *where* is not the same as knowing *how*.

A related issue concerns relating cognitive functions and cognitive neuroscience. Functions precede localizationism. For instance, creating target and reference tasks depends on a pre-existing functional analysis of cognitive processing. Furthermore, cognitive neuroscience cannot use neural observations to generate functional descriptions. "Trying to understand perception by studying only neurons is like trying to understand bird flight by studying only feathers: It just cannot be done" (Marr, 1982, p. 27).

Bennett and Hacker (2003, 2013) offer one final concern about how cognitive neuroscience relates the brain to cognition. They recognize that the brain causes psychological states but argue that we make a logical error when we attribute psychological states to the brain. They claim that we can only ascribe psychological states to whole organisms and not to parts of whole organisms (e.g., the brain). In Section 5.9, I examine Bennett and Hacker's critique in more detail.

Given the various concerns raised above, what can cognitive neuroscience contribute to cognitive psychology? Cognitive neuroscience encounters problems when trying to reduce cognition to brain processes. We can view cognitive neuroscience more pragmatically by claiming that it contributes to cognitive psychology's functional analyses. Cognitive psychologists cannot directly observe cognitive processes, so they must infer functions from empirical observations. Cognitive neuroscience offers new observations to support functional analysis.

Cognitive neuroscientists frequently use ERPs to study attention (Woodman, 2010). ERPs can measure changes in brain activity occurring 1 millisecond to the next. We can reliably associate different ERP components with different kinds of attentional processes, such as shifting attention during a visual search. Participants do not have to shift attention away from a task to respond to it, another advantage of measuring attentional processing with ERPs. We can also combine ERPs with other spatial measures of brain processing, such as fMRI (Heinze et al., 1994; Hopfinger et al., 2000; Mangun et al., 1998).

Functional analysis requires more than merely identifying potential functions. When we perform functional analysis, we decompose higher-order functions into organized systems of sub-functions. Cognitive neuroscience can help to guide functional decomposition, as illustrated by cognitive neuroscience's study of human memory. Some of the earliest evidence for analyzing memory into different subsystems arose from studies of memory deficits associated with brain lesions (Scoville & Milner, 1957; Squire, 2009). More recent brain imaging studies associate different patterns of brain activity with different kinds of memory (Cabeza & Nyberg, 2000; Milner et al., 1998; Squire & Wixted, 2011). Cognitive neuroscience's ability to guide functional decomposition does not require localizationism. We need not correlate a cognitive function with a local brain region. We only need to observe reliable differences in activation patterns, realizing that multiple brain regions might produce the differences.

Cognitive neuroscience can also aid functional decomposition by exploring domains that cognitive psychologists might not ordinarily study. For instance, we will see in Section 5.10 that cognitive psychologists rarely study emotion. However, cognitive neuroscientists have studied the relationship between emotion and memory (Eichenbaum, 2002). Thus, cognitive neuroscience can expand the typical domain of a functional analysis conducted by cognitive psychologists.

We cannot complete a functional analysis without evidence of primitive sub-functions. Because biological mechanisms bring to life the primitives of human or animal cognition, cognitive neuroscience can help to subsume a functional analysis. In all likelihood, cognitive neuroscience's support for the subsumption of functional primitives requires a microscopic perspective of the sort favoured by Uttal (2011). We can find one example in current accounts of Hebbian learning. In his theory of cell assemblies, Hebb (1949) proposed that, if two neurons generated action potentials at the same time, then the excitatory connection between them would strengthen. His idea inspired many models of associative learning (Hinton & Anderson, 1981; Milner, 1957; Rochester et al., 1956).

We can subsume Hebbian learning. The biological phenomenon of long-term potentiation, dependent on N-methyl-D-aspartate (NMDA) receptors in hippocampal neurons, provides a biological account of Hebb's learning rule (Bliss & Lomo, 1973; Brown, 1990; Lynch, 1986; Martinez & Derrick, 1996). NMDA receptors only permit ions to pass through membranes when both pre- and post-synaptic activity occur at the same time. Furthermore, blocking NMDA receptor sites prevents the hippocampus from establishing memories, indicating that NMDA receptors relate to learning (Morris et al., 1986). NMDA receptors explain Hebbian learning (Brown & Milner, 2003; Klein, 1999; van Hemmen & Senn, 2002).

Many controversies emerge when we treat the goal of cognitive neuroscience as reducing psychological functions to neural processes. We find fewer controversies when we view the goal as providing additional observations to support functional analysis. The methods of cognitive neuroscience complement the methods of experimental cognitive psychologists, aiding the broader effort of performing functional analyses of cognition.

5.9 Do Brains Think?

Do brains think? Almost every modern cognitive psychologist would answer "Yes." However, other scholars would not (Bennett et al., 2007; Bennett & Hacker, 2003, 2013). Bennett and Hacker argue that brains do not think and that cognitive neuroscientists should not attribute psychological properties to the brain. Bennett and Hacker argue that brains do not think because thinking is a characteristic of whole organisms and not of their parts: "We deny that it makes sense to say that the brain is conscious, feel[s] sensations, perceives, thinks, knows or wants anything—for these are attributes of animals, not of their brains" (2013, p. 242).

Bennett and Hacker (2013) take inspiration from Ludwig Wittgenstein's *Philosophical Investigations*, drawing from a particular passage in that book: "Only of a human being and of what resembles (behaves like) a living human being can one say: it has sensations; it sees, is blind; hears, is deaf; is conscious or unconscious" (1953, §281). Bennett and Hacker argue that claiming brains think provides an example of the *mereological fallacy*. We commit that fallacy when we attribute a property to a part that we should attribute to the whole organism.

Bennett and Hacker's (2013) position seems to return to behaviorism. For instance, on what basis would they attribute consciousness to a whole organism? "*The concept* of consciousness is bound up with the behavioral grounds for ascribing consciousness to the animal" (p. 245). They say that we can only attribute psychological states to organisms when organisms display proper behaviour. Brains do not behave, and therefore we cannot say that brains have psychological properties.

The mereological fallacy challenges widely accepted views of brains and minds. Not surprisingly, the fallacy faces considerable criticism (Churchland, 2005; Dennett, 2007; Searle, 2007), some of which arises from the computer metaphor.

Churchland (2005, p. 470) describes digital computers as devices *"deliberately built* to engage in the 'rule-governed manipulation of complex symbols.'" Computer engineers explain how computers work by appealing to information processing. To computer designers, computers store, manipulate, and retrieve information by following formal rules. "Such talk now makes perfect sense, at least to computer scientists" (p. 470).

Bennett and Hacker respond by applying the mereological fallacy to digital computers:

> It is true that we do, in casual parlance, say that computers remember, that they search their memory, that they calculate, and sometimes, when they take a long time, we jocularly say that they are thinking things over. But this is merely a *façon de parler*. It is not a literal application of the terms "remember," "calculate" and "think." Computers are devices designed to fulfil certain functions for us. We can store information in a computer, as we can in a filing cabinet. But filing cabinets cannot remember anything, and neither can computers. We use computers to produce the results of a calculation—just as we used to use a slide rule or a cylindrical mechanical calculator. Those results are produced without anyone or anything literally calculating—as is evident in the case of a slide rule or a mechanical calculator. (2013, p. 248)

However, their criticism of digital computers abandons the behaviorism that they apply to the brain by admitting that computers generate the right behaviour: "Computers are devices designed to fulfil certain functions for us." Bennett and Hacker dismiss behavioural evidence, however, because computers do not generate behaviour in the right way:

> Computers were not built to "engage in the rule-governed manipulation of symbols," they were built to produce results that will *coincide* with rule-governed, correct manipulation of symbols. Further, computers can no more *follow* a rule than can a mechanical calculator. A machine can execute operations that accord with the rule, provided all the causal links built into it function as designed and assuming that the design ensures the generation of a regularity in accordance with the chosen rule or rules. But for something to constitute

following a rule, the mere production of a regularity in accordance with the rule is not sufficient. (2013, p. 256)

What, in addition to behaviour, do Bennett and Hacker require to support the claim that computers follow rules? As they suggest,

A being can be said to be following a rule only in the context of a complex practice involving actual and potential activities of justifying, noticing mistakes and correcting them by reference to the rule, criticizing deviations from the rule, and, if called upon, explaining an action as being in accordance with the rule and teaching others what counts as following a rule. (2013, p. 256)

Similarly, "In order literally to calculate, one must have a grasp of a wide range of concepts, follow a multitude of rules that one must know, and understand a variety of operations. Computers do not and cannot" (p. 248).

Thus, when the internal causal links of a computer cause it to perform calculations, it does not perform "true" calculation. True calculation requires additional, semantic properties: grasping concepts or understanding operations.

Bennett and Hacker's (2013) response to Churchland restates the Chinese room problem (Section 5.7). When Bennett and Hacker look inside computers, they fail to see the expected calculation processes. Similarly, when they look inside the brain, they fail to see the expected thinking processes. However, they have incorrect expectations. Functional analysis decomposes behaviour into an organized system of primitives, which themselves neither resemble nor reveal the whole system's behaviour. Although we might describe a whole brain as understanding English, we cannot describe individual neurons in the same way (Churchland & Churchland, 1990). When we look inside a system, we can explain it using functional analysis; we should not see whole behaviour. We should see instead the primitives for bringing the whole behaviour into being.

Churchland's (2005) rebuttal damages Bennett and Hacker's (2013) position because we can explain computers using functional analysis, which dictates a computer's design (Kidder, 1981). When a designer explains how she engineers computer behaviour, the explanation takes a different form from what Bennett and Hacker would like. Churchland's critique demonstrates that the mereological fallacy does not always have problems. By hypothesis, cognitivists argue that we can explain thinking, and ultimately brain function, in the same way that we can explain computers. The mereological hypothesis will apply to neither computers nor brains when the hypothesis is true.

One further puzzle created by Bennett and Hacker's position concerns the purpose of cognitive neuroscience. Bennett and Hacker admit that we require brain processes for thinking to occur, and they describe cognitive neuroscience as aiming "to illuminate those mechanisms in the brain that must function normally in order for us to be able to exercise our psychological faculties, such as perception and memory" (2013, p. 1). However, the mereological fallacy dictates that we cannot accomplish the stated aim by ascribing psychological states to brain states. How, then, can cognitive neuroscience relate brain function to psychological faculties?

Functional analysis provides an answer. We explain information processing systems at different levels (e.g., computational, algorithmic, architectural, and implementational; see Section 1.7) (Dawson, 2013; Marr, 1982; Pylyshyn, 1984). We can describe electric circuits physically or as computing a complex Boolean function (Shannon, 1938). However, we expect differences between explaining a system at one level and explaining the same system at another level. The biological account of centre-surround cells in the lateral geniculate nucleus differs dramatically from the mathematical derivation of a difference of Gaussians function.

Nevertheless, we can relate different levels to one another. Both centre-surround cells and differences of Gaussians describe edge detection. The empirical successes of cognitivism show that we can sensibly claim that brains think. However, we must expect differences between accounting for a system at the implementational level and accounting for a system at the algorithmic level. The brain mechanisms for thinking differ from thinking itself.

5.10 Which Topics Are Important to Cognitive Psychology?

In Sections 5.2 through 5.9, I discussed architectural challenges to traditional cognitive psychology from connectionism, architectural challenges from embodied cognition, and philosophical issues raised by cognitive neuroscience. In the final two sections of this chapter, I step back to consider broadly the nature of cognitive psychology. How can we define cognitive psychology? In Section 5.10, I attempt to define it by exploring how textbooks have presented the discipline in different decades. We will see that the definition of cognitive psychology seems to change over time. In Section 5.11, I propose a more general, but hopefully more lasting, definition by moving away from cognitive psychology's topics and by moving toward its methods. I begin by exploring how cognitive psychology textbooks present the discipline as the study of specific topics and by observing changes in such topics over decades.

Which topics are important to cognitive psychology? Let us explore how textbooks have introduced students to the discipline over the past several decades. Thomas Verner Moore (1939) wrote the first book, titled simply *Cognitive Psychology*. Moore discussed topics often seen in modern texts: perception, imagery, memory, judgment, and reasoning. However, his book had little impact (Knapp, 1985; Surprenant & Neath, 1997). Surprenant and Neath note that other important books, aligned with more prominent schools of psychology (functionalism and behaviorism) overshadowed Moore (Hilgard & Marquis, 1940; Hull et al., 1940; McGeoch, 1942; Woodworth, 1938). Moore did not spark the cognitive revolution.

Important texts appeared after the cognitive revolution. *Cognition and Thought* (Reitman, 1965) introduced information processing to psychologists and included an appendix on how to program computers to simulate psychological models. *Cognitive Psychology* (Neisser, 1967), usually described as the field's founding text, defined cognitive psychology as the study of "all the processes by which the sensory input is transformed, reduced, elaborated, stored, recovered and used" (p. 4).

Cognitive psychology texts became more common in the 1970s. *An Introduction to Cognitive Psychology* (Manis, 1971) discussed topics ranging from learning and memory to cognitive consistency and social judgment. *Cognitive Psychology: The Study of Knowing, Learning and Thinking* (Anderson, 1975) placed cognitive psychology into an idiosyncratic context of cybernetics, systems theory, and control theory. The variety of topics covered by early texts suggests that a unified understanding of cognitive psychology had not yet emerged. However, by the late 1970s, cognitive psychology texts had become more standardized and adopted an organization still seen in modern books (Reynolds & Flagg, 1977; Solso, 1979).

For example, *Cognitive Psychology* (Reynolds & Flagg, 1977) begins by placing the cognitive approach in a historical context. Early chapters discuss peripheral processes (sensory memory, pattern recognition), middle chapters describe memory, and final chapters focus on language. The cognitive psychology textbooks of the 1980s elaborate Reynolds and Flagg's organization by adding later chapters on higher-order processing, such as problem solving, reasoning, and judgment and decision making (Anderson, 1980, 1985; Dodd & White, 1980; Reed, 1982, 1988). From the 1990s on, such organization becomes the norm, although more modern texts also include an early chapter on neuroscience.

To gain insight into the contents of cognitive psychology textbooks, as well as into the changes in contents over time, let us explore the contents of several books. We can examine chapter titles and lengths, and classify each chapter as covering a general topic, adopting a methodology similar to earlier analyses of cognitive psychology texts (Lewandowsky & Dunbar, 1983; Marek & Griggs, 2001). I consider two texts from the 1960s (Neisser, 1967; Reitman, 1965); five from the 1970s (Bourne et al., 1979; Lachman et al., 1979; Manis, 1971; Reynolds & Flagg, 1977; Solso, 1979); six from the 1980s (Anderson, 1980, 1985; Dodd & White, 1980; Reed, 1982, 1988; Solso, 1988); and six from the 1990s (Haberlandt, 1994; Kellogg, 1995; Martindale, 1991; Medin & Ross, 1992; Reed, 1996; Solso, 1995). The remaining 12 appeared in 2000 or later (Anderson, 2000, 2020; Braisby & Gellatly, 2012; Eysenck & Keane, 2020; Farmer & Matlin, 2019; Goldstein, 2011, 2015; Groome, 2014; McBride & Cutting, 2019; Reisberg, 2013, 2018; Sinnett et al., 2016).

I process each book as follows. First, I record the title of each chapter and the total number of pages. Second, I examine the contents of each chapter and then classify the chapter as presenting one of the 22 finer-detailed topics in the left column of Table 5-1. When I could conceivably assign a chapter to more than one category, I use only one category (e.g., I code "language acquisition" as "language," not as "learning"); I use a consistent coding. Third, I calculate the total number of pages for each category by summing up the number of pages for all chapters belonging to that category.

After I code each book, I collapse topics into a coarser set of categories by combining several finer categories to define a more general category. For instance, category 5 in the coarser scheme ("Problem Solving, Reasoning") was created by combining four finer categories ("Problem Solving," "Reasoning," "Judgment, Decision Making," "Intelligence, Creativity"). The layout of Table 5-1 shows the finer categories that I combined into each coarser category. The coarser coding scheme is very similar to the one used by Marek and Griggs (2001). The processing represents each textbook in terms of the number of pages devoted to both the finer and the coarser topics listed in Table 5-1. I convert the number of pages into proportions by dividing each by the total number of pages in a text.

This textbook representation permits us to see easily which topics are important to cognitive psychology, which topics are more important than others, and how topic coverage changes over time. For example, Figure 5-5 presents a *treemap* of the text contents from Table 5-1's coarser topics. We can create the treemap by averaging the proportion of pages devoted to a topic over the books representing four different time periods: the 1970s, 1980s, 1990s, and 2000s (any book published

Table 5-1 Two sets of categories used to classify the contents of book chapters

Finer Topics	Coarser Topics
1. Foundations, History	1. Foundations, History
2. Neuroscience	2. Neuroscience, Physiology
3. Sensation	3. Perception, Attention, Consciousness
4. Attention	
5. Perception	
6. Consciousness	
7. Primary Memory	4. Memory
8. Secondary Memory	
9. Levels of Processing	
10. Representational Format	
11. Mental Imagery	
12. Problem Solving	5. Problem Solving, Reasoning
13. Reasoning	
14. Judgment, Decision Making	
15. Intelligence, Creativity	
16. Language	6. Language
17. Development	7. Development
18. Learning	8. Other
19. Emotion	
20. Social	
21. Models, Simulation	
22. Other	

after 2000). A treemap represents proportions hierarchically. Figure 5-5's first level in the hierarchy represents book topics; the second level organizes topics by book eras.

In Figure 5-5, I represent the upper part of the hierarchy (the set of eight topics from the coarse coding scheme) using a large rectangle of a uniform colour. For instance, the large white rectangle at the top left of the treemap represents the

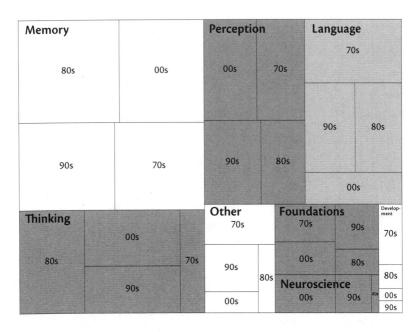

Figure 5-5 A treemap of how cognitive psychology textbooks cover the coarse set of topics from Table 5-1. The books belong to the 1970s (1970–1979), the 1980s (1980–1989), the 1990s (1990–1999), or the 2000s (2000–2020).

topic "Memory." The rectangle's size represents the proportion of pages in texts that we can classify as covering "Memory." I represent the hierarchy's next level (book era) by dividing a large rectangle into components. For instance, I divide the large white rectangle for the topic "Memory" into four smaller rectangles. I label each smaller rectangle by era; each rectangle's size represents a topic's coverage by a subset of books (i.e., all books belonging to the same era).

When we inspect the large rectangles in Figure 5-5, we find that the topic "Memory" receives the most coverage, because the rectangle for "Memory" has the largest area. The next most covered topics are "Perception," "Language," and "Thinking," each of which has roughly equal coverage. We find less coverage for "Foundations" and "Other." "Neuroscience" has little coverage, followed by "Development."

We can also see, from Figure 5-5, how topic coverage changes over the four different eras. "Memory" and "Perception" receive equal coverage over all four eras, but "Language" receives less coverage beginning in 2000. Most coverage of "Neuroscience" occurs after 2000 and receives little coverage prior to the 1990s. The coverage of "Development" has decreased since the 1980s. "Thinking" receives more treatment after the 1980s. The 1980s stand out for having less coverage of "Foundations."

We should also consider topics *absent* from Figure 5-5 (unless they belong to "Other"). Social cognition has its own textbooks (Fiske & Taylor, 2020; Kunda, 1999) and receives little coverage in cognitive psychology texts. The same is true for comparative cognition, a field absent from Figure 5-5 but covered by its own texts (Menzel & Fischer, 2012; Olmstead & Kuhlmeier, 2015; Shettleworth, 2013). Figure 5-5 reveals a discipline that focuses on cognition in individual adult humans. The figure also reveals that the coverage of unique topics ("Other") decreases after 2000, suggesting a growing uniformity of topic coverage in modern texts.

We can consider the similarities between individual texts in more detail by computing correlations between texts. We can calculate using the values for each text for the finer set of topics from Table 5-1. (This analysis excluded an extreme outlier, the Reitman [1965] text, which produced negative correlations with all other texts.)

We can use our correlations to conduct a multi-dimensional scaling (MDS) analysis. MDS, a statistical tool, positions different objects in a map. MDS places similar objects near one another and dissimilar objects farther apart. Figure 5-6 plots a three-dimensional MDS solution derived from the textbook correlations. The MDS solution provides an excellent fit to the data; the solution produces a correlation of 0.975 for distances among the books in Figure 5-6 and the original correlations. What does Figure 5-6 reveal about the relationships among individual textbooks? Each dimension of the graph represents different topic combinations.

The first dimension ("Perception/Neuroscience vs Language/Memory") arranges books in terms of their combined treatment of four different topics. Books having a more positive position along this dimension (Braisby & Gellatly, 2012; Goldstein, 2011; Groome, 2014) have more coverage of both perception and neuroscience and less coverage of both language and memory. In contrast, books having a more negative position along this dimension (Anderson, 2020; Haberlandt, 1994; Reed, 1996) have less coverage of both perception and neuroscience and more coverage of both language and memory.

We can provide a similar account for the second dimension ("Language/ Neuroscience vs Memory/Problem Solving"), which provides the *y* axis of the top plot, and the *x* axis of the bottom plot, of Figure 5-6. Books with a more positive position along this dimension (Dodd & White, 1980; Goldstein, 2011, 2015) have more coverage of both language and neuroscience and less coverage of both memory and problem solving. In contrast, books with a more negative position along this

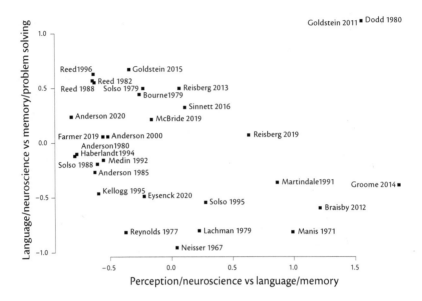

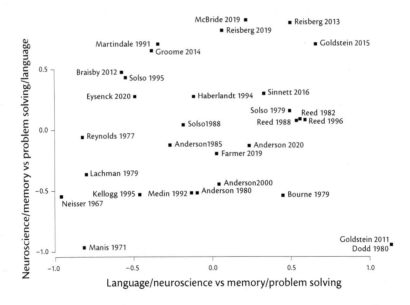

Figure 5-6 A plot of the three-dimensional MDS solution for correlations among textbooks based upon the 22 finer topics from Table 5-1. The top plot uses the first and second dimensions as the coordinates of the books. The bottom plot uses the second and third dimensions as the coordinates of the books.

dimension (Lachman et al., 1979; Manis, 1971; Neisser, 1967; Reynolds & Flagg, 1977) have less coverage of both language and neuroscience and more coverage of both memory and problem solving.

We can also provide a similar account for the third dimension ("Neuroscience/Memory vs Problem Solving/Language"), which provides the y axis of the bottom plot of Figure 5-6. Books with a more positive position along this dimension (McBride & Cutting, 2019; Reisberg, 2013, 2018) have more coverage of both neuroscience and memory and less coverage of both problem solving and language. In contrast, books with a more negative position along this dimension (Dodd & White, 1980; Goldstein, 2011; Manis, 1971) have less coverage of both neuroscience and memory and more coverage of both problem solving and language.

Which topics are important to cognitive psychology? Figure 5-5 indicates that the core topics are memory, followed by thinking, perception, and language. However, a topic's importance changes over time. For instance, modern texts, but not earlier texts, have high coverage of neuroscience. Figure 5-6 indicates that different textbooks emphasize different topic combinations. Books with more coverage of neuroscience and perception, or of neuroscience and memory, have less coverage of language and problem solving.

In summary, cognitive psychology texts cover similar topics but still differ noticeably from one another. The average correlation used for the MDS analysis is 0.431. A correlation so large suggests a strong commonality of topics in texts through the decades. However, a correlation so small also suggests great variability of topic coverage. Some variation suggests that the definition of cognitive psychology has changed over time, as I discuss in Section 5.11.

5.11 What Is Cognitive Psychology?

What is cognitive psychology? To answer that question, we might consider textbook definitions. The definition of cognitive psychology has evolved over the decades. Moore (1939, p. v) provided the first textbook definition of cognitive psychology: "Cognitive psychology is the branch of general psychology which studies the way in which the human mind receives impressions from the external world and interprets the impressions thus received." Moore's definition highlights a common theme of cognitive psychology's later reaction to behaviorism: replacing the passive responder with the active information processing agent.

Neisser (1967) defines cognitive psychology in two parts. He first restates Moore's (1939) definition but introduces information processing ideas: "The term 'cognition' refers to all the processes by which the sensory input is transformed, reduced, elaborated, stored, recovered, and used" (p. 4). Neisser then lists cognitive psychology's prototypical topics: "Such terms as *sensation, perception, imagery, retention, recall, problem-solving,* and *thinking,* among many others, refer to hypothetical stages or aspects of cognition" (p. 4). Let us call his definition the information processing definition.

We find that definition in many cognitive psychology textbooks published after Neisser's (1967) (Anderson, 1980; Haberlandt, 1994; Reed, 1982, 1988, 1996; Reynolds & Flagg, 1977). For example, Reynolds and Flagg write that "cognitive psychology is defined partly by what it does (the information processing approach to be described shortly) and by its subject matter, the higher mental processes" (p. 11).

Importantly, an alternative, broader definition appears in more modern texts. It places less emphasis on information processing and more emphasis on research methods or approaches. Let us call this the methodological definition. One example is provided by Eysenck (2020, p. 37):

> Cognitive psychology used to be unified by an approach based on an analogy between the mind and the computer. This information-processing approach viewed the mind as a general-purpose, symbol processing system of limited capacity. Today there are four main approaches to human cognition: cognitive psychology, cognitive neuropsychology, cognitive neuroscience, and computational cognitive science. These four approaches are increasingly combined to provide an enriched understanding of human cognition.

We can find Eysenck's methodological definition in several modern textbooks (Farmer & Matlin, 2019; Groome, 2014; McBride & Cutting, 2019). That definition includes other fields' contributions to studying cognition. Cognitive neuropsychology studies deficits in cognitive performance associated with brain injuries. Cognitive neuroscience uses brain imaging techniques to explore the relationship between normal brain function and cognition. Computational cognitive science produces computer models of cognitive phenomena. The methodological definition modernizes cognitive psychology by including the latest methodologies.

Unfortunately, the methodological definition fails to consider any overarching approach to cognition. Defining cognitive psychology only in terms of methodological approaches seems to be too inclusive. For example, Skinner (1957) studied a core cognitive topic, language, but his theory was not cognitive (Chomsky,

1959), and Skinner (1977) was not a cognitive psychologist. Modern simulations, such as deep belief networks, successfully solve many tasks involving images or language (LeCun et al., 2015), but they do not produce cognitive theory. The cognitive neuroscience promoted by some (Bennett & Hacker, 2003, 2013) provides details about brain processes but excludes psychological terms. Such examples conform to the methodological definition but do not belong to cognitive psychology.

A better definition must include the *nature* of cognition. It must also include the kind of explanations that cognitive psychologists seek. For instance, *cognitive psychology is the branch of general psychology which explains psychological phenomena by using functional analysis to describe information processing.* This definition appeals to a theory about cognition (information processing) and refers to the type of explanation sought (i.e., functional analyses). Neither the information processing hypothesis nor the practice of conducting functional analysis restricts the variety of theories or topics characterized by the definition.

Furthermore, by emphasizing the kind of explanation that cognitive psychologists seek, the definition forces Eysenck's (2020) four approaches to be included in cognitive psychology only by contributing to functional analysis. For instance, the definition includes computer simulations only compared to human performance in the search for strong equivalence. Similarly, the definition includes studies from cognitive neuropsychology or cognitive neuroscience only for guiding functional decomposition or for providing evidence for causal subsumption.

Some might argue that this candidate definition excludes too much from cognitive psychology. But cognitive psychology proceeds by adopting a strong theory—the information processing hypothesis—and then by exploring the topics that the hypothesis can explain (Pylyshyn, 1980, 1984). "It is no less true of cognitive science than of other fields that we start off with the clear cases and work out, *modifying our view of the domain of the theory as we find where the theory works*" (Pylyshyn, 1980, p. 119; italics added). The theoretical perspective persists while cognitive psychology's topics and methods evolve.

References

Ackley, D. H., Hinton, G. E., & Sejnowski, T. J. (1985). A learning algorithm for Boltzman machines. *Cognitive Science, 9*, 147–169.

Adams, F., & Aizawa, K. (2008). *The bounds of cognition.* Blackwell.

Adler, I. (1961). *Thinking machines.* Signet Science Library.

Agullo, M., Carlson, D., Clague, K., Ferrari, G., Ferrari, M., Yabuki, H., & Hempel, R. (2003). *LEGO mindstorms masterpieces.* Syngress Publishing.

Anderson, B. F. (1975). *Cognitive psychology: The study of knowing, learning, and thinking.* Academic Press.

Anderson, J. A., Silverstein, J. W., Ritz, S. A., & Jones, R. S. (1977). Distinctive features, categorical perception and probability learning: Some applications of a neural model. *Psychological Review, 84*, 413–451.

Anderson, J. R. (1980). *Cognitive psychology and its implications.* W. H. Freeman.

Anderson, J. R. (1983). *The architecture of cognition.* Harvard University Press.

Anderson, J. R. (1985). *Cognitive psychology and its implications, 2nd edition.* W. H. Freeman.

Anderson, J. R. (1990). *The adaptive character of thought.* Lawrence Erlbaum Associates.

Anderson, J. R. (2000). *Cognitive psychology and its implications* (5th ed.). Worth Publishers.

Anderson, J. R. (2015). *Cognitive psychology and its implications* (8th ed.). Worth Publishers.

Anderson, J. R. (2020). *Cognitive psychology and its implications* (9th ed.). Worth Publishers.

Anderson, J. R., Bothell, D., Byrne, M. D., Douglass, S., Lebiere, C., & Qin, Y. L. (2004). An integrated theory of the mind. *Psychological Review, 111*(4), 1036–1060.

Anderson, J. R., & Bower, G. H. (1973). *Human associative memory.* Lawrence Erlbaum Associates.

Anderson, J. R., & Matessa, M. (1997). A production system theory of serial memory. *Psychological Review, 104*(4), 728–748.

Anderson, M. L., Richardson, M. J., & Chemero, A. (2012). Eroding the boundaries of Cognition: Implications of embodiment. *Topics in Cognitive Science, 4*(4), 717–730. https://doi.org/10.1111/j.1756-8765.2012.01211.x

Andresen, J. (1991). Skinner and Chomsky 30 years later on or, the return of the repressed. *Behavior Analyst, 14*(1), 49–60. https://doi.org/10.1007/bf03392552

Arrieta, A. B., Diaz-Rodriguez, N., Del Ser, J., Bennetot, A., Tabik, S., Barbado, A., . . . & Herrera, F. (2020). Explainable Artificial Intelligence (XAI): Concepts, taxonomies, opportunities and challenges toward responsible AI. *Information Fusion, 58*, 82–115. https://doi.org/10.1016/j.inffus.2019.12.012

Ashby, W. R. (1956). *An introduction to cybernetics.* Chapman & Hall.

Ashby, W. R. (1960). *Design for a brain* (2nd ed.). John Wiley & Sons.

Ashcraft, M. H. (1976). Priming and property dominance effects in semantic memory. *Memory & Cognition, 4*(5), 490–500. https://doi.org/10.3758/bf03213209

Ashcraft, M. H. (1978). Property dominance and typicality effects in property statement verification. *Journal of Verbal Learning and Verbal Behavior, 17*(2), 155–164. https://doi.org/10.1016/s0022-5371(78)90119-6

Baddeley, A. D. (1966). Short-term memory for word sequences as a function of acoustic semantic and formal similarity. *Quarterly Journal of Experimental Psychology, 18*, 362–365. https://doi.org/10.1080/14640746608400055

Baddeley, A. D. (1986). *Working memory.* Oxford University Press.

Baddeley, A. D. (1990). *Human memory: Theory and practice.* Allyn & Bacon.

Baddeley, A. D., & Dale, H. C. A. (1966). Effect of semantic similarity on retroactive interference in long- and short-term memory. *Journal of Verbal Learning and Verbal Behavior, 5*(5), 417–420. https://doi.org/10.1016/s0022-5371(66)80054-3

Bandettini, P. A. (2012). Twenty years of functional MRI: The science and the stories. *Neuroimage, 62*(2), 575–588. https://doi.org/10.1016/j.neuroimage.2012.04.026

Bateson, G. (1972). *Steps to an ecology of mind.* Ballantine Books.

Bechtel, W., & Abrahamsen, A. (1991). *Connectionism and the mind.* Blackwell.

Bechtel, W., & Abrahamsen, A. A. (2002). *Connectionism and the mind: Parallel processing, dynamics, and evolution in networks* (2nd ed.). Blackwell.

Bell, D. A. (1962). *Intelligent machines: An introduction to cybernetics.* Blaisdell.

Bender, A., & Beller, S. (2012). Nature and culture of finger counting: Diversity and representational effects of an embodied cognitive tool. *Cognition, 124*(2), 156–182. https://doi.org/10.1016/j.cognition.2012.05.005

Bengio, Y. (2009). Learning deep architectures for AI. *Foundations and Trends in Machine Learning, 2*(1), 1–127.

Bengio, Y., Courville, A., & Vincent, P. (2013). Representation learning: A review and new perspectives. *IEEE Transactions on Pattern Analysis and Machine Intelligence, 35*(8), 1798–1828. https://doi.org/10.1109/tpami.2013.50

Benjamin, L. T. (2019). *A brief history of modern psychology* (3rd ed.). Blackwell.

Bennett, M. R., Dennett, D., Hacker, P., & Searle, J. R. (2007). *Neuroscience and philosophy: Brain, mind, and language.* Columbia University Press.

Bennett, M. R., & Hacker, P. M. S. (2003). *Philosophical foundations of neuroscience.* Blackwell.

Bennett, M. R., & Hacker, P. M. S. (2013). *History of cognitive neuroscience*. Wiley-Blackwell.

Berkeley, E. C. (1949). *Giant brains: Or, Machines that think*. Wiley.

Berkeley, I. S. N., Dawson, M. R. W., Medler, D. A., Schopflocher, D. P., & Hornsby, L. (1995). Density plots of hidden value unit activations reveal interpretable bands. *Connection Science, 7*, 167–186.

Bertalanffy, L. V. (1967). *Robots, men, and minds*. Braziller.

Bever, T. G., Fodor, J. A., & Garrett, M. (1968). A formal limitation of associationism. In T. R. Dixon & D. L. Horton (Eds.), *Verbal behavior and general behavior theory* (pp. 582–585). Prentice-Hall.

Bharucha, J. J. (1999). Neural nets, temporal composites, and tonality. In D. Deutsch (Ed.), *The psychology of music* (2nd ed., pp. 413–440). Academic Press.

Biederman, I. (1987). Recognition by components: A theory of human image understanding. *Psychological Review, 94*, 115–147.

Bliss, T. V. P., & Lomo, T. (1973). Long-lasting potentiation of synaptic transmission in dentate area of anesthetized rabbit following stimulation of perforant path. *Journal of Physiology—London, 232*(2), 331–356.

Block, N. (1981). *Imagery*. MIT Press.

Bock, R. D., & Jones, L. V. (1968). *The measurement and prediction of judgment and choice*. Holden-Day.

Boden, M. (1977). *Artificial intelligence and natural man*. Basic Books.

Boole, G. (1854/2003). *The laws of thought*. Prometheus Books.

Boring, E. G. (1950). *A history of experimental psychology*. Appleton-Century-Crofts.

Bourne, L. E., Dominowski, R. L., & Loftus, E. F. (1979). *Cognitive processes*. Prentice-Hall.

Bousfield, W. A., & Cowan, T. M. (1964). Immediate memory spans for CVC trigrams. *Journal of General Psychology, 70*(2), 283–293. https://doi.org/10.1080/00221309.1964.9920599

Braisby, N., & Gellatly, A. (2012). *Cognitive psychology* (2nd ed.). Oxford University Press.

Braitenberg, V. (1984). *Vehicles: Explorations in synthetic psychology*. MIT Press.

Bransford, J. D., Barclay, J. R., & Franks, J. J. (1972). Sentence memory: Constructive versus interpretive approach. *Cognitive Psychology, 3*(2), 193–209.

Breazeal, C. (2003). Toward sociable robots. *Robotics and Autonomous Systems, 42*(3–4), 167–175. https://doi.org/10.1016/s0921-8890(02)00373-1

Breazeal, C. (2004). Social interactions in HRI: The robot view. *IEEE Transactions on Systems Man and Cybernetics Part C—Applications and Reviews, 34*(2), 181–186. https://doi.org/10.1109/tsmcc.2004.826268

Breazeal C., Dautenhahn K., Kanda T. (2016) Social Robotics. In: Siciliano B., Khatib O. (eds) *Springer Handbook of Robotics*. Springer Handbooks. Springer.

Breazeal, C., Gray, J., & Berlin, M. (2009). An embodied cognition approach to mindreading skills for socially intelligent robots. *International Journal of Robotics Research, 28*(5), 656–680. https://doi.org/10.1177/0278364909102796

Breazeal, C. L. (2002). *Designing sociable robots*. MIT Press.

Brentano, F. C. (1874/1995). *Psychology from an empirical standpoint* (Paperback ed.). Routledge.

Broadbent, D. E. (1958). *Perception and communication*. Pergamon Press.

Bronowski, J. (1973). *The ascent of man*. British Broadcasting Corporation.

Brooks, R. A. (1991). Intelligence without representation. *Artificial Intelligence, 47*, 139–159.

Brooks, R. A. (1997). The Cog project. *Journal of the Robotics Society of Japan, 15*(7), 969–970.

Brooks, R. A. (1999). *Cambrian intelligence: The early history of the new AI*. MIT Press.

Brooks, R. A. (2002). *Flesh and machines: How robots will change us*. Pantheon Books.

Brooks, R. A., Breazeal, C., Marjanovic, M., Scasselati, B., & Williamson, M. M. (1999). The Cog project: Building a humanoid robot. In C. Nehaniv. (Ed.), *Computation for metaphors, analogy, and agents. CMAA 1998. Lecture notes in computer science, vol. 1562*. Springer.

Brooks, R. A., & Stein, L. A. (1994). Building brains for bodies. *Autonomous Robots, 1*(1), 7–25. https://doi.org/10.1007/BF00735340

Brown, R. E., & Milner, P. M. (2003). Timeline—The legacy of Donald O. Hebb: More than the Hebb synapse. *Nature Reviews Neuroscience, 4*(12), 1013–1019. https://doi.org/10.1038/nrn1257

Brown, T. H. (1990). Hebbian synapses: Biophysical mechanisms and algorithms. *Annual Review of Neuroscience, 13*, 475–511.

Bruner, J. S. (1957). On perceptual readiness. *Psychological Review, 64*, 123–152.

Bruner, J. S. (1990). *Acts of meaning*. Harvard University Press.

Bruner, J. S. (1992). Another look at New Look 1. *American Psychologist, 47*(6), 780–783.

Bruner, J. S., Postman, L., & Rodrigues, J. (1951). Expectation and the perception of color. *American Journal of Psychology, 64*(2), 216–227.

Cabeza, R., & Nyberg, L. (1997). Imaging cognition: An empirical review of PET studies with normal subjects. *Journal of Cognitive Neuroscience, 9*(1), 1–26.

Cabeza, R., & Nyberg, L. (2000). Imaging cognition II: An empirical review of 275 PET and fMRI studies. *Journal of Cognitive Neuroscience, 12*(1), 1–47. https://doi.org/10.1162/08989290051137585

Calvo, P., & Gomila, A. (2008). *Handbook of cognitive science: An embodied approach*. Elsevier.

Campbell, M., Hoane, A. J., & Hsu, F. H. (2002). Deep Blue. *Artificial Intelligence, 134*(1–2), 57–83. https://doi.org/10.1016/s0004-3702(01)00129-1

Carruthers, P. (2006). *The architecture of the mind: Massive modularity and the flexibility of thought*. Oxford University Press.

Cermak, L. S., & Craik, F. I. M. (1979). *Levels of processing in human memory*. Lawrence Erlbaum Associates.

Chemero, A. (2000). Anti-representationalism and the dynamical stance. *Philosophy of Science, 67*(4), 625–647. https://doi.org/10.1086/392858

Chemero, A. (2009). *Radical embodied cognitive science*. MIT Press.

Ching, T., Himmelstein, D. S., Beaulieu-Jones, B. K., Kalinin, A. A., Do, B. T., Way, G. P., . . . & Greene, C. S. (2018). Opportunities and obstacles for deep learning in biology and medicine. *Journal of the Royal Society Interface, 15*(141). https://doi.org/10.1098/rsif.2017.0387

Chomsky, N. (1957). *Syntactic structures* (2nd ed.). Mouton de Gruyter.

Chomsky, N. (1959). A review of B. F. Skinner's *Verbal behavior*. *Language, 35*, 26–58.

Chomsky, N. (1965). *Aspects of the theory of syntax*. MIT Press.

Chomsky, N. (1966). *Cartesian linguistics: A chapter in the history of rationalist thought*. Harper & Row.

Chomsky, N. (1995). *The minimalist program*. MIT Press.

Chomsky, N., Mukherji, N., Patnaik, B. N., & Agnihotri, R. K. (2000). *The architecture of language*. Oxford University Press.

Chrisomalis, S. (2013). Constraint, cognition, and written numeration. *Pragmatics & Cognition, 21*(3), 552–572. https://doi.org/10.1075/pc.21.3.08chr

Churchland, P. M. (2005). Cleansing science. *Inquiry—An Interdisciplinary Journal of Philosophy, 48*(5), 464–477. https://doi.org/10.1080/00201740500242001

Churchland, P. M., & Churchland, P. S. (1990). Could a machine think? *Scientific American, 262*, 32–37.

Churchland, P. S., Koch, C., & Sejnowski, T. J. (1990). What is computational neuroscience? In E. L. Schwartz (Ed.), *Computational neuroscience* (pp. 46–55). MIT Press.

Clark, A. (1989). *Microcognition*. MIT Press.

Clark, A. (1993). *Associative engines*. MIT Press.

Clark, A. (1997). *Being there: Putting brain, body, and world together again*. MIT Press.

Clark, A. (1999). An embodied cognitive science? *Trends in Cognitive Sciences, 3*(9), 345–351.

Clark, A. (2003). *Natural-born cyborgs*. Oxford University Press.

Clark, A. (2008). *Supersizing the mind: Embodiment, action, and cognitive extension*. Oxford University Press.

Clark, A. (2016). *Surfing uncertainty: Prediction, action, and the embodied mind*. Oxford University Press.

Clark, A., & Chalmers, D. (1998). The extended mind (active externalism). *Analysis, 58*(1), 7–19.

Cofer, C. N. (1978). Origins of the *Journal of Verbal Learning and Verbal Behavior*. *Journal of Verbal Learning and Verbal Behavior, 17*(1), 113–126. https://doi.org/10.1016/s0022-5371(78)90573-x

Cohen, J. D., Dunbar, K., & McClelland, J. L. (1991). On the control of automatic processes: A parallel distributed processing account of the Stroop effect. *Psychological Review, 97,* 332–361.

Colby, K. M., Hilf, F. D., Weber, S., & Kraemer, H. C. (1972). Turing-like indistinguishability tests for validation of a computer simulation of paranoid processes. *Artificial Intelligence, 3*(2), 199–221.

Collins, A. M., & Loftus, E. F. (1975). Spreading activation theory of semantic processing. *Psychological Review, 82*(6), 407–428. https://doi.org/10.1037//0033-295x .82.6.407

Collins, A. M., & Quillian, M. R. (1969). Retrieval time from semantic memory. *Journal of Verbal Learning and Verbal Behavior, 8,* 240–247.

Coltheart, M., Rastle, K., Perry, C., Langdon, R., & Ziegler, J. (2001). DRC: A dual route cascaded model of visual word recognition and reading aloud. *Psychological Review, 108*(1), 204–256. https://doi.org/10.1037//0033-295x.108.1.204

Conrad, R. (1964). Acoustic confusions in immediate memory. *British Journal of Psychology, 55*(1), 75–84.

Conway, F., & Siegelman, J. (2005). *Dark hero of the information age: In search of Norbert Wiener, the father of cybernetics.* Basic Books.

Conway, M. A. (1997). *Cognitive models of memory* (1st MIT Press ed.). MIT Press.

Cook, V. J., & Newson, M. (1996). *Chomsky's universal grammar: An introduction.* Blackwell.

Cooper, L. A., & Shepard, R. N. (1973a). Chronometric studies of the rotation of mental images. In W. G. Chase (Ed.), *Visual information processing* (pp. 75–176). Academic Press.

Cooper, L. A., & Shepard, R. N. (1973b). The time required to prepare for a rotated stimulus. *Memory & Cognition, 1*(3), 246–250.

Cooter, R. (2014). Neural veils and the will to historical critique: Why historians of science need to take the neuro-turn seriously. *Isis, 105*(1), 145–154. https://doi.org/10 .1086/675556

Cox, R. R., & Evarts, E. V. (1961). An evoked response detector. *Electroencephalography and Clinical Neurophysiology, 13*(3), 478–480 https://doi.org/10.1016/0013-4694 (61)90023-2

Craik, F. I. M. (2002). Levels of processing: Past, present . . . and future? *Memory, 10*(5–6), 305–318. https://doi.org/10.1080/09658210244000135

Craik, F. I. M., & Lockhart, R. S. (1972). Levels of processing: A framework for memory research. *Journal of Verbal Learning and Verbal Behavior, 11,* 671–684.

Cramer, P. (1968). *Word association.* Academic Press.

Cummins, R. (1975). Functional analysis. *Journal of Philosophy, 72,* 741–760.

Cummins, R. (1983). *The nature of psychological explanation.* MIT Press.

Cummins, R. (1989). *Meaning and mental representation.* MIT Press.

Dartnall, H. J. A., Bowmaker, J. K., & Molino, J. D. (1983). Human visual pigments: Microspectrophotometric results from the eyes of seven persons. *Proceedings of the Royal Society of London Series B—Biological Sciences, 220*, 115–130.

Dawson, G. D. (1954). A summation technique for the detection of small evoked potentials. *Electroencephalography and Clinical Neurophysiology, 6*(1), 65–84. https://doi.org/10.1016/0013-4694(54)90007-3

Dawson, M. R. W. (1991). The how and why of what went where in apparent motion: Modeling solutions to the motion correspondence process. *Psychological Review, 98*, 569–603.

Dawson, M. R. W. (1998). *Understanding cognitive science*. Blackwell.

Dawson, M. R. W. (2004). *Minds and machines: Connectionism and psychological modeling*. Blackwell.

Dawson, M. R. W. (2009). Computation, cognition—and connectionism. In D. Dedrick & L. Trick (Eds.), *Cognition, computation, and Pylyshyn* (pp. 175–199). MIT Press.

Dawson, M. R. W. (2013). *Mind, body, world: Foundations of cognitive science*. Athabasca University Press.

Dawson, M. R. W. (2018). *Connectionist representations of tonal music: Discovering musical patterns by interpreting artificial neural networks*. Athabasca University Press.

Dawson, M. R. W. (2022). Probability learning by perceptrons and people. *Comparative Cognition and Behavior Reviews, 15* (monograph), 1–188.

Dawson, M. R. W., Dupuis, B., & Wilson, M. (2010). *From bricks to brains: The embodied cognitive science of LEGO robots*. Athabasca University Press.

Dawson, M. R. W., & Harshman, R. A. (1986). The multidimensional analysis of asymmetries in alphabetic confusion matrices: Evidence for global-to-local and local-to-global processing. *Perception & Psychophysics, 40*(6), 370–383. https://doi.org/10.3758/bf03208196

Dawson, M. R. W., Medler, D. A., McCaughan, D. B., Willson, L., & Carbonaro, M. (2000). Using extra output learning to insert a symbolic theory into a connectionist network. *Minds and Machines, 10*, 171–201.

Dawson, M. R. W., Perez, A., & Sylvestre, S. (2020). Artificial neural networks solve musical problems with Fourier phase spaces. *Scientific Reports, 10*(1), 7151. https://doi.org/10.1038/s41598-020-64229-4

de Oliveira, G. S., Raja, V., & Chemero, A. (2019). Radical embodied cognitive science and "Real Cognition." *Synthese (198)*, 1–22. https://doi.org/10.1007/s11229-019-02475-4

Deeks, A. (2019). The judicial demand for explainable artificial intelligence. *Columbia Law Review, 119*(7), 1829–1850.

Deese, J. (1965). *The structure of associations in language and thought*. Johns Hopkins University Press.

Deese, J., & Hulse, S. H. (1967). *The psychology of learning* (3rd ed.). McGraw-Hill.

Dehaene, S. (2011). *The number sense: How the mind creates mathematics* (Rev. and updated ed.). Oxford University Press.

Dennett, D. C. (2007). Philosophy as naive anthropology: Comment on Bennett and Hacker. In M. R. Bennett, D. C. Dennett, P. M. S. Hacker, & J. R. Searle (Eds.), *Neuroscience and Philosophy: Brain, Mind, and Language* (pp. 73–96). Columbia University Press.

Descartes, R. (1637/1960). *Discourse on method and meditations.* Bobbs-Merrill.

Dodd, D. H., & White, R. M. (1980). *Cognition: Mental structures and processes.* Allyn & Bacon.

Doidge, N. (2007). *The brain that changes itself: Stories of personal triumph from the frontiers of brain science.* Viking.

Donders, F. C. (1869/1969). On the speed of mental processes. *Acta Psychologica, 30,* 412–431. https://doi.org/10.1016/0001-6918(69)90065-1

Dove, G. (2014). Thinking in words: Language as an embodied medium of thought. *Topics in Cognitive Science, 6*(3), 371–389. https://doi.org/10.1111/tops.12102

Dreyfus, H. L. (1967). Why computers must have bodies in order to be intelligent. *Review of Metaphysics, 21*(1), 13–32.

Dreyfus, H. L. (1972). *What computers can't do: A critique of artificial reason.* Harper & Row.

Dreyfus, H. L. (1992). *What computers still can't do.* MIT Press.

Dreyfus, H. L., & Dreyfus, S. E. (1988). Making a mind versus modeling the brain: Artificial intelligence back at the branchpoint. In S. Graubard (Ed.), *The artificial intelligence debate* (pp 15–44). MIT Press.

Dudai, Y. (1989). *The neurobiology of memory.* Oxford University Press.

Duncker, K. (1945). On problem-solving. *Psychological Monographs, 58*(5), 1–112.

Dutton, J. M., & Briggs, W. G. (1971). Simulation model construction. In J. M. Dutton & W. H. Starbuck (Eds.), *Computer simulation of human behavior* (pp. 103–126). John Wiley & Sons.

Dutton, J. M., & Starbuck, W. H. (1971). *Computer simulation of human behavior.* John Wiley & Sons.

Dyer, F. N. (1973). The Stroop phenomenon and its use in study of perceptual, cognitive, and response processes. *Memory & Cognition, 1*(2), 106–120. https://doi.org/10.3758/bf03198078

Eichenbaum, H. (2002). *The cognitive neuroscience of memory: An introduction.* Oxford University Press.

Elman, J. L., Bates, E. A., Johnson, M. H., Karmiloff-Smith, A., Parisi, D., & Plunkett, K. (1996). *Rethinking innateness.* MIT Press.

Erhan, D., Courville, A., & Bengio, Y. (2010). Understanding representations learned in deep architectures. Technical Report 1355, Departement d'informatique et recherche operationnelle, Université de Montréal.

Ericsson, K. A., & Simon, H. A. (1984). *Protocol analysis: Verbal reports as data*. MIT Press.

Ericsson, K. A., & Simon, H. A. (1993). *Protocol analysis* (Rev. ed.). MIT Press.

Estes, W. K. (1975). Some targets for mathematical psychology. *Journal of Mathematical Psychology, 12*, 263–282.

Eysenck, M. W., & Keane, M. T. (2020). *Cognitive psychology: A student's handbook* (8th ed.). Routledge.

Farah, M. J. (1994). Neuropsychological inference with an interactive brain: A critique of the "locality" assumption. *Behavioral and Brain Sciences, 17*, 43–104.

Farina, M. V. (1970). *Flowcharting*. Prentice-Hall.

Farmer, T. A., & Matlin, M. W. (2019). *Cognition* (10th ed.). Wiley.

Feigenbaum, E. A., & Feldman, J. (1963). *Computers and thought*. McGraw-Hill.

Feigenbaum, E. A., & McCorduck, P. (1983). *The fifth generation*. Addison-Wesley.

Ferrari, G. (2006). Masterpiece 3—The LEGO Turing machine. In K. Clague (Ed.), *Classic LEGO mindstorms projects and software tools* (pp. 105–150). Syngress.

Figdor, C. (2013). What is the "cognitive" in cognitive neuroscience? *Neuroethics, 6*(1), 105–114. https://doi.org/10.1007/s12152-012-9157-5

Finke, R.A., & Pinker, S. (1982). Spontaneous imagery scanning in mental extrapolation. *Journal of Experimental Psychology: Learning, Memory, and Cognition, 8*, 142-147.

Fischer, M. H., & Brugger, P. (2011). When digits help digits: Spatial-numerical associations point to finger counting as prime example of embodied cognition. *Frontiers in Psychology, 2*. https://doi.org/10.3389/fpsyg.2011.00260

Fischer, M. H., & Zwaan, R. A. (2008). Embodied language: A review of the role of the motor system in language comprehension. *Quarterly Journal of Experimental Psychology, 61*(6), 825–850. https://doi.org/10.1080/17470210701623605

Fiske, S. T., & Taylor, S. E. (2020). *Social cognition: From brains to culture* (4th ed.). SAGE Publications.

Flanagan, O. J. (1984). *The science of the mind*. MIT Press.

Fodor, J. A. (1968). *Psychological explanation: An introduction to the philosophy of psychology*. Random House.

Fodor, J. A. (1975). *The language of thought*. Harvard University Press.

Fodor, J. A. (1983). *The modularity of mind*. MIT Press.

Fodor, J. A., & Pylyshyn, Z. W. (1988). Connectionism and cognitive architecture. *Cognition, 28*(1–2), 3–71.

Ford, K. M., & Pylyshyn, Z. W. (1996). *The robot's dilemma revisited: The frame problem in artificial intelligence*. Ablex.

Forte, A. (1973). *The structure of atonal music*. Yale University Press.

Frisch, S. (2014). How cognitive neuroscience could be more biological—and what it might learn from clinical neuropsychology. *Frontiers in Human Neuroscience, 8*. https://doi.org/10.3389/fnhum.2014.00541

Fukushima, K. (1986). A neural network model for selective attention in visual pattern recognition. *Biological Cybernetics, 55*, 5–15.

Gallese, V., & Goldman, A. (1998). Mirror neurons and the simulation theory of mind-reading. *Trends in Cognitive Sciences, 2*(12), 493–501.

Gallese, V., Keysers, C., & Rizzolatti, G. (2004). A unifying view of the basis of social cognition. *Trends in Cognitive Sciences, 8*(9), 396–403.

Gallese, V., & Sinigaglia, C. (2011). What is so special about embodied simulation? *Trends in Cognitive Sciences, 15*(11), 512–519. https://doi.org/10.1016/j.tics.2011.09 .003

Gardner, H. (1984). *The mind's new science.* Basic Books.

Gates, A. I. (1916). The mnemonic span for visual and auditory digits. *Journal of Experimental Psychology, 1*, 393–403. https://doi.org/10.1037/h0071265

Gawehn, E., Hiss, J. A., & Schneider, G. (2016). Deep learning in drug discovery. *Molecular Informatics, 35*(1), 3–14. https://doi.org/10.1002/minf.201501008

Gentner, D., Holyoak, K. J., & Kokinov, B. N. (2001). *The analogical mind: Perspectives from cognitive science.* MIT Press.

Gerrissen, J. F. (1991). On the network-based emulation of human visual search. *Neural Networks, 4*, 543–564.

Gibson, J. J. (1979). *The ecological approach to visual perception.* Houghton Mifflin.

Gick, M. L., & Holyoak, K. J. (1980). Analogical problem solving. *Cognitive Psychology, 12*(3), 306–355. https://doi.org/10.1016/0010-0285(80)90013-4

Glanzer, M., & Cunitz, A. R. (1966). Two storage mechanisms in free recall. *Journal of Verbal Learning and Verbal Behavior, 5*(4), 351–360.

Glenberg, A. M., Witt, J. K., & Metcalfe, J. (2013). From the revolution to embodiment: 25 years of cognitive psychology. *Perspectives on Psychological Science, 8*(5), 573–585. https://doi.org/10.1177/1745691613498098

Gluck, M. A., & Myers, C. (2001). *Gateway to memory: An introduction to neural network modeling of the hippocampus and learning.* MIT Press.

Goh, G. B., Hodas, N. O., & Vishnu, A. (2017). Deep learning for computational chemistry. *Journal of Computational Chemistry, 38*(16), 1291–1307. https://doi.org/10 .1002/jcc.24764

Gold, E. M. (1967). Language identification in the limit. *Information and Control, 10*, 447–474.

Goldstein, E. B. (2011). *Cognitive psychology: Connecting mind, research, and everyday experience* (3rd ed.). Cengage Learning.

Goldstein, E. B. (2015). *Cognitive psychology: Connecting mind, research, and everyday experience* (4th ed., student ed.). Cengage Learning.

Goldstine, H. H. (1993). *The computer—From Pascal to von Neumann.* Princeton University Press.

Goldstine, H. H., & von Neumann, J. (1947). *Planning and coding of problems for an electronic computing instrument* (Vol. 1, Part 2, pp. 1–194). Institute for Advanced Study, Princeton University.

Goss, A. E., & Nodine, C. F. (1965). *Paired-associates learning: The role of meaningfulness, similarity, and familiarization*. Academic Press.

Grasse, P. P. (1959). La reconstruction du nid et les coordinations interindividuelles chez *Bellicositermes natalensis* et *Cubitermes sp.* la théorie de la stigmergie: Essai d'interprétation du comportement des termites constructeurs. *Insectes Sociaux, 6*(1), 41–80.

Gregory, R. L. (1970). *The intelligent eye*. Weidenfeld & Nicolson.

Gregory, R. L. (1978). *Eye and brain*. McGraw-Hill.

Grier, D.A. (2013). Edward Feigenbaum. *IEEE Annals of the History of Computing, 35(4)*, 74-81. doi.org/10.1109/MAHC.2013.49

Grenville, B. (2001). *The uncanny: Experiments in cyborg culture*. Vancouver Art Gallery; Arsenal Pulp Press.

Grey Walter, W. (1963). *The living brain*. W. W. Norton.

Griffith, N., & Todd, P. M. (1999). *Musical networks: Parallel distributed perception and performance*. MIT Press.

Groome, D. (2014). *An introduction to cognitive psychology: Processes and disorders* (3rd ed.). Psychology Press, Taylor & Francis Group.

Haberlandt, K. (1994). *Cognitive psychology*. Allyn & Bacon.

Hanson, S. J., & Burr, D. J. (1990). What connectionist models learn: Learning and representation in connectionist networks. *Behavioral and Brain Sciences, 13*, 471–518.

Haugeland, J. (1985). *Artificial intelligence: The very idea*. MIT Press.

Hebb, D. O. (1949). *The organization of behavior: A neuropsychological theory*. Wiley.

Hecht-Nielsen, R. (1987). *Neurocomputing*. Addison-Wesley.

Heidbreder, E. (1933). *Seven psychologies* (Student's ed.). Appleton-Century-Crofts.

Heinze, H. J., Mangun, G. R., Burchert, W., Hinrichs, H., Scholz, M., Munte, T. F., . . . & Hillyard, S. A. (1994). Combined spatial and temporal imaging of brain activity during visual selective attention in humans. *Nature, 372*(6506), 543-546. https://doi.org/10.1038/372543a0

Helmholtz, H. (1868/1968). The recent progress of the theory of vision. In R. M. Warren & R. P. Warren (Eds.), *Helmholtz on perception: Its Physiology and Development* (pp. 61-136). John Wiley & Sons.

Hilgard, E. R., & Marquis, D. G. (1940). *Conditioning and learning*. Appleton-Century.

Hillis, W. D. (1998). *The pattern on the stone*. Basic Books.

Hinton, G. E. (2007). Learning multiple layers of representation. *Trends in Cognitive Sciences, 11*(10), 428–434. https://doi.org/10.1016/j.tics.2007.09.004

Hinton, G. E., & Anderson, J. A. (1981). *Parallel models of associative memory.* Lawrence Erlbaum Associates.

Hinton, G. E., Osindero, S., & Teh, Y. (2006). A fast learning algorithm for deep belief nets. *Neural Computation, 18*(7), 1527–1554. https://doi.org/10.1162/neco.2006.18.7.1527

Hinton, G. E., & Salakhutdinov, R. R. (2006). Reducing the dimensionality of data with neural networks. *Science, 313*(5786), 504–507. https://doi.org/10.1126/science.1127647

Hobbes, T. (1651/1967). *Hobbes's leviathan.* Clarendon Press.

Hodges, A. (1983). *Alan Turing: The enigma of intelligence.* Unwin Paperbacks.

Hofstadter, D. R. (1979). *Godel, Escher, Bach: An eternal golden braid.* Basic Books.

Holyoak, K. J., & Thagard, P. (1995). *Mental leaps: Analogy in creative thought.* MIT Press.

Hopfield, J. J. (1982). Neural networks and physical systems with emergent collective computational abilities. *Proceedings of the National Academy of Sciences, 79,* 2554–2558.

Hopfinger, J. B., Buonocore, M. H., & Mangun, G. R. (2000). The neural mechanisms of top-down attentional control. *Nature Neuroscience, 3*(3), 284–291.

Horgan, T., & Tienson, J. (1996). *Connectionism and the philosophy of psychology.* MIT Press.

Hubel, D. H., & Wiesel, T. N. (1959). Receptive fields of single neurones in the cat's striate cortex. *Journal of Physiology, 148,* 574–591.

Hubel, D. H., & Wiesel, T. N. (1962). Receptive fields, binocular interaction and functional architecture in the cat's visual cortex. *Journal of Physiology, 160,* 106–154.

Hull, C. L., Hovland, C. I., Ross, R. T., Hall, M., Perkins, D. T., & Fitch, F. B. (1940). *Mathematico deductive theory of rote learning: A study in scientific methodology.* Yale University Press.

Hunt, E. (1971). What kind of computer is man? *Cognitive Psychology, 2*(1), 57–98. https://doi.org/10.1016/0010-0285(71)90003-x

Hurley, S. (2001). Perception and action: Alternative views. *Synthese, 129*(1), 3–40.

Hutchins, E. (1995). *Cognition in the wild.* MIT Press.

James, W. (1890). *The principles of psychology, volume one.* Dover Publications.

Jensen, A. R., & Rohwer, W. D. (1966). Stroop color-word test: A review. *Acta Psychologica, 25*(1), 36–93. https://doi.org/10.1016/0001-6918(66)90004-7

Jevons, W. S. (1870). On the mechanical performance of logical inference. *Philosophical Transactions of the Royal Society of London, 160,* 497–518.

Joanisse, M. F., & McClelland, J. L. (2015). Connectionist perspectives on language learning, representation and processing. *Wiley Interdisciplinary Reviews: Cognitive Science, 6*(3), 235–247. https://doi.org/10.1002/wcs.1340

Johnson-Laird, P. N. (1983). *Mental models.* Harvard University Press.

Jones, E. G., & Mendell, L. M. (1999). Assessing the decade of the brain. *Science, 284*(5415), 739. https://doi.org/10.1126/science.284.5415.739

Kahneman, D., Treisman, A., & Gibbs, B. J. (1992). The reviewing of object files: Object-specific integration of information. *Cognitive Psychology, 24*(2), 175–219.

Kamilaris, A., & Prenafeta-Boldu, F. X. (2018). Deep learning in agriculture: A survey. *Computers and Electronics in Agriculture, 147*, 70–90. https://doi.org/10.1016/j.compag.2018.02.016

Kellogg, R. T. (1995). *Cognitive psychology.* SAGE Publications.

Kidder, T. (1981). *The soul of a new machine.* Avon Books.

Kirsh, D. (1995). The intelligent use of space. *Artificial Intelligence, 73*(1–2), 31–68. https://doi.org/10.1016/0004-3702(94)00017-u

Klein, R. M. (1999). The Hebb legacy. *Canadian Journal of Experimental Psychology, 53*(1), 1–3.

Knapp, T. J. (1985). Contributions to the history of psychology: Moore, T. V., and his "Cognitive Psychology" of 1939. *Psychological Reports, 57*(3), 1311–1316. https://doi.org/10.2466/pr0.1985.57.3f.1311

Köhler, W. (1947). *Gestalt psychology, an introduction to new concepts in modern psychology.* Liveright.

Köhler, W. (1925/2018). *The mentality of apes* (E. Winter, Trans.). Routledge.

Kohonen, T. (1977). *Associative memory: A system-theoretical approach.* Springer-Verlag.

Kok, A. (2020). *Functions of the brain: A conceptual approach to cognitive neuroscience.* Routledge.

Kolb, B. (1995). *Brain plasticity and behavior.* Lawrence Erlbaum Associates.

Kosslyn, S. M. (1980). *Image and mind.* Harvard University Press.

Kosslyn, S. M. (1987). Seeing and imagining in the cerebral hemispheres: A computational approach. *Psychological Review, 94*(2), 148–175.

Kosslyn, S. M. (1994). *Image and brain.* MIT Press.

Kosslyn, S. M., Ball, T. M., & Reiser, B. J. (1978). Visual images preserve metric spatial information: Evidence from studies of image scanning. *Journal of Experimental Psychology: Human Perception and Performance, 4*(1), 47–60.

Kosslyn, S. M., Brunn, J., Cave, K. R., & Wallach, R. W. (1984). Individual differences in mental imagery ability: A computational analysis. *Cognition, 18*(1–3), 195–243.

Kosslyn, S. M., Farah, M. J., Holtzman, J. D., & Gazzaniga, M. S. (1985). A computational analysis of mental image generation: Evidence from functional dissociations in split-brain patients. *Journal of Experimental Psychology: General, 114*(3), 311–341.

Kosslyn, S. M., & Shwartz, S. P. (1977). A simulation of visual imagery. *Cognitive Science, 1*, 265–295.

Kosslyn, S. M., Thompson, W. L., & Ganis, G. (2006). *The case for mental imagery.* Oxford University Press.

Kruschke, J. K. (1992). ALCOVE: An exemplar-based connectionist model of category learning. *Psychological Review, 99*, 22–44.

Külpe, O., & Titchener, E. B. (1895). *Outlines of psychology, based upon the results of experimental investigation*. Macmillan.

Kunda, Z. (1999). *Social cognition: Making sense of people*. MIT Press.

Kurzweil, R. (1990). *The age of intelligent machines*. MIT Press.

La Mettrie, J. O. D. (1750). *Man a machine* (2nd ed.). Printed for G. Smith.

Lachman, R., Lachman, J. L., & Butterfield, E. C. (1979). *Cognitive psychology and information processing*. Lawrence Erlbaum Associates.

Laird, J. E., Newell, A., & Rosenbloom, P. S. (1987). Soar: An architecture for general intelligence. *Artificial Intelligence, 33*(1), 1–64. https://doi.org/10.1016/0004-3702 (87)90050-6

Lakoff, G., & Johnson, M. (1999). *Philosophy in the flesh: The embodied mind and its challenge to Western thought*. Basic Books.

Lakoff, G., & Núñez, R. E. (2000). *Where mathematics comes from: How the embodied mind brings mathematics into being*. Basic Books.

Langenecker, S. A., Nielson, K. A., & Rao, S. M. (2004). fMRI of healthy older adults during Stroop interference. *Neuroimage, 21*(1), 192–200. https://doi.org/10.1016/j .neuroimage.2003.08.027

Larochelle, H., Mandel, M., Pascanu, R., & Bengio, Y. (2012). Learning algorithms for the classification restricted Boltzmann machine. *Journal of Machine Learning Research, 13*, 643–669.

Lauterbur, P. C. (1973). Image formation by induced local interactions: Examples employing nuclear magnetic resonance. *Nature, 242*(5394), 190–191. https://doi.org/ 10.1038/242190a0

Leahey, T. H. (1987). *A history of psychology* (2nd ed.). Prentice-Hall.

Leahey, T. H. (1992). The mythical revolutions of American psychology. *American Psychologist, 47*(2), 308–318.

LeCun, Y., Bengio, Y., & Hinton, G. (2015). Deep learning. *Nature, 521*(7553), 436–444. https://doi.org/10.1038/nature14539

Leighton, J. P., & Sternberg, R. J. (2004). *The nature of reasoning*. Cambridge University Press.

Lewandowsky, S. (1993). The rewards and hazards of computer simulations. *Psychological Science, 4*, 236–243.

Lewandowsky, S., & Dunbar, K. (1983). Cognitive psychology: A comparative review of textbooks. *American Journal of Psychology, 96*(3), 391–403. https://doi.org/10.2307/ 1422320

Lippmann, R. P. (1989). Pattern classification using neural networks. *IEEE Communications Magazine, November*, 47–64.

Livingstone, M., & Hubel, D. (1988). Segregation of form, color, movement and depth: Anatomy, physiology, and perception. *Science, 240* (4853), 740–750.

Locke, J. (1706/1977). *An essay concerning human understanding.* J. M. Dent & Sons.

Lockhart, R. S., & Craik, F. I. M. (1990). Levels of processing: A retrospective commentary on a framework for memory research. *Canadian Journal of Psychology, 44*(1), 87–112. https://doi.org/10.1037/h0084237

Lorayne, H., & Lucas, J. (1974). *The memory book.* Stein & Day.

Luce, R. D. (1986). *Response times: Their role in inferring elementary mental organization.* Oxford University Press.

Lynch, G. (1986). *Synapses, circuits, and the beginnings of memory.* MIT Press.

Macleod, C. M. (1991). Half a century of research on the Stroop effect: An integrative review. *Psychological Bulletin, 109*(2), 163–203. https://doi.org/10.1037/0033-2909.109.2.163

Macleod, C. M. (2015). Attention: Beyond Stroop's (1935) colour-word interference phenomenon. In D. Groome & M. W. Eysenck (Eds.), *Cognitive psychology: Revisiting the classic studies* (pp. 60–70). SAGE Publications.

Mandler, G. (2002). Origins of the cognitive (r)evolution. *Journal of the History of the Behavioral Sciences, 38*(4), 339–353. https://doi.org/10.1002/jhbs.10066

Mangun, G. R., Buonocore, M. H., Girelli, M., & Jha, A. P. (1998). ERP and fMRI measures of visual spatial selective attention. *Human Brain Mapping, 6*(5–6), 383–389. https://doi.org/10.1002/(sici)1097-0193(1998)6:5/6<383::aid-hbm10>3.3.co;2-q

Manis, M. (1971). *An introduction to cognitive psychology.* Brooks/Cole.

Marek, P., & Griggs, R. A. (2001). Useful analyses for selecting a cognitive psychology textbook. *Teaching of Psychology, 28*(1), 40–44.

Marquand, A. (1885). A new logical machine. *Proceedings of the American Academy of Arts and Sciences, 21*, 303–307.

Marr, D. (1982). *Vision.* W. H. Freeman.

Martindale, C. (1991). *Cognitive psychology: A neural-network approach.* Brooks/Cole.

Martinez, J. L., & Derrick, B. E. (1996). Long-term potentiation and learning. *Annual Review of Psychology, 47*, 173–203.

Martinez, J. L., & Kesner, R. (1998). *Neurobiology of learning and memory.* Academic Press.

Maunsell, J. H. R., & Newsome, W. T. (1987). Visual processing in monkey extrastriate cortex. *Annual Review of Neuroscience, 10*, 363–401.

Mayer, R. E. (1977). *Thinking and problem solving.* Scott, Foresman & Company.

Mays, W. (1953). The first circuit for an electrical logic-machine. *Science, 118*(3062), 281–282.

McBeath, M. K., Shaffer, D. M., & Kaiser, M. K. (1995). How baseball outfielders determine where to run to catch fly balls. *Science, 268*(5210), 569–573. https://doi.org/10.1126/science.7725104

McBride, D. M., & Cutting, J. C. (2019). *Cognitive psychology: Theory, process, and methodology* (2nd ed.). SAGE Publications.

McClelland, J. L. (1979). Time relations of mental processes: Examination of systems of processes in cascade. *Psychological Review, 86*(4), 287–330. https://doi.org/10.1037/0033-295x.86.4.287

McClelland, J. L., & Rumelhart, D. E. (1986). *Parallel distributed processing. Volume 2: Psychological and biological models.* MIT Press.

McCloskey, M. (1991). Networks and theories: The place of connectionism in cognitive science. *Psychological Science, 2,* 387–395.

McCorduck, P. (1979). *Machines who think: A personal inquiry into the history and prospects of artificial intelligence.* W. H. Freeman.

McCulloch, W. S., & Pitts, W. (1943). A logical calculus of the ideas immanent in nervous activity. *Bulletin of Mathematical Biophysics, 5,* 115–133.

McGeoch, J. A. (1942). *The psychology of human learning, an introduction.* Longmans, Green and Company.

Mechanic, A. (1964). Responses involved in rote learning of verbal materials. *Journal of Verbal Learning and Verbal Behavior, 3*(1), 30–36. https://doi.org/10.1016/s0022-5371(64)80056-6

Medin, D. L., & Ross, B. H. (1992). *Cognitive psychology.* Harcourt Brace Jovanovich College Publishers.

Medler, D. A. (1998). A brief history of connectionism. *Neural Computing Surveys, 1,* 18–72.

Medler, D. A., Dawson, M. R. W., & Kingstone, A. (2005). Functional localization and double dissociations: The relationship between internal structure and behavior. *Brain and Cognition, 57,* 146–150.

Menary, R. (2008). *Cognitive integration: Mind and cognition unbounded.* Palgrave Macmillan.

Menary, R. (2010). *The extended mind.* MIT Press.

Menzel, R., & Fischer, J. (2012). *Animal thinking: Contemporary issues in comparative cognition.* MIT Press.

Meyer, D. E., Glass, J. M., Mueller, S. T., Seymour, T. L., & Kieras, D. E. (2001). Executive-process interactive control: A unified computational theory for answering 20 questions (and more) about cognitive ageing. *European Journal of Cognitive Psychology, 13*(1–2), 123–164.

Meyer, D. E., & Kieras, D. E. (1997a). A computational theory of executive cognitive processes and multiple-task performance. 1. Basic mechanisms. *Psychological Review, 104*(1), 3–65.

Meyer, D. E., & Kieras, D. E. (1997b). A computational theory of executive cognitive processes and multiple-task performance. 2. Accounts of psychological refractory-period phenomena. *Psychological Review, 104*(4), 749–791.

Miller, G. A. (1951). *Language and communication.* McGraw-Hill.

Miller, G. A. (1956). The magical number seven, plus or minus two: Some limits on our capacity for processing information. *Psychological Review, 63*(2), 81–97. https://doi .org/10.1037/h0043158

Miller, G. A. (2003). The cognitive revolution: A historical perspective. *Trends in Cognitive Sciences, 7*(3), 141–144.

Miller, G. A., Galanter, E., & Pribram, K. H. (1960). *Plans and the structure of behavior.* Henry Holt & Company.

Milner, B., Squire, L. R., & Kandel, E. R. (1998). Cognitive neuroscience and the study of memory. *Neuron, 20*(3), 445–468. https://doi.org/10.1016/s0896-6273(00)80987-3

Milner, P. M. (1957). The cell assembly: Mark II. *Psychological Review, 64*(4), 242–252.

Minsky, M. L. (1985). *The society of mind.* Simon & Schuster.

Minsky, M. L. (2006). *The emotion machine: Commensense thinking, artificial intelligence, and the future of the human mind.* Simon & Schuster.

Minsky, M. L., & Papert, S. (1969). *Perceptrons: An introduction to computational geometry.* MIT Press.

Mohamed, A., Dahl, G. E., & Hinton, G. E. (2012). Acoustic modeling using deep belief networks. *IEEE Transactions on Audio Speech and Language Processing, 20*(1), 14–22. https://doi.org/10.1109/tasl.2011.2109382

Mollon, J. D. (1982). Colour vision and colour blindness. In H. B. Barlow & J. D. Mollon (Eds.), *The senses* (pp. 165–191). Cambridge University Press.

Moore, T. V. (1939). *Cognitive psychology.* Lippincott.

Moravec, H. (1999). *Robot.* Oxford University Press.

Morris, R. G. M., Anderson, E., Lynch, G. S., & Baudry, M. (1986). Selective impairment of learning and blockade of long-term potentiation by an N-methyl-D-aspartate receptor antagonist, AP5. *Nature, 319*(6056), 774–776. https://doi.org/10.1038/319774a0

Mozer, M. C., & Smolensky, P. (1989). Using relevance to reduce network size automatically. *Connection Science, 1*, 3–16.

Murdock, B. B. (1962). The serial position effect of free recall. *Journal of Experimental Psychology, 64*(5), 482–488. https://doi.org/10.1037/h0045106

Neisser, U. (1967). *Cognitive psychology.* Appleton-Century-Crofts.

Newell, A. (1973). Production systems: Models of control structures. In W. G. Chase (Ed.), *Visual information processing* (pp. 463–526). Academic Press.

Newell, A. (1980). Physical symbol systems. *Cognitive Science, 4*, 135–183.

Newell, A. (1990). *Unified theories of cognition.* Harvard University Press.

Newell, A., Shaw, J. C., & Simon, H. A. (1958). Elements of a theory of human problem solving. *Psychological Review, 65*, 151–166.

Newell, A., & Simon, H. A. (1956). The logic theory machine: A complex information-processing system. *IRE Transactions on Information Theory, 2*(3), 61–79. https://doi .org/10.1109/tit.1956.1056797

Newell, A., & Simon, H. A. (1961). Computer simulation of human thinking. *Science, 134*(349), 2011–2017.

Newell, A., & Simon, H. A. (1972). *Human problem solving*. Prentice-Hall.

Newell, A., & Simon, H. A. (1976). Computer science as empirical inquiry—Symbols and search. *Communications of the ACM, 19*(3), 113–126.

Nicholls, J. G., Martin, A. R., & Wallace, B. G. (1992). *From neuron to brain* (3rd ed.). Sinauer Associates.

Nilsson, N. J. (1984). *Shakey the robot*. Stanford Research Institute.

Nilsson, N. J. (2010). *The quest for artificial intelligence: A history of ideas and achievements*. Cambridge University Press.

Noble, C. E. (1952). An analysis of meaning. *Psychological Review, 59*(6), 421–430. https://doi.org/10.1037/h0054087

Noë, A. (2004). *Action in perception*. MIT Press.

Noë, A. (2009). *Out of our heads*. Hill and Wang.

Olmstead, M. C., & Kuhlmeier, V. A. (2015). *Comparative cognition*. Cambridge University Press.

Osbeck, L. M. (2019). *Values in psychological science: Re-imagining epistemic priorities at a new frontier*. Cambridge University Press.

Paivio, A. (1969). Mental imagery in associative learning and memory. *Psychological Review, 76*, 241–263.

Paivio, A. (1971). *Imagery and verbal processes*. Holt, Rinehart & Winston.

Paivio, A. (1986). *Mental representations: A dual-coding approach*. Oxford University Press.

Paivio, A., & Csapo, K. (1969). Concrete image and verbal memory codes. *Journal of Experimental Psychology, 80*(2P1), 279–285. https://doi.org/10.1037/h0027273

Paivio, A., Smythe, P. C., & Yuille, J. C. (1968). Imagery versus meaningfulness of nouns in paired-associate learning. *Canadian Journal of Psychology, 22*(6), 427–441. https://doi.org/10.1037/h0082782

Paivio, A., Yuille, J. C., & Madigan, S. A. (1968). Concreteness imagery and meaningfulness values for 925 nouns. *Journal of Experimental Psychology, 76*(1 Monograph Supplement), 1–25. https://doi.org/10.1037/h0025327

Papert, S. (1988). One AI or many? *Daedalus, 117*(1), 1–14.

Pedersen, D. B. (2011). Revisiting the neuro-turn in the humanities and natural sciences. *Pensamiento, 67*(254), 767–786.

Pennington, L. A., & Waters, R. H. (1938). The anticipation method in paired associate learning. *Journal of Psychology, 6*(2), 281–283. https://doi.org/10.1080/00223980.1938.9917605

Peterson, L. R., & Peterson, M. J. (1959). Short-term retention of individual verbal items. *Journal of Experimental Psychology, 58*, 193–198.

Pinker, S. (1979). Formal models of language learning. *Cognition, 7*, 217–283.

Pinker, S. (1997). *How the mind works*. W. W. Norton.

Pinker, S., & Prince, A. (1988). On language and connectionism: Analysis of a parallel distributed processing model of language acquisition. *Cognition, 28*, 73–193.

Polger, T. W. (2012). Functionalism as a philosophical theory of the cognitive sciences. *Wiley Interdisciplinary Reviews: Cognitive Science, 3*(3), 337–348. https://doi.org/10.1002/wcs.1170

Polger, T. W., & Shapiro, L. A. (2016). *The multiple realization book*. Oxford University Press.

Popper, K. (1978). Natural selection and the emergence of mind. *Dialectica, 32*, 339–355.

Posner, M. I. (1978). *Chronometric explorations of mind*. Lawrence Erlbaum Associates.

Posner, M. I., & Snyder, C. R. R. (1975). Attention and cognitive control. In R. L. Solso (Ed.), *Information processing and cognition: The Loyola symposium* (pp. 55–85). Lawrence Erlbaum Associates.

Putnam, H. (1975a). The nature of mental states. In H. Putnam (Ed.), *Mind, language and reality: Philosophical papers* (Vol. 2, pp. 51–58). Cambridge University Press.

Putnam, H. (1975b). Philosophy and our mental life. In H. Putnam (Ed.), *Mind, language and reality: Philosophical papers* (Vol. 2, pp. 291–303). Cambridge University Press.

Pylyshyn, Z. W. (1973). What the mind's eye tells the mind's brain: A critique of mental imagery. *Psychological Bulletin, 80*, 1–24.

Pylyshyn, Z. W. (1980). Computation and cognition: Issues in the foundations of cognitive science. *Behavioral and Brain Sciences, 3*(1), 111–132.

Pylyshyn, Z. W. (1981a). The imagery debate: Analogue media versus tacit knowledge. *Psychological Review, 88*(1), 16–45.

Pylyshyn, Z. W. (1981b). Psychological explanations and knowledge-dependent processes. *Cognition, 10*(1–3), 267–274.

Pylyshyn, Z. W. (1984). *Computation and cognition*. MIT Press.

Pylyshyn, Z. W. (1987). *The robot's dilemma: The frame problem in artificial intelligence*. Ablex.

Pylyshyn, Z. W. (2001). Visual indexes, preconceptual objects, and situated vision. *Cognition, 80*(1–2), 127–158.

Pylyshyn, Z. W. (2003a). *Seeing and visualizing: It's not what you think*. MIT Press.

Pylyshyn, Z. W. (2003b). Explaining mental imagery: Now you see it, now you don't—Reply to Kosslyn et al. *Trends in Cognitive Sciences, 7*(3), 111–112.

Pylyshyn, Z. W. (2003c). Return of the mental image: Are there really pictures in the brain? *Trends in Cognitive Sciences, 7*(3), 113–118.

Pylyshyn, Z. W. (2007). *Things and places: How the mind connects with the world*. MIT Press.

Pylyshyn, Z. W., Haladjian, H. H., King, C. E., & Reilly, J. E. (2008). Selective nontarget inhibition in Multiple Object Tracking. *Visual Cognition, 16*(8), 1011–1021. https://doi .org/10.1080/13506280802247486

Quillian, M. R. (1967). Word concepts: A theory and simulation of some basic semantic capabilities. *Behavioral Science, 12*(5), 410–430. https://doi.org/10.1002/bs.3830120511

Quillian, M. R. (1969). Teachable language comprehender: A simulation program and theory of language. *Communications of the ACM, 12*(8), 459–476. https://doi.org/10 .1145/363196.363214

Ratcliff, R. (1990). Connectionist models of recognition memory—Constraints imposed by learning and forgetting functions. *Psychological Review, 97*(2), 285–308.

Reed, S. K. (1982). *Cognition: Theory and applications.* Brooks/Cole.

Reed, S. K. (1988). *Cognition: Theory and applications* (2nd ed.). Brooks/Cole.

Reed, S. K. (1996). *Cognition: Theory and applications.* Wadsworth Publishing.

Reisberg, D. (2013). *Cognition: Exploring the science of the mind* (5th ed.). W. W. Norton & Company.

Reisberg, D. (2018). *Cognition: Exploring the science of the mind* (7th ed.). W. W. Norton & Company.

Reitman, W. R. (1965). *Cognition and thought: An information processing approach.* John Wiley & Sons.

Restle, F., & Greeno, J. G. (1970). *Introduction to mathematical psychology.* Addison-Wesley.

Reynolds, A. G., & Flagg, P. W. (1977). *Cognitive psychology.* Winthrop Publishers.

Rips, L., Shoben, E. J., & Smith, E. E. (1973). Semantic distance and verification of semantic relations. *Journal of Verbal Learning and Verbal Behavior, 12*, 1–20.

Rizzuto, D. S., & Kahana, M. J. (2001). An autoassociative neural network model of paired-associate learning. *Neural Computation, 13*(9), 2075–2092.

Robbins, P., & Aydede, M. (2009). *The Cambridge handbook of situated cognition.* Cambridge University Press.

Rochester, N., Holland, J. H., Haibt, L. H., & Duda, W. L. (1956). Tests on a cell assembly theory of the action of the brain, using a large digital computer. *IRE Transactions on Information Theory, IT-2*, 80–93.

Rock, I. (1983). *The logic of perception.* MIT Press.

Rosch, E. (1975). Cognitive reference points. *Cognitive Psychology, 7*(4), 532–547.

Rosch, E., & Mervis, C. B. (1975). Family resemblances: Studies in the internal structure of categories. *Cognitive Psychology, 7*, 573–605.

Rosenblatt, F. (1958). The perceptron: A probabilistic model for information storage and organization in the brain. *Psychological Review, 65*(6), 386–408.

Rosenblatt, F. (1962). *Principles of neurodynamics.* Spartan Books.

Rowlands, M. (2010). *The new science of the mind: From extended mind to embodied phenomenology.* MIT Press.

Rumelhart, D. E., Hinton, G. E., & Williams, R. J. (1986). Learning representations by back-propagating errors. *Nature, 323*(6088), 533–536.

Rumelhart, D. E., & McClelland, J. L. (1986a). On learning the past tenses of English verbs. In J. L. McClelland & D. E. Rumelhart (Eds.), *Parallel distributed processing, V.2.* (pp. 216–271). MIT Press.

Rumelhart, D. E., & McClelland, J. L. (1986b). *Parallel distributed processing, V.1.* MIT Press.

Rundus, D. (1971). Analysis of rehearsal processes in free recall. *Journal of Experimental Psychology, 89*(1), 63–77. https://doi.org/10.1037/h0031185

Rupert, R. D. (2009). *Cognitive systems and the extended mind.* Oxford University Press.

Ryle, G. (1949). *The concept of mind.* Hutchinson & Company.

Samuel, A. L. (1959). Some studies in machine learning using the game of checkers. *IBM Journal of Research and Development, 3*(3), 211–229. https://doi.org/10.1147/rd.33.0210

Sarikaya, R., Hinton, G. E., & Deoras, A. (2014). Application of deep belief networks for natural language understanding. *IEEE-ACM Transactions on Audio Speech and Language Processing, 22*(4), 778–784. https://doi.org/10.1109/taslp.2014.2303296

Saxberg, B. V. H. (1987a). Projected free fall trajectories. 1. Theory and simulation. *Biological Cybernetics, 56*(2–3), 159–175. https://doi.org/10.1007/bf00317991

Saxberg, B. V. H. (1987b). Projected free fall trajectories. 2. Human experiments. *Biological Cybernetics, 56*(2–3), 177–184. https://doi.org/10.1007/bf00317992

Schaeffer, J., Culberson, J., Treloar, N., Knight, B., Lu, P., & Szafron, D. (1992). A world championship caliber checkers program. *Artificial Intelligence, 53*(2–3), 273–289. https://doi.org/10.1016/0004-3702(92)90074-8

Schaeffer, J., Lake, R., Lu, P., & Bryant, M. (1995). Chinook: The world man-machine checkers champion. *AI Magazine, 17*(1), 21–29.

Schaeffer, J., Treloar, N., Lu, P., & Lake, R. (1993). Man versus machine . . . for the world checkers championship. *AI Magazine, 14*(2), 28–35.

Schlimmer, J. S. (1987). *Concept acquisition through representational adjustment* (Unpublished doctoral dissertation). University of California Irvine.

Schnapf, J. L., Nunn, B. J., Meister, M., & Baylor, D. A. (1990). Visual transductions in cones of the monkey *Macaca fascicularis. Journal of Physiology, 427*, 681–713.

Schneider, W. (1987). Connectionism: Is it a paradigm shift for psychology? *Behavior Research Methods, Instruments, & Computers, 19*, 73–83.

Schneider, W., & Shiffrin, R. M. (1977). Controlled and automatic human information-processing. 1. Detection, search, and attention. *Psychological Review, 84*(1), 1–66. https://doi.org/10.1037/0033-295x.84.1.1

Schriber, T. J. (1969). *Fundamentals of flowcharting.* Wiley.

Scoville, W. B., & Milner, B. (1957). Loss of recent memory after bilateral hippocampal lesions. *Journal of Neurology, Neurosurgery and Psychiatry, 20*, 11–21.

Scribner, S., & Tobach, E. (1997). *Mind and social practice: Selected writings of Sylvia Scribner*. Cambridge University Press.

Searle, J. R. (1980). Minds, brains, and programs. *Behavioral and Brain Sciences, 3*, 417–424.

Searle, J. R. (1984). *Minds, brains and science*. Harvard University Press.

Searle, J. R. (1990). Is the brain's mind a computer program? *Scientific American, 262*, 26–31.

Searle, J. R. (2007). Putting consciousness back in the brain: Reply to Bennett and Hacker. In M. R. Bennett, D. C. Dennett, P. M. S. Hacker, & J. R. Searle (Eds.), *Neuroscience and philosophy: Brain, mind, and language* (pp. 97–126). Columbia University Press.

Seidenberg, M. (1993). Connectionist models and cognitive theory. *Psychological Science, 4*, 228–235.

Shannon, C. E. (1938). A symbolic analysis of relay and switching circuits. *Transactions of the American Institute of Electrical Engineers, 57*, 713–723.

Shapiro, L. A. (2011). *Embodied cognition*. Routledge.

Shapiro, L. A. (2014). *The Routledge handbook of embodied cognition*. Routledge.

Shapiro, L. A. (2019). *Embodied cognition* (2nd ed.). Routledge.

Shen, D. G., Wu, G. R., & Suk, H. I. (2017). Deep learning in medical image analysis. *Annual Review of Biomedical Engineering, 19(1)*, 221–248.

Shepard, R. N., & Cooper, L. A. (1982). *Mental images and their transformations*. MIT Press.

Shepard, R. N., & Metzler, J. (1971). Mental rotation of three-dimensional objects. *Science, 171(3972)*, 701–703.

Shettleworth, S. J. (2013). *Fundamentals of comparative cognition*. Oxford University Press.

Shiffrin, R. M., & Atkinson, R. C. (1969). Storage and retrieval processes in long-term memory. *Psychological Review, 76(2)*, 179–193.

Shiffrin, R. M., & Schneider, W. (1977). Controlled and automatic human information-processing. 2. Perceptual learning, automatic attending, and a general theory. *Psychological Review, 84(2)*, 127–190. https://doi.org/10.1037/0033-295x.84.2.127

Simon, H. A. (1969). *The sciences of the artificial*. MIT Press.

Simon, H. A. (1979). *Models of thought*. Yale University Press.

Simon, H. A. (2007). Karl Duncker and cognitive science. In J. Valsiner (Ed.), *Thinking in psychological science: Ideas and their makers* (pp. 3–16). Transaction Publishers.

Simon, H. A., & Newell, A. (1958). Heuristic problem solving: The next advance in operations research. *Operations Research, 6*, 1–10.

Simpson, D. (2005). Phrenology and the neurosciences: Contributions of F. J. Gall and J. G. Spurzheim. *ANZ Journal of Surgery, 75(6)*, 475–482. https://doi.org/10.1111/j.1445-2197.2005.03426.x

Sinnett, S., Smilek, D., & Kingstone, A. (2016). *Cognition* (6th ed.). Oxford University Press.

Skinner, B. F. (1950). Are theories of learning necessary? *Psychological Review, 57*(4), 193–216. https://doi.org/10.1037/h0054367

Skinner, B. F. (1957). *Verbal behavior.* Appleton-Century-Crofts.

Skinner, B. F. (1977). Why I am not a cognitive psychologist. *Behaviorism, 5*(2), 1–10.

Skinner, B. F. (1990). Can psychology be a science of mind? *American Psychologist, 45*(11), 1206–1210. https://doi.org/10.1037//0003-066x.45.11.1206

Smolensky, P. (1988). On the proper treatment of connectionism. *Behavioral and Brain Sciences, 11,* 1–74.

Solso, R. L. (1979). *Cognitive psychology.* Harcourt, Brace, Jovanovich.

Solso, R. L. (1988). *Cognitive psychology* (2nd ed.). Allyn & Bacon.

Solso, R. L. (1995). *Cognitive psychology* (4th ed.). Allyn & Bacon.

Sorabji, R. (2006). *Aristotle on memory* (2nd ed.). University of Chicago Press.

Sperling, G. (1960). The information available in brief visual presentations. *Psychological Monographs, 74*(11), 1–29. https://doi.org/10.1037/h0093759

Sperry, R. W. (1993). The impact and promise of the cognitive revolution. *American Psychologist, 48*(8), 878–885.

Squire, L. R. (1987). *Memory and brain.* Oxford University Press.

Squire, L. R. (1992). Declarative and nondeclarative memory: Multiple brain systems supporting learning and memory. *Journal of Cognitive Neuroscience, 4,* 232–243.

Squire, L. R. (2009). The legacy of patient H. M. for neuroscience. *Neuron, 61*(1), 6–9. https://doi.org/10.1016/j.neuron.2008.12.023

Squire, L. R., & Wixted, J. T. (2011). The cognitive neuroscience of human memory since HM., *Annual Review of Neuroscience, 34*(1) 259–288.

Sternberg, S. (1969a). Discovery of processing stages: Extensions of Donders' method. *Acta Psychologica, 30,* 276–315. https://doi.org/10.1016/0001-6918(69)90055-9

Sternberg, S. (1969b). Memory-scanning: Mental processes revealed by reaction-time experiments. *American Scientist, 4,* 421–457.

Stewart, I. (1994). A subway named Turing. *Scientific American, 271,* 104–107.

Stone, J. L., & Hughes, J. R. (2013). Early history of electroencephalography and establishment of the American Clinical Neurophysiology Society. *Journal of Clinical Neurophysiology, 30*(1), 28–44. https://doi.org/10.1097/WNP.0b013e31827edb2d

Stroop, J. R. (1935). Studies of interference in serial verbal reactions. *Journal of Experimental Psychology, 18,* 643–662. https://doi.org/10.1037/0096-3445.121.1.15

Surprenant, A. M., & Neath, I. (1997). T. V. Moore's (1939) *Cognitive psychology. Psychonomic Bulletin & Review, 4*(3), 342–349. https://doi.org/10.3758/bf03210791

Swade, D. D. (1993). Redeeming Charles Babbage's mechanical computer. *Scientific American, 268,* 86–91.

Theraulaz, G., & Bonabeau, E. (1999). A brief history of stigmergy. *Artificial Life, 5,* 97–116.

Thorndike, E. L. (1932). *The fundamentals of learning.* Bureau of Publications, Teachers College, Columbia University.

Todd, P. M., & Loy, D. G. (1991). *Music and connectionism.* MIT Press.

Townsend, J. T. (1971). Note on identifiability of parallel and serial processes. *Perception & Psychophysics, 10*(3), 161–163.

Townsend, J. T. (1990). Serial vs parallel processing: Sometimes they look like Tweedledum and Tweedledee but they can (and should) be distinguished. *Psychological Science, 1*(1), 46–54.

Treisman, A. M. (1985). Preattentive processing in vision. *Computer Vision, Graphics, and Image Processing, 31,* 156–177.

Treisman, A. M. (1986). Features and objects in visual processing. *Scientific American, 254,* 114–124.

Treisman, A. M. (1988). Features and objects: The fourteenth Bartlett memorial lecture. *Quarterly Journal of Experimental Psychology, 40A,* 201–237.

Treisman, A. M., & Gelade, G. (1980). A feature integration theory of attention. *Cognitive Psychology, 12*(1), 97–136.

Treisman, A. M., & Gormican, S. (1988). Feature analysis in early vision: Evidence from search asymmetries. *Psychological Review, 95,* 14–48.

Treisman, A. M., Sykes, M., & Gelade, G. (1977). Selective attention and stimulus integration. In S. Dornic (Ed.), *Attention and performance VI.* Lawrence Erlbaum Associates.

Tschentscher, N., Hauk, O., Fischer, M. H., & Pulvermuller, F. (2012). You can count on the motor cortex: Finger counting habits modulate motor cortex activation evoked by numbers. *Neuroimage, 59*(4), 3139–3148. https://doi.org/10.1016/j.neuroimage.2011.11.037

Tulving, E. (1983). *Elements of episodic memory.* Oxford University Press.

Tulving, E., Donaldson, W., & Bower, G. H. (1972). *Organization of memory.* Academic Press.

Turing, A. M. (1936). On computable numbers, with an application to the Entscheidungsproblem. *Proceedings of the London Mathematical Society, Series 2h, 42,* 230–265.

Turing, A. M. (1950). Computing machinery and intelligence. *Mind, 59,* 433–460.

Turner, B. M., Miletic, S., & Forstmann, B. U. (2018). Outlook on deep neural networks in computational cognitive neuroscience. *Neuroimage, 180,* 117–118. https://doi.org/10.1016/j.neuroimage.2017.12.078

Tversky, A. (1977). Features of similarity. *Psychological Review, 84,* 327–352.

Tye, M. (1991). *The imagery debate.* MIT Press.

Uexküll, J. V. (1957). A stroll through the worlds of animals and men: A picture book of invisible worlds. In C. H. Schiller (Ed.), *Instinctive behavior: The development of a modern concept* (Vol. 134, pp. 5–80). International Universities Press.

Uexküll, J. V. (2001). An introduction to *umwelt. Semiotica, 134*(1–4), 107–110.

Underwood, B. J., & Schulz, R. W. (1960). *Meaningfulness and verbal learning.* Lippincott.

Ungerleider, L. G., & Mishkin, M. (1982). Two cortical visual systems. In D. Ingle, M. A. Goodale, & R. J. W. Mansfield (Eds.), *Analysis of visual behavior* (pp. 549–586). MIT Press.

Uttal, W. R. (2011). *Mind and brain: A critical appraisal of cognitive neuroscience.* MIT Press.

van Essen, D. C., Anderson, C. H., & Felleman, D. J. (1992). Information processing in the primate visual system: An integrated systems perspective. *Science, 255*(5043), 419–423.

van Hemmen, J. L., & Senn, W. (2002). Hebb in perspective. *Biological Cybernetics, 87,* 317–318.

VanLehn, K. (1991). *Architectures for intelligence.* Lawrence Erlbaum Associates.

Varela, F. J., Thompson, E., & Rosch, E. (1991). *The embodied mind: Cognitive science and human experience.* MIT Press.

Vico, G. (1710/1988). *On the most ancient wisdom of the Italians.* Ithaca: Cornell University Press.

Vidal, F., & Ortega, F. (2017). *Being brains: Making the cerebral subject.* Fordham University Press.

Virues-Ortega, J. (2006). The case against B. F. Skinner 45 years later: An encounter with N. Chomsky. *Behavior Analyst, 29*(2), 243–251. https://doi.org/10.1007/bf03392133

von Neumann, J. (1958). *The computer and the brain.* Yale University Press.

Vygotsky, L. S. (1986). *Thought and language* (Translation newly rev. and ed.). MIT Press.

Warren, H. C. (1921). *A history of the association psychology.* Charles Scribner's Sons.

Wasner, M., Moeller, K., Fischer, M. H., & Nuerk, H. C. (2014). Aspects of situated cognition in embodied numerosity: The case of finger counting. *Cognitive Processing, 15*(3), 317–328. https://doi.org/10.1007/s10339-014-0599-z

Wason, P. C. (1966). *Reasoning.* Penguin.

Wason, P. C., & Johnson-Laird, P. N. (1972). *Psychology of reasoning: Structure and content.* Batsford.

Wasserman, G. S. (1978). *Color vision: An historical introduction.* John Wiley & Sons.

Watson, J. B. (1913). Psychology as the behaviorist views it. *Psychological Review, 20,* 158–177.

Waugh, N. C., & Norman, D. A. (1965). Primary memory. *Psychological Review, 72*, 89–104.

Weizenbaum, J. (1966). Eliza—A computer program for the study of natural language communication between man and machine. *Communications of the ACM, 9*(1), 36–45.

Weizenbaum, J. (1976). *Computer power and human reason*. W. H. Freeman.

Wertheimer, M., & Asch, S. E. (1945). *Productive thinking*. Harper & Brothers.

Wheeler, W. M. (1911). The ant colony as an organism. *Journal of Morphology, 22*(2), 307–325.

Widrow, B., & Hoff, M. E. (1960). Adaptive switching circuits. *Institute of Radio Engineers, Wester Electronic Show and Convention, Convention Record, Part 4*, 96–104.

Wiener, N. (1948). *Cybernetics: Or control and communication in the animal and the machine*. MIT Press.

Wiener, N. (1950). *The human use of human beings: Cybernetics and society*. Houghton Mifflin.

Wilkins, A. J. (1971). Conjoint frequency, category size, and categorization time. *Journal of Verbal Learning and Verbal Behavior, 10*(4), 382–385. https://doi.org/10.1016/s0022-5371(71)80036-1

Wilson, M. (2002). Six views of embodied cognition. *Psychonomic Bulletin & Review, 9*(4), 625–636. https://doi.org/10.3758/bf03196322

Wilson, R. A. (2004). *Boundaries of the mind: The individual in the fragile sciences—Cognition*. Cambridge University Press.

Wilson, R. A. (2005). *Genes and the agents of life: The individual in the fragile sciences—Biology*. Cambridge University Press.

Winograd, T. (1972). *Understanding natural language*. Academic Press.

Winograd, T. (1983). *Language as a cognitive process. Volume 1: Syntax*. Addison-Wesley.

Winograd, T., & Flores, F. (1987). *Understanding computers and cognition*. Addison-Wesley.

Wittgenstein, L. (1953). *Philosophical investigations* (G. E. M. Anscombe, Trans.). Blackwell.

Wolfe, J. M. (1994). Guided search 2.0: A revised model of visual search. *Psychonomic Bulletin & Review, 1*(2), 202–238.

Wolfe, J. M., Cave, K. R., & Franzel, S. L. (1989). Guided search: An alternative to the feature integration model for visual search. *Journal of Experimental Psychology: Human Perception and Performance, 15*(3), 419–433.

Wolfe, J. M., Franzel, S. L., & Cave, K. R. (1988). Parallel visual search for conjunctions of color and form. *Journal of the Optical Society of America, 4*, 95.

Wood, G. (2002). *Living dolls: A magical history of the quest for artificial life*. Faber & Faber.

Woodman, G. F. (2010). A brief introduction to the use of event-related potentials in studies of perception and attention. *Attention Perception & Psychophysics, 72*(8), 2031–2046. https://doi.org/10.3758/app.72.8.2031

Woodworth, R. S. (1938). *Experimental psychology*. H. Holt & Company.

Yates, F. A. (1966). *The art of memory*. University of Chicago Press.